your baby's first year

month by month

what to expect and how to care for your baby

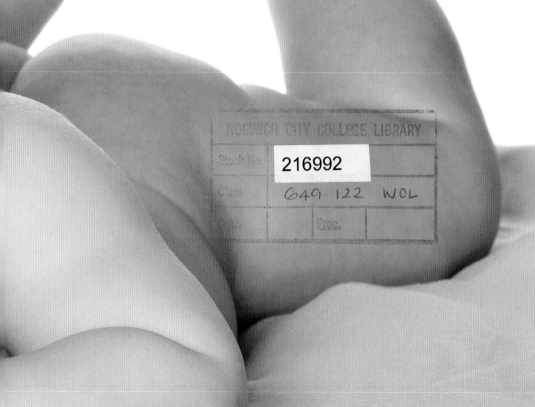

PRACTICAL
parenting

hamlyn

An Hachette Livre UK company
www.hachettelivre.co.uk

First published in Great Britain in 2008 by
Hamlyn, a division of Octopus Publishing Group Ltd
2–4 Heron Quays, London E14 4JP
www.octopusbooks.co.uk

Copyright © Octopus Publishing Group Ltd 2008

ISBN: 978-0-600-61716-7

A CIP catalogue record for this book is available from the British Library

Printed and bound in China

10 9 8 7 6 5 4 3 2 1

Your Baby's First Year has been produced in association with *Practical Parenting* magazine

Practical Parenting® is a registered trademark © IPC Magicalia Publishing Ltd 2008

To subscribe to **Practical Parenting** call 01689 899200 or log on to **www.practicalparenting.co.uk**

contents

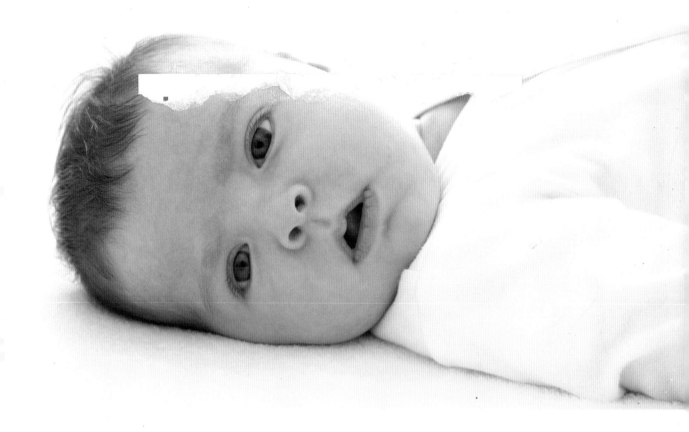

your baby's
first year
month by month

introduction

Congratulations on the arrival (or imminent arrival) of your new little person!

This is one of the most amazing moments of your life, yet this can also be one of the most overwhelming and, at times, daunting experiences you'll ever know. After all that practical help and support during the delivery, bringing home your new bundle of joy and tears, then shutting the door behind you, can make you feel as if you're now completely on your own.

In fact, the important thing to realize is that you're definitely not alone. There's a wealth of help around you, from friends and family to health visitors and GPs, as well as books such as this.

Of course, you wouldn't be human if you didn't have dreams and doubts, hopes, fears and feelings, as well as hundreds of questions that change and develop as your little one changes and develops in front of your eyes.

But whatever your queries, concerns or anxieties, you won't find a more useful guide than this. With its mix of expert advice, practical tips, shared experiences and real-life stories, this book can really help to give you the confidence to be a fantastic mum and to love the first 12 months of your baby's life.

Simply use the book to suit you – you can dip in as every stage brings a new challenge or dilemma, or read it from cover to cover so that you feel better prepared for what tomorrow holds.

It's a long and exciting journey, and this is just the first step, so relax in the knowledge that you've got help at your fingertips.

I wish you and your baby a truly unforgettable first year.

SUSIE BOONE
Editor-in-Chief, *Practical Parenting*

chapter 1

your new baby

The moment you have been waiting for has finally arrived: you are about to meet your baby. Many anxieties of pregnancy are now cast aside as you hold your newborn in your arms; this may also be the first time you discover his sex. As the reality of being a mum sinks in, make the most of the support to hand, and take time to focus on getting to know your baby, setting the all-important bonding process in motion.

meeting
your new baby

During your pregnancy you will have tried to imagine how you will feel when you see your baby for the first time and, of course, what he will look like. The way in which you meet your baby will depend on the type of birth you have had. If you've experienced a vaginal birth, your baby will probably be placed straight on to your skin; if you've had an emergency caesarean section, he may be handed straight to the paediatrician to be checked before you get to hold him.

' When everyone left the room, I gazed at Millie in my arms and talked softly to her. She was looking straight into my eyes and I felt the most enormous rush of love. Nothing had prepared me for how I would feel. '

Kate, mother of
Millie (10 days)

shared experience

discovering the sex

Once your baby has been born, there's no reason why you and your partner can't discover the sex of your child for yourselves. Just make sure you tell your midwife or doctor that this is what you would like to do so that they don't spoil the surprise!

To begin with, some parents feel shock and disappointment when they discover the sex of their baby. They may have been told by the sonographer to expect a girl and have planned for this, only to find that the ultrasound results were wrong. Others may have secretly hoped for a son, but now realize that they have another daughter. These feelings are normal, but often parents daren't admit how they feel. This doesn't mean that they aren't happy or don't love their baby – they just have an initial feeling of disappointment.

Although during your pregnancy you may have spent a lot of time wondering about the sex of your baby, once he or she is born, you'll probably find that you don't even think about this again – your baby is just your baby.

Holding your baby in your arms for the first time is a truly unique moment and one that many mothers find quite overwhelming.

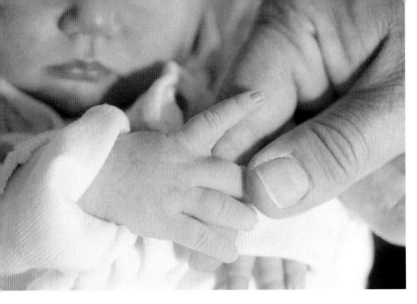

So tiny is your baby that it seems impossible for him to be so complete – a version of you and your partner, but in miniature.

getting close

You or your partner might choose to cut the umbilical cord, and some parents place a great deal of emphasis on this act as symbolizing the time when their baby begins to exist independently. It's a good idea to have skin-to-skin contact with your baby as early as possible. Your heartbeat, voice, body warmth and the smell of your skin will comfort him and encourage him to feel secure and warm, as well as help to initiate breast-feeding.

first feelings

Nothing and nobody can prepare you for how you will feel when you meet your baby for the first time, simply because no one knows how you will feel.

Some women immediately experience an instinctive rush of love and protection for their new baby, while others feel nothing but sheer exhaustion, are not very interested in meeting their baby and take time to get to know and love him. Neither of these 'meetings' is right or wrong; they are just different. You will get to know and love your baby in your own time.

Some women feel too shaky to hold their baby immediately following the birth and so their partner will have the first cuddle. Even if you have to have some stitches or feel a bit wobbly, your baby should be kept close by so that you can still see him.

getting to know him

It's important to have some quiet time together with your baby soon after the birth. These moments are very precious and should be respected as your time, when you get to know each other and enjoy the first feelings of being a family. With a full-term healthy baby, there should be no rush to weigh and measure him: these things aren't going to change over the next few hours! You and your partner should be left to enjoy your baby. Peel off the blankets, look at his body, feel his skin on yours, examine his tiny fingers and toes, talk to him and watch him turn his head towards you as he recognizes your voice.

Keeping your baby close to you will help him to feel secure and reassured. Newborns sleep for around 20 hours out of every 24, so make the most of your baby's waking time by talking to him and really getting to know each other. It's normal to feel anxious about holding him 'properly' or to wonder how you will recognize his cry as a message that it's time to feed, but the confidence will come. You might hold him differently to the way your partner does, or not change his nappy in the same way as the midwife, but this doesn't matter. There are different ways of doing lots of things, but this doesn't necessarily mean that one way is better than another.

'I felt like the only woman in the world who had ever had a baby – if I could, I would have left the delivery room door open and invited everyone in to meet my baby. I wanted to let everyone know how brilliant I was for having given birth to this beautiful baby!'

Michele, mother of Jacob (3 weeks)

shared experience

your baby's
appearance

New parents are often surprised by their newborn baby's appearance and worry that something may be wrong. Your baby may look a little 'bruised' or blemished, and she may be covered in creamy-white vernix and smears of blood. Her head will probably look slightly longer than normal due to the pressure of the birth. These things settle soon afterwards, but be prepared for the fact that your baby may not look as if she's come straight off the cover of a glossy magazine.

Blemishes on the face and puffiness around the eyes usually disappear in the first few days after birth.

your baby's head

The bones of your newborn's head are soft and will overlap slightly as she is squeezed down the birth canal. This is called 'moulding', and your baby's head will return to its normal shape within a few days. It probably looks quite large and out of proportion to the rest of her, and this is totally normal.

The fontanelles or 'soft spots' on your baby's head are two areas where the bones have not yet joined together. The most obvious one is diamond shaped and is found on the top of her head; it closes at around 3 months. The other is triangular and located at the back; it closes at around 18 months. There is a tough membrane covering the fontanelles, so don't worry that you'll hurt your baby when you cuddle her or wash her hair.

Bumps on your baby's head are common. An egg-shaped bump called a cephalhaematoma is formed by bleeding between the scalp skin and the bone, due to pressure during the birth. Such bumps generally appear within 24 hours and do not cause problems, but can sometimes take a few months to disappear completely.

Marks on the side of the head or a dark circular bruise on the scalp are common following a forceps or ventouse delivery, and will disappear within 48 hours.

Eyes The eyes are nearly always blue in Caucasian newborns, but may change colour after a few months. Darker-skinned babies usually have brown eyes, but these too may change later on. Your baby's eyes may look a bit puffy and swollen after the birth, and it's also common to have a burst blood vessel in the white of the eye from the pressure of the birth, which will disappear in time.

At birth, your baby's eyes are about three-quarters of the size of an adult's eyes. Your newborn baby can focus the distance from the breast to your face, so as you hold her, talk to her and watch how intently she looks at you.

your baby's body

Skin Your newborn baby's skin will probably be mottled and may turn white and blue in patches due to her immature circulation. It may still be covered in sticky white vernix, which usually disappears after a day or two. Don't rush to wash it off, as it will help to moisturize her skin. She may also have some fine hair over her body, known as lanugo, and this too will disappear. Some babies have dry skin, which will probably correct itself; if not, try gently rubbing in some olive oil.

Cord A short length of umbilical cord will still be attached to your baby's navel and your midwife or doctor will have applied a plastic clamp where it was separated. On the first day the remaining cord will still be soft, but by the following day it will have become hard, shrivelling and gradually turning black before dropping off, usually by the time your baby is 10 days old. Fold the top of his nappy back so that air can get to it and help with the process of separation.

The amount of vernix or lanugo still present at birth depends on the baby, and traces of both will be gone within a day or two.

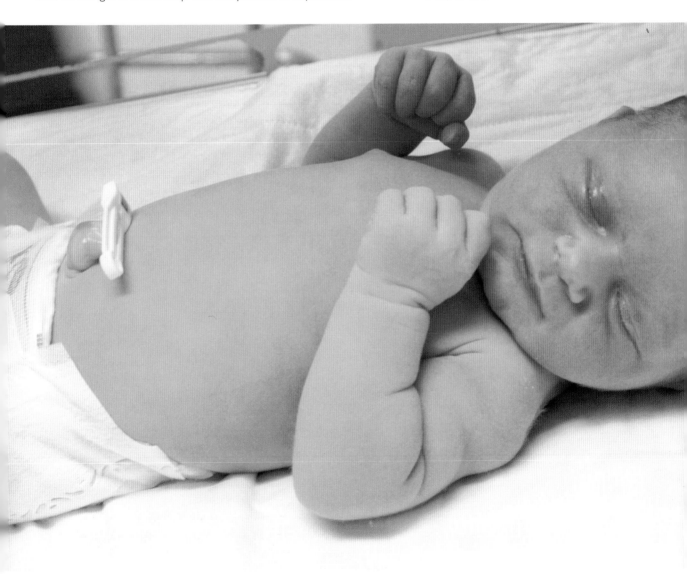

Your baby is born with a grasping reflex that is very strong at birth. If you lay a finger across her palm, her fingers will automatically close around it.

Breasts These are often swollen, but this subsides by the time your baby is 4 weeks old.

Genitals These often look red and swollen in both boys and girls. In girls it is common to have some vaginal discharge, sometimes streaked with blood, due to the hormones present at birth.

Hands Babies' hands (and feet) often feel cooler than the rest of the body. However, as long as your baby's abdomen is warm, her temperature is fine. Sometimes both hands and feet are a little blue in colour, as a newborn's circulation is immature.

Feet Babies' feet often turn in because of their position while curled up in the womb. By six months of age, however, your baby's feet will have become straighter.

bodily functions

Meconium For the first 2 or 3 days, your baby's bowel movements will consist of a black/green tar-like substance called meconium, which is composed of materials ingested while she was in the womb. Gradually this faecal matter will change to a yellow colour, as your baby's feeding becomes established.

Breathing Newborn babies often make funny noises while breathing and can 'snort' as though they have a blocked nose. The bridge of your baby's nose is low and this is why she may make snuffly sounds, as the air travels through the tiny nasal passages. Her breathing may also appear irregular at times and for a few breaths will seem quite fast before returning to normal.

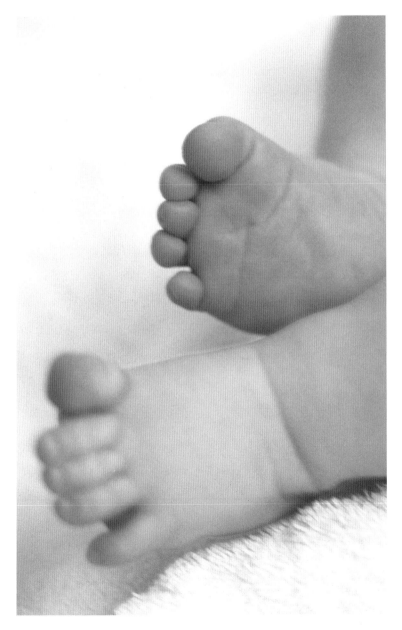

A newborn baby's toes are often curled after birth, but will flare out if you run a finger along the sole of her foot. This is known as the plantar reflex.

spots and birthmarks

Babies commonly have spots and marks on their skin, some of which will come and go, particularly on their face.

- Pink birthmarks, commonly referred to as 'stork marks', often appear on the eyelids, forehead or neck. Although they will fade over time, they sometimes become apparent when your baby cries.
- 'Strawberry marks' are red and raised, and they too will fade over time.
- Dark-skinned babies often have a mark called a 'Mongolian blue spot', usually on the lower back, which looks like a bruise. This is harmless and will have disappeared by puberty.
- Some babies have tiny white spots around their nose called 'milia' or 'milk spots', caused by blocked sweat and oil glands, which disappear within a few weeks.

first tests
and checks

Your midwife or doctor will automatically assess your baby as soon as he is born, and at 1 minute of age he will be given a 'score' out of 10 for his well-being. This test is called the Apgar (after the doctor who devised it) and is repeated again at 5 minutes.

newborn health checks

A short while after the birth, the midwife will examine your baby for any obvious problems or abnormalities as she weighs and measures him. Within the first few days of birth, a more thorough check will be performed, usually by the paediatrician or your own doctor if you are at home.

Head and neck The doctor will check your baby's skull bones and fontanelles, and examine the roof of his mouth to make sure that the palate is properly formed. His eyes, ears and nose will be checked, and his neck examined for any signs of cysts.

Immediately after birth your baby is weighed and measured, and these checks continue at regular intervals throughout his first year.

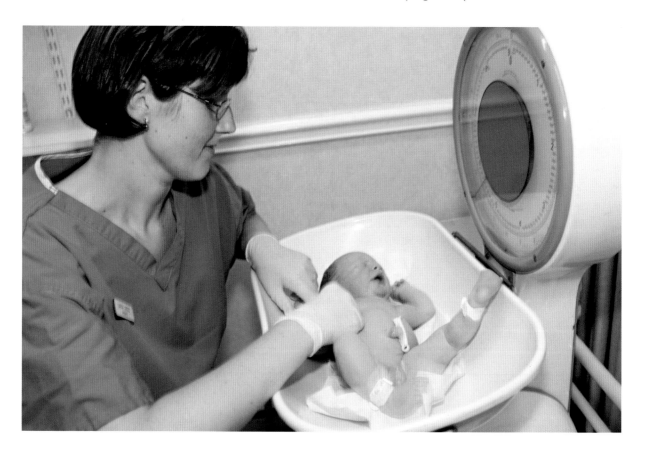

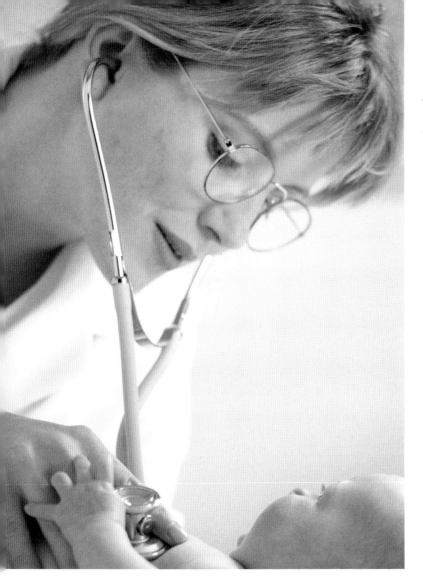

A baby's heart beats at some 180 beats per minute at birth, but drops to 120 within a couple of hours.

the Apgar score

Five categories are assessed in this test, each of which is given a score of 0, 1 or 2. The checks cover:

Colour Babies are often tinged with blue when first born, but they do pink up quickly after arrival! In dark-skinned babies, the inside of the mouth, whites of the eyes, soles of the feet and palms are examined.

Heart rate Your newborn baby should have a heart rate of over 100 beats per minute.

Breathing This should be strong and regular – if your baby is crying, then it will be.

Muscle tone Your baby should be able to move his arms and legs in an active way.

Response/reflex Your baby should respond to stimulation, such as being dried with a towel or handled.

A healthy baby will have a score of 7 or higher. A baby with a slightly lower score may need time to recover from the birth – if the score is very low, he may need medical attention.

Heart sounds and breathing Your baby's heart rate should be around 120 beats per minute. It is fairly common to find an 'innocent' heart murmur within the first few hours of birth as his immature circulatory system adjusts. If the murmur continues, then a scan of your baby's heart may be arranged before you leave hospital.

Spine The doctor will hold your baby and run their thumb down the bones in his back (vertebrae), to check that they are in the right place and for any obvious abnormalities of the spinal cord.

Hips Very gently, the doctor will bend your baby's legs up and turn them out to check for signs of a condition called congenital dislocation of the hips (CDH) or development dysplasia of the hips (DDH). This is when the ball at the top of the thigh bone (femur) doesn't fit properly into the socket of the pelvis or dislocates. One or two babies in every hundred will have some kind of hip problem and some babies are more prone than others, including those who have a family history of hip problems, were in a breech position or had very little fluid around them (oligohydramnios). If this is the case with your baby, the paediatrician may suggest an ultrasound scan within the first few weeks of birth to check for any problems.

The palmar (grasp) reflex is so strong at birth that it is possible to raise a baby as he grasps your thumbs.

Abdominal organs The doctor will gently feel your baby's abdomen, to check the size of the organs.

Feet, hands, arms and legs The doctor will look at your baby's feet to see if there is any sign that they turn in excessively (talipes). This is often due to the position of the baby in the womb and will correct itself later on. The creases on your baby's palms will be checked: usually there are two. A single crease can sometimes be an indication of Down's syndrome (see page 235), in which case further investigations will be carried out, including a blood test. The tone and strength in your baby's limbs will also be observed.

Genitals and anus It is common for babies to have swollen genitals following birth and a baby girl may have some vaginal discharge for a couple of days. The doctor will check that the genitals are properly formed and that a boy's testicles are in his scrotum. If they are not (undescended testicles), the chances are that this will happen in the weeks or months following birth. The doctor will also ask you whether your baby has opened his bowels (passed meconium, see page 15) and passed urine.

Reflexes The doctor will check your baby's reflexes (involuntary actions), which are present at birth and indicate that the central nervous system is working correctly.

His reflexes include:

Rooting If you gently stroke your baby's cheek, he will turn towards it and open his mouth, as if searching for the breast.

Sucking Your baby will suck not only the nipple but also your finger or his own fist. This reflex is extremely strong.

Swallowing Your baby is able to swallow colostrum or milk immediately after birth.

Stepping When your baby is held upright underneath the arms, he will make stepping movements as his feet brush against a surface.

Grasp When your finger is placed in your newborn's hand, he will automatically curl his fingers around it.

Startle or Moro A sudden movement as though he is falling will cause your baby to throw his arms out wide, spreading his fingers.

'heel prick' blood screening

A blood test is offered in the first week after birth to screen your baby for rare but serious conditions, which may include:

Phenylketonuria Babies with this condition are unable to process a substance in their food called phenylalanine, and if untreated it can cause mental disability. However, if identified early, a special diet can make a huge difference and prevent severe disability.

Congenital hypothyroidism Babies who do not have enough of the hormone thyroxine do not grow properly, and their physical and mental development can be severely affected. However, if this condition is detected early enough, medication can be used to prevent serious disability.

Cystic fibrosis This condition primarily affects the lungs and digestive system. Although there is no cure, early treatment can result in the child living a longer, healthier life (see page 234).

Sickle cell disorder This is an inherited disorder that affects the red blood cells and can be extremely serious. Sickle cell anaemia is one such disorder and is found mainly in families originating from the Caribbean, Eastern Mediterranean, Middle East, Africa and Asia. Early treatment has huge benefits, reducing illness and allowing the child to live a much healthier life (see page 235).

MCADD (Medium Chain Acyl-CoA Dehydrogenase Deficiency) Babies with this condition have a problem making energy for the body, due to a problem in breaking down fats. If this is detected early, close attention can be paid to the diet in order to prevent serious illness.

hearing test

Your baby's hearing may be tested within a few days of birth, either in hospital or at home. This takes just a few minutes and is carried out by placing a small, soft-tipped earpiece in the outer part of your baby's ear. Sometimes the test needs to be repeated, not because there is a problem but because your baby has fluid in his ear following the birth.

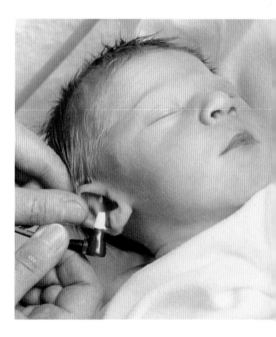

Hearing tests are routine within the first few weeks of birth, and are usually performed at home by a health professional.

how will you feel?

Giving birth can be exhilarating, empowering, bewildering, frightening, sensual, shocking, exhausting – the list goes on. Many women feel a combination of these emotions and are completely unprepared for this experience. There is no right way to feel after the birth of your baby, and you will probably find that when the hormones kick in, you'll be on a rollercoaster of emotions.

'I never dared tell anyone at the time, but I didn't feel love for Martha when she was first born. I thought she was lovely, but mainly I felt shocked by the birth. When she was about 4 weeks old and crying, I picked her up and she immediately stopped. I realized then that I had fallen in love with her.'

Sarah, mother of Martha (5 months)

shared experience

becoming a mother

After the birth, when the medical staff have established that you and your baby are well, you will finally be left alone with her. It is often then that the reality of becoming a mother hits home. The responsibility can seem overwhelming, as you hold this tiny person who for the last 9 months has been your 'bump'. It can be frightening, but also exciting.

There is no expectation that you will immediately 'know' your baby. When she cries, she may need feeding, cuddling or a nappy change, and it takes a few weeks before you can work out what the different cries mean. Gradually you will get to know her.

Whether you feel under- or overwhelmed by the experience, you can be certain that your life will change dramatically following the birth of your baby.

new emotions

For many women, it is only as they get to know their baby that they start to love her. A lot of emphasis is placed on a woman bonding immediately with her baby and feeling overwhelming love, but it's not uncommon to feel completely exhausted and disappointed that initially you have very little interest in your baby. This is completely normal and you are not alone in feeling this way. It is often the father who is more emotional at the birth of his child. He may describe feeling not only wonder at seeing his baby being born but also an enormous sense of relief that after all these months of anticipation his baby and partner are safe. For more information on bonding, see pages 58–59.

Following the birth, it's not unusual to feel guilt that you didn't 'cope' with labour or couldn't follow your carefully prepared birth plan, and your partner may also feel guilty that he wasn't able to do more during labour to provide support. However, the most important thing is that you and your baby come through the birth safely, whatever 'type' of birth that is.

If you have a history of miscarriages, infertility treatment or any other loss, you can be hit unexpectedly by emotions that reappear from the past. You may need to talk these feelings through with your partner, midwife or doctor.

recovery

The experience of birth can be a shock and it's not surprising that this can have an impact on the way you feel afterwards. You may have had an image in your mind of a tranquil water birth with immediate skin-to-skin contact, but in reality you might have had a forceps delivery or been rushed to the operating theatre for a caesarean section.

If you've had an instrumental birth (ventouse or forceps), you might be feeling very bruised and sore, and also guilty that you are not able to do all the things with your baby that you had initially hoped. However, there is plenty of time for taking your baby out and showing her off, so for now you should concentrate on your own recovery and avoid being hard on yourself. Have a lavender bath (see box right) to reduce the soreness caused by stitches.

Although the rates for caesarean sections are increasing, it should still be considered major surgery. With any other surgery the emphasis would be on your recovery, but as you've also had a baby the focus is inevitably on her welfare and it's very easy for you to be neglected. Following a caesarean section, you should concentrate on feeding your baby and very little else. Try to make sure that you have some support at home, and rest whenever you can. For more information on recovering from the birth of your baby, see pages 52–53.

It's useful to consider whether or not you have anyone you could call upon for extra support just in case things don't go to plan and you need some extra help. Many men take paternity leave nowadays; just make sure you make the most of the help when it's available.

'I never expected to see Rob so emotional, and it came as a huge shock to me. As soon as Billy was born, he sobbed as though his heart was breaking. He told me that he felt full of love and admiration for what I'd gone through, but he was also so relieved that we were both OK.'

Janine, mother of
Billy (4 weeks)

shared experience

'survival' strategies

- Keep a jug of water by the toilet to pour between your legs as you pass urine, as it may sting.
- Keep stitches clean — frequent baths with four drops of lavender oil added will help with healing.
- Sleep when your baby sleeps, even if it's in the middle of the afternoon.
- If you're feeling low, talk to your partner about it and also your midwife or doctor.

bringing your baby home

After 9 months of preparation, you will probably feel very excited about bringing your baby home for the first time. Many new parents are surprised to discover that they also feel nervous, a little overwhelmed and worried about how they are going to cope. This is completely normal, especially if you are feeling tired and uncomfortable after the birth. Fortunately, there is lots of help and support available to help you adjust, and you will soon feel much more confident and relaxed.

don't forget the car seat

If you have given birth in hospital and will be travelling home by car, you will need a baby car seat. Most hospitals won't let you leave until they have seen your baby strapped safely into his car seat, so it's a good idea to purchase one well in advance. Newborns need a rear-facing car seat, so it's important to check that you have the right one for you baby's age and weight, and make sure you know how to install it (see pages 230–231).

leaving hospital

If you have given birth in hospital, the length of your stay will be determined by the type of delivery you had, how well you and your baby are doing and how busy the hospital is at the time. Whether you return home within hours or days of the birth, it's important to take it easy and relax for the first few days.

- If you have had a straightforward vaginal delivery and both you and your baby are well, most hospitals will discharge you within a few hours, if you wish.
- Following a caesarean section, you are likely to stay for 3–5 days.
- If your baby is premature or has difficulties such as breathing problems, he may need to be cared for in a special care unit for a few days or weeks before he is ready to go home.

Many new mothers are keen to get home as soon as they can, but if you have the option to spend a few days in hospital, it's usually a good idea to do so. Not only will you have the opportunity to rest and recover but you will also have a team of midwives on hand to teach you how to feed and care for your baby, which is invaluable during the first few days.

Before you leave hospital, a midwife will check that you are feeling well and recovering from the birth, and your baby will be given a full examination (see pages 16–19). If you are breast-feeding, a midwife will make sure that your baby is latching on correctly. If you have had a home birth, your midwife or doctor will carry out these checks.

what happens next?

The day after you have been discharged from hospital you should be visited at home by a community midwife. She will weigh your baby, ensure feeding is well established, look out for common problems like jaundice, check that the umbilical stump is healing, take the 'heel prick' blood tests a few days after the birth (see page 19) and make sure that you are well, both physically and emotionally.

Some mothers are able to take their babies home within hours of birth.

Health professionals carry out routine checks at regular intervals throughout your baby's first year, although these are more frequent during the early months.

registering the birth

You will need to register your baby's birth as soon as possible. In the UK, you must do so within 6 weeks of the date he was born. This can be done at any register office, although the process will take a few days longer if you go to one in a different district to that in which your baby was born. If you were married at the time of the conception or birth, either parent can register the birth. If you were not married but would like the father's details to be entered in the register, you will have to sign the birth register together. When this is done, you will be given a free short birth certificate, which contains your baby's details. Once you have this, you will be entitled to the various monetary benefits available to parents of young children.

It is important to monitor your baby's growth and development in the days and weeks following the birth. In the UK, some time between 10 and 28 days after the birth a health visitor will take over your care. She will visit you at home, before arranging for you to take your baby to the baby clinic for future check-ups. You will be given a health record book for your baby, which will record his changing height, weight and head circumference, along with details of vaccinations and any concerns that you discuss with your doctor or health visitor.

It is perfectly normal for your baby to lose weight during the first few days after birth. As long as there are no problems with feeding, he should be back to his birth weight within a week to 10 days, and from then on should gain weight steadily.

adapting to life with your
new arrival

Nothing turns your life upside down as much as the arrival of a new baby, and the first few days can be a particularly anxious and difficult time. It's very common to feel that you don't know what you're doing or worry that you won't be a good parent, especially when you are given conflicting advice by well-meaning friends and relatives. Trust your instincts and try not to compare yourself to other mothers. No matter how confident they appear, they probably have exactly the same concerns as you.

Q **How soon can I take my baby outside?**

A Most newborns first experience the outside world on their way home from hospital, so there's no need to worry about taking your baby out too soon. The most important thing is to ensure that she is suitably dressed. Newborn babies cannot regulate their body temperature properly, so it's best to dress her in several layers, which you can add or remove as necessary. Use your common sense: if it's very warm or very cold, it's best not to stay outside for too long.

common concerns

Many new parents have never even held a newborn before, let alone changed a nappy, bathed a baby or soothed a crying one. Even these day-to-day tasks can seem difficult at first, but over the coming weeks and months you will discover what works best for you.

holding your baby

Although newborn babies seem very fragile, they are more robust than they look. As long as you are gentle, take care to support your baby's head and neck and avoid any sudden movements, you're unlikely to hurt or upset her accidentally. It's important to overcome your nerves and hold her confidently so that she feels safe and secure.

Holding your baby securely and with confidence encourages the bonding process to start. She will already recognize your voice and smell.

coping with crying

Crying is the only way that your baby can communicate her needs and feelings. She'll cry when she is:

- Hungry
- Tired
- Hot or cold
- Ready for a nappy change

– and sometimes for no reason at all. In time, you will learn to distinguish between cries and work out exactly what she's asking for. Until then, run through the list of her basic needs until you discover why she is upset.

mood swings

During the first few days of your baby's life, you are likely to feel very tired and uncomfortable after the birth. Many women also feel upset and tearful, which can add to the pressure. These mood swings are caused by the hormonal changes that occur after birth and are completely normal. Give yourself time to adjust and don't be afraid to ask for help and support if you need it.

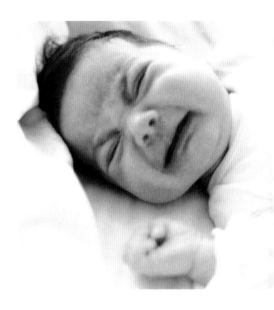

A baby cries for an average of 2 hours a day, every day, for the first 6 weeks.

coping with tiredness

Sleep deprivation is one of the most difficult aspects of being a new parent. In the early days, you will be getting up several times in the night to feed, change and settle your baby, and broken sleep can leave you feeling absolutely exhausted. At this stage, don't succumb to the pressure to 'get back to normal' straight away. If your partner is taking paternity leave, make the most of the opportunity to share responsibility for taking care of your baby, and don't refuse offers of help from family and friends.

If you are struggling with tiredness, these suggestions might help:

- Don't worry about keeping your house perfectly clean and tidy. Ask friends or family for help with the washing and ironing or, if you can afford it, hire a cleaner.
- Stay in bed after the early-morning feed. If your baby goes back to sleep, you can too.
- Resist the urge to 'get things done' when your baby naps. Instead, put your feet up and read a magazine, have a hot bath or catch up on some much-needed sleep.
- Eat a sensible, balanced diet. It's too soon to worry about losing the extra baby weight.
- Ask your partner to take your baby out in the pram so that you can have a short break.
- Get some fresh air. Taking a break from the chaos will help you to relax and clear your head.
- Dress your baby in sleepsuits at first. These are easy to change and will cut down on the washing and ironing.
- After 4 weeks, you could try to express milk so that your partner can take responsibility for one of the night feeds (see pages 192–193).

coping with visitors

Friends and family are usually very keen to visit as soon as possible after the birth of your baby. This can be exhausting, so it's best to limit visitors at first so that you and your partner have plenty of quiet time with your newborn. When you do have visitors, don't feel that you have to play the perfect hostess. They are coming to see you and your baby, not to have endless cups of tea and plates of biscuits. If they ask if you would like them to bring anything, be honest. Usually they will be only too happy to pick up some shopping on the way.

baby equipment

Most new parents can't wait to start shopping for their baby, but there is such a bewildering array of products available that it's often hard to know where to start. Nursery equipment can be very expensive, so don't feel pressurized into buying things you don't really need. If you can, ask other parents for advice before you buy so that you can avoid any potentially expensive mistakes.

Q **Is it cheaper if you buy reusable nappies?**

A You can save a great deal of money over the years if you use reusable nappies, although it does cost more at first, as you will need to buy 15–20 nappies. If you don't want to wash your own nappies, you can use a nappy-laundering service, which will deliver clean nappies to your door, but this won't work out much cheaper than using disposables. (See also page 137.)

essential equipment

Do your shopping for essential items several weeks before your baby is due. Once you have these, you can decide which other items you need when your baby arrives.

Car seat You will need this in order to transport your baby home from hospital by car. Some are available as part of a 'travel system' and clip straight on to the pram base.

Pram or pushchair This is likely to be your biggest investment, so make sure that it's the right size, shape and weight to suit your requirements. If you use the car a lot, buy one that is easy to fold. If you rely on public transport, opt for one that is light and easy to steer. The pram or pushchair should allow your baby to lie flat for the first 6 months. Some come with a detachable carrycot that can be converted into a pushchair later.

Nappies are essential, whether disposable or reusable, and you can make changing easier and more comfortable by using baby wipes, cotton wool and a barrier cream.

Cot Look for a cot that allows you to adjust the height of the mattress as your baby grows. A drop-side mechanism will also make it easier to lift him in and out. Alternatively, buy a cot-bed, which converts into a small bed as your child grows.

Mattress, sheets and blankets It's very important to choose a supportive mattress that fits snugly into the cot. Always buy new, to protect your baby from dust mites that might trigger allergies. You will also need several fitted sheets, flat sheets and cellular blankets.

Feeding equipment The equipment you will need depends on whether you plan to breast-feed or bottle-feed. If you are breast-feeding but plan to give your baby expressed milk from time to time, you will need a breast pump, bottles, teats and sterilizing equipment; if you are bottle-feeding, you will also need formula milk (see pages 192–193 and 196–199). Bibs and muslin squares are essential for mopping up, but there is no need to buy a high chair until your baby is around 6 months old.

Nappies and changing equipment You have a choice of disposable or reusable nappies, but it's best not to buy too many to begin with so that you can experiment with different brands and sizes when your baby is born. You will also need a changing mat, cotton wool, baby wipes and a barrier cream to help prevent and soothe nappy rash (see page 137).

Clothing At first, your baby will need only cotton vests and sleepsuits, socks or bootees, a hat and, if he's a winter baby, a warm all-in-one for going outside (see pages 154–155).

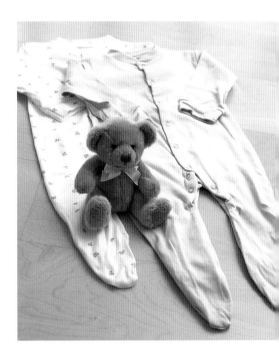

Most babies are adequately dressed in a sleepsuit for time spent in the home, both during the day and night.

non-essential equipment

If you have extra money to spend, there is plenty more useful equipment you can buy for your baby.

Baby bath Handy in the first few weeks, but a non-slip bathmat in your usual bath works just as well.

Changing table Does make it easier to change your baby's nappy, but it takes up a lot of room and is only safe to use until your baby learns to roll over.

Moses basket Can be convenient for the first few weeks as an alternative place for your baby to sleep, as it can be moved easily from room to room. If you have a pram that comes with a detachable carrycot, you can use this instead.

Baby sleeping bag Very useful if your baby tends to kick off his sheets and blankets.

Sling or papoose Handy for carrying your baby when it's not possible or convenient to use a pram.

Baby changing bag Some stylish changing bags are available with useful insulated pockets and fold-out changing mats.

Bouncy chair Great for keeping your baby occupied for a few minutes when you have things to do.

Baby monitor May be unnecessary at first if your baby sleeps in your room, but it is useful if and when he sleeps in his own room.

buying second-hand

You can find great bargains in charity shops, online auctions, car boot sales and classified advertisements. However, you should never buy a second-hand car seat unless you know the person selling it, as it may have been damaged in an accident. You should also check that second-hand prams and toys carry the relevant safety marks.

if your baby is premature

A premature or pre-term baby is one who is born before 37 weeks' gestation. There are different degrees of prematurity, and there's a big difference between a baby born at 24 weeks and one born at 36 weeks. Premature babies of whatever gestation are far more likely to survive today than in even the recent past, although some of them will have long-term problems.

reasons for premature birth

In one-third of cases, there appears to be no reason for premature birth. In the remaining cases, reasons include:

- Conditions such as pre-eclampsia (shortage of blood affecting both mother and baby, caused by a defect in the placenta), obstetric cholestasis (a liver disorder in the mother) or gestational diabetes.
- An infection of the bladder or of the vagina.
- Twins or other multiple pregnancies.
- An emergency, such as a heavy bleed or very high blood pressure.
- Previous surgery to the cervix.
- Lifestyle, including recreational drugs, smoking, poor diet and high caffeine intake.
- Concerns over the baby's growth, leading to induced labour.

your baby's appearance

Babies born at less than 28 weeks' gestation will look very fragile and their skin almost transparent, as they have so little fat. The older your baby's gestational age, the less fragile she will look, as she will be bigger and will have started to lay down some fat. Your baby's head won't be in proportion to her body and will seem relatively large. She will also appear quite hairy due to the soft down covering her skin. She won't have very much energy and will sleep for a lot of the time.

how you will feel

When your baby is taken away from you at birth and transferred to the special care baby unit, it can be a massive shock. Although you have been through labour or undergone a caesarean section, it may have come as a huge surprise due to the prematurity, and then suddenly you have no baby with you as 'proof' of what you have just been through. If you are unable to visit your baby immediately, it's important that you are given a photograph of her and are then taken to see her as soon as possible.

Understandably, many parents find it very difficult to see their babies in intensive care, particularly as they feel powerless to help them.

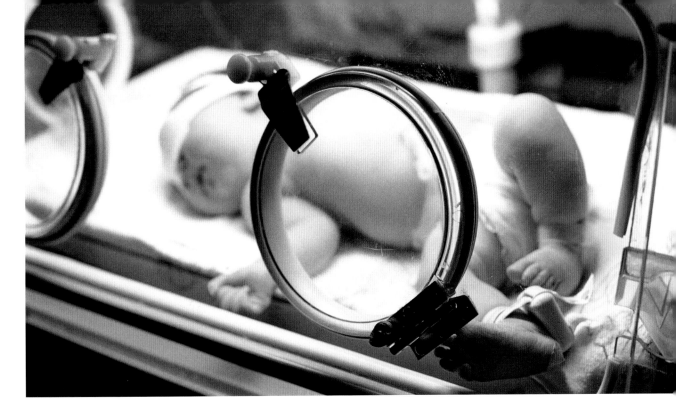

In the special care unit, it can feel as though the incubator is a barrier between you and your baby, but there will be 'portholes' in it through which you can stroke your baby. Once her health is stable, many units encourage 'kangaroo care' whereby even tiny babies spend periods of time against their mother's bare chest, tucked inside her clothing. Babies are known to thrive on this, listening to their mother's heartbeat and smelling her skin. Spending intimate time like this cuddling and talking to your baby, telling her how much she is loved, can also help with bonding, in an environment where it's easy to feel that you are just a visitor when others are looking after your baby. You should be encouraged to provide some of the care for your baby, including feeding, changing and washing. During this time, life outside the unit may seem unreal. You will probably become angry at other people carrying on with their everyday lives and feel intolerant of their problems. All this is absolutely normal when you have a tiny baby being cared for away from you.

In the beginning, the focus will be very much on your baby, especially her weight gain and feeding. Even once you have brought her home, you will probably feel anxious for a while. It can take time to gain confidence in providing care for your baby when there have been so many other 'experts' involved at the hospital. Once you know your baby is fine and the focus on her health is less intense, it is common to start feeling depressed or anxious, which is a reasonable reaction considering the events that have taken place. It's important to talk about how you feel with your partner or health professional. It's particularly worthwhile to talk to others who have had a similar experience, as it can be very reassuring to know that you are not alone. It's natural to feel guilt, anger and shock, and important that you are supported as you work through this period.

Physical contact with your baby is vital for both you and her at this time, so make the most of every opportunity.

development milestones

For a premature baby, when it comes to monitoring her progress there are two important dates: the day on which she was born, and the day on which she was due to be born. Don't expect her to catch up with other babies as soon as she leaves hospital. This will take time, but by the age of 3 years most infants born prematurely will have caught up with other children.

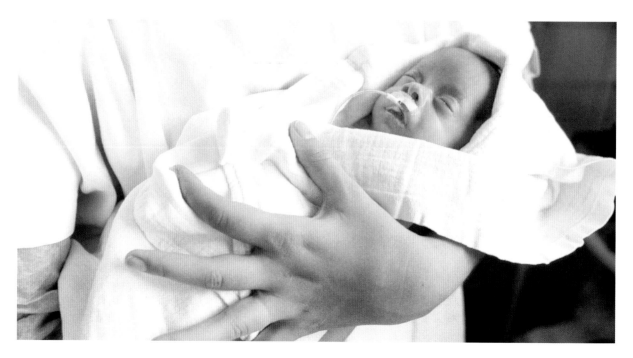

Having a baby prematurely does not make it impossible to breast-feed when you take your baby home, but breast-feeding may be harder to establish.

specialized equipment

The equipment on the special care unit might seem intimidating, but premature babies need help with warmth, feeding and breathing, and the beeping, flashing machines provide this. Ask what the various machines are for – they will seem far less scary once you understand what they do (see pages 32–33).

feeding your baby

The way your premature baby is fed will depend upon her size and gestation time.

intravenous Initially, a very tiny baby (23–28 weeks' gestation) who is too small or poorly to digest milk will have her requirements for calories and nutrition given intravenously (IV). However, you will still be encouraged to use a breast pump to stimulate the production of milk, ready for when she is able to be given this at a feed. Even if you did not intend to breast-feed, you will nevertheless be encouraged to do so with a premature baby due to the high volume of antibodies present in colostrum and breast milk, which will help to protect her from infections and illness.

tube feeding When very small babies start to feed, the milk is given via a naso-gastric tube – a fine plastic tube that is passed into the stomach via the nose. The milk is then inserted into the tube through a syringe. For tiny babies, a transpyloric tube is inserted through the stomach and into the small intestine, and small amounts of milk are passed through it continuously.

How long your baby is tube fed will depend upon her size and health. Some babies feed like this for only a matter of days, but for others it can be months. As your baby becomes stronger, you should be encouraged to hold her to your breast, letting her smell your skin, before her tube feed. She may try to lick at the milk, gradually learning how to feed at the breast. You might also be encouraged to give her a dummy when she is tube fed, so that she can develop the coordination of sucking and breathing while swallowing.

cup feeding As your baby gets stronger, some units will encourage cup feeding so that she has the opportunity to smell and taste the milk by 'lapping' it out of a tiny cup. Gradually she will take a bit more and you can try holding her against your skin as you offer her the cup. She might still need extra milk given via a tube, as she will probably only take tiny amounts from a cup to begin with. However, once she has worked out how to suck, swallow and breathe, she can be introduced to the breast or bottle.

health problems

A premature baby is more vulnerable to health problems – commonly infections and breathing difficulties, as her immune system is immature and the lungs are the last part of the body to develop. Some babies will need help with their breathing for just a few days, but for others it can be months. Antibiotics can clear most bacterial infections, but reducing the risk of these is important via thorough hand washing for anyone who comes into contact with your baby.

If your fragile newborn develops health problems, you will most likely feel extremely frightened to see her struggling to overcome them. You will need to feel that the staff to whom you have entrusted her care are approachable and will keep you up to date with any changes. You will probably find it helpful to have all the information on the various problems your baby may face, and the unit can usually supply this for you.

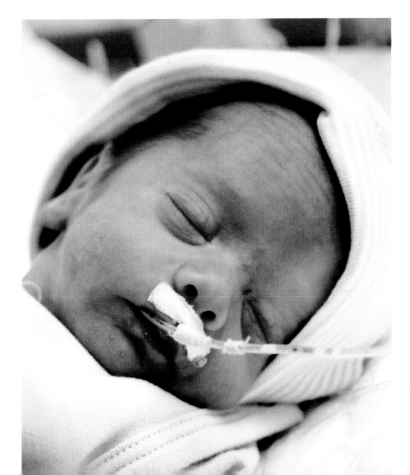

‘ When Rosie was on the special care unit, it felt as though I was having to share her with all the staff. It was wonderful to think that by breast-feeding I could provide something for her that nobody else could. ’

Debbie, mother of
Rosie (10 months, born at 30 weeks)

‘ It seemed so wrong going home at night – I felt as though the umbilical cord was still attached to Alfie and I didn't want to leave him. I spent hours sitting with him, talking to him and stroking him. He looked so tiny and vulnerable, like a baby bird, and I felt as though I needed to be there all the time, though of course I couldn't. ’

Ngaio, mother of
Alfie (3 months, born at 25 weeks)

shared
experiences

The special care unit works hard to prevent your baby's exposure to additional risks, such as infections, and will monitor her health very closely.

special care baby

Babies don't have to be premature to be transferred to the special care baby unit: other reasons include breathing difficulties, infection screening and various medical conditions. The unit will have a high ratio of specialized staff to babies so that close and appropriate care can be given.

Special care babies are well looked after in purpose-designed units, complete with all the latest technology.

equipment

Special care units look very high tech and can be a bit unnerving, with an array of monitors and machines that beep and flash every time a baby moves. Most of it is designed to help your baby with warmth, feeding and breathing, which is what you will have provided for him while he was in your womb.

incubator

This is a small plastic cot with a lid, which has a temperature control and keeps your baby warm. It can also control the humidity in the air around him, preventing his skin from becoming too dry. Most incubators have 'portholes' through which you can touch your baby. An open incubator has no lid or portholes.

vital signs monitors

There may be several of these monitors attached to your baby, each with a different function:
- Tiny sensor pads are placed on your baby's chest to monitor his breathing and heart rate. An alarm will sound if these readings move out of the normal range.
- A sensor is attached to your baby's foot or hand to monitor the level of oxygen in his blood. This can drop in a baby who is experiencing breathing difficulties.
- A machine will measure your baby's blood pressure via a tiny cuff on his arm.

phototherapy unit or bilibed

This type of incubator shines a bright light on to your baby in order to treat jaundice (see left).

IV line

This is a fine tube that is connected to a vein and provides your baby with fluid or medication. A fine tube can also be passed through your baby's umbilicus (navel) to provide him with nutrients, medication or fluid, or in order to take a blood sample.

why might my baby need special care?

There are several common reasons for a baby to be moved to the special care unit.

jaundice

The majority of newborns will develop some degree of jaundice, which causes a slight yellow tinge to the skin and eyes. Babies are born with an excess of red blood cells, which when broken down produce a pigment called bilirubin. A baby's immature liver cannot remove the bilirubin quickly, and the build-up causes a yellowish colour to develop under the skin.

In most cases jaundice does not cause a problem, but occasionally it can result in a baby becoming drowsy, which in turn causes feeding problems, and then the jaundice becomes worse. Severe jaundice can cause brain damage, so it's important that any incidence that is not within a normal range is treated. Where there are concerns, a blood test from your baby will monitor the levels of jaundice and if necessary he will be given phototherapy, in which bright lights are used to help break down the bilirubin. He can still be lifted out of the incubator for you to cuddle and feed him.

infections

Although premature babies are more prone to infections, any baby can be born with or develop one, and a series of investigations will be recommended if this is suspected. Tests can include taking samples of your baby's blood, urine and spinal fluid. Swabs may be taken from his umbilical cord and ears, and a chest X-ray might be needed. Infections can cause a baby to become ill very quickly, and it may be advised that your baby begins treatment with antibiotics even before an infection has been confirmed.

breathing problems

With some babies, it is obvious as soon as they are born that they have breathing difficulties, whereas others may develop them within the first few hours. A baby who has difficulties with breathing will usually need oxygen and it's important that the levels are measured carefully, as too much or too little can be dangerous. Equipment used to help your baby with breathing may include:

Ventilator This machine can take over the breathing in a baby who is very poorly, or where the lungs need time to mature. Depending on the problems your baby has, he may only need help from the ventilator for a day; less commonly, such help may extend for several months.

Continuous positive airway pressure (CPAP) A machine helps to keep your baby's lungs slightly inflated after each breath so that they do not collapse. This is beneficial for small or poorly babies, as they do not have to make quite so much effort to breathe.

Nasal cannula This is a flexible plastic tube inserted via the nose through which extra oxygen is passed into your baby's lungs.

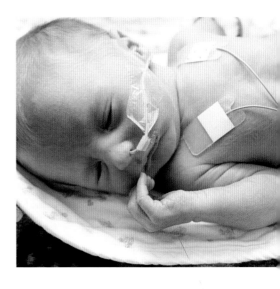

A number of babies that enter special care need to have their breathing monitored.

' Jordan was born with a heart defect that hadn't been picked up before the birth. Although he was on the special care unit for the first 2 days while the diagnosis was made, he was then moved to a specialist unit in another hospital. Luckily, I was able to go with him and stayed with him until he'd had surgery. I'd never even considered that there could be a problem with my baby, and in some ways I'm glad I hadn't known, as otherwise I would have spent the whole pregnancy worrying. '

Annie, mother of
Jordan (8 months)

shared experience

special needs

The majority of babies are healthy and born without problems, but some parents will discover that their child has a condition, disease or disability. This might mean that her life is significantly affected, which inevitably means that yours will be too, with frequent trips to the hospital and child-development centre. You will also naturally experience concerns for the future.

Awaiting the diagnosis of a specific condition can be as traumatic as having your suspicions confirmed.

attitudes

Friends and family may not know how to react when they first discover that your baby has a condition such as Down's syndrome or spina bifida, and can sometimes act inappropriately. It is inevitable that someone will say the wrong thing, but it won't be intentional — such remarks stem most often from ignorance or embarrassment. Be open about the condition your baby has, since people are often interested and want to know more but are afraid to ask.

diagnosis

Even if you decided to take up all the screening tests during your pregnancy, there is never a guarantee that your baby will be born without any problems. Some conditions, such as a cleft lip and palate, may be obvious at birth. Others, such as Down's syndrome, may be suspected but require confirmation with a chromosomal blood test. Still others are not suspected until a problem suddenly becomes apparent, such as a baby with a heart condition who starts to experience breathing difficulties after the birth.

All babies are checked initially at birth and then undergo a more thorough examination within a few days (see pages 16–19). If you have concerns about your baby's well-being or suspect that there might be a problem, let a member of staff know, as mothers' instincts are often correct. Any tests that need to be done to confirm a diagnosis will be acted upon quickly, as the staff will understand how upsetting and unsettling it is not to have a firm diagnosis when a specific condition is suspected. Your baby will probably need to be seen by more than one doctor, as the paediatrician will be called for an opinion. Sometimes a medical opinion is then requested from yet another doctor.

coming to terms

Even parents who were prepared for the diagnosis of a condition detected during pregnancy may wonder if it was wrong, and when their baby is born they will look for further confirmation. Some may feel prepared, while those who had no idea that there was a problem will need time to adjust to the shock. Many parents describe the emotions as similar to those following bereavement.

Once your baby's condition has been diagnosed, you will probably experience a rollercoaster of emotions, including:

Disbelief or denial when the diagnosis is first made. You may find yourself asking for a second opinion or believing that the situation will change and improve.

Anger that the problem wasn't picked up antenatally or that it has happened to your baby, aimed not only at others but also at yourself.

Guilt that there was something you did or didn't do during pregnancy that is to blame, even when doctors reassure you that this would not have made any difference. You might also feel guilt at how you felt initially on being told the news, or the way you feel now on seeing the disability your baby has.

Depression at what has happened, and a huge sense of loss that you do not have the baby you thought you had. She is still your baby, but a different one from the child you had imagined when you pictured the future with her.

Acceptance, which for a minority of parents may come almost immediately or, more usually, take months or even years.

support systems

Most parents of a child with special needs will require support, which can come in various forms. It might be from family and friends offering practical help, although the help that many parents find most useful is the opportunity to talk to others who have children with the same condition. Your midwife, doctor or social worker should be able to give you details of support groups and other organizations, and if there isn't one locally, then you may want to think about starting one. The internet can be a source of information, with forums set up for parents of children with special needs to 'chat', support each other and share information. Support groups aren't just a wonderful source of emotional support but also invaluable in gathering practical tips.

'I could see immediately that Max had Down's syndrome and although we had to wait for the result of blood tests we knew what the diagnosis would be. What really hurt was that lots of people didn't say 'congratulations' to me – they all looked really sorry for us and embarrassed. Yes, we were shocked, but he was still our son and we were proud of him.'

Ceri, mother of
Max (6 months)

shared experience

Parents of babies with special needs find there is a tremendous amount of support available to them, both from the medical profession and parents in similar situations.

coping with
twins

It probably seems a long time since you first discovered you were pregnant with twins and now finally they have arrived. Your feelings are probably pretty similar to how you reacted then: wonderful though it is, you might also be concerned about how you're going to cope with the practicalities of caring for two babies.

Q **My twins cry a lot and never feed at the same time. What am I doing wrong?**

A You're not doing anything wrong: life with twins will always be demanding, particularly when they are tiny. You could try creating a routine by waking one baby and trying to encourage them to feed together so that hopefully they'll sleep together too, gradually developing a pattern. If they are unsettled, try taking them out in the pram – often the motion, plus the stimulation of the change of temperature and different sounds outside, will make them sleepy. If your babies are crying and you need to 'escape', put them safely in their cot and walk away. Make yourself a warm drink and then go back to them. They won't come to any harm being left alone for 10 minutes, and it will give you a chance to recharge your batteries.

preparation

It is important to do the necessary groundwork during your pregnancy and set up as much support as possible in advance, ready for the time when you finally come home with your babies. Statistically, you are more likely to have a caesarean section with twins, so you need to consider that you may not be as mobile as you hoped after the birth and will be in some discomfort for a while. When people offer to help, it's usually because they genuinely want to. It can be difficult if you're not used to accepting support from others, but when you have two babies to look after – and perhaps a toddler or older child as well – you will probably appreciate anything that's offered.

sleeping arrangements

There is no evidence to suggest that it's any safer for your babies to sleep in separate cots, and during the early days and weeks they will often settle better cuddled up together, as they are already used to sharing a small space in the womb. The same guidelines apply as for any baby: details are provided on pages 168–169. Although it's usually not long before twins end up in their own cots, if yours do settle well together, there are some extra-wide cots available that are specifically designed for twins. For more information on twins' sleeping arrangements, see page 171.

It is safe, even practical, for twins to sleep in the same cot until about 3 months old.

out and about

Getting out and about with twins can involve some serious organization, but it's important that you gain the confidence to do this or the days can seem very long! There are lots of prams and pushchairs available for twins, some side by side and others tandem, and three-seaters for triplets. If you have a toddler, you might want to have a board on wheels that attaches to your buggy for your toddler to ride on. Getting in touch with your local twins club and asking other mothers which equipment they found most useful can be invaluable. Another option is to have one baby in a pushchair and the other in a sling. Don't be afraid to have a play with the various pieces of equipment in stores, checking how quickly each folds up, its weight and how well it manoeuvres through narrow spaces and up and down steps.

feeding twins

You are the only person who can decide on the right way to feed your twins. Some mothers find it easier to breast-feed exclusively, as although the onus is entirely on them to do the feeding, there are no bottles to make up, no sterilization of equipment and a lot less to carry on a day out! Alternatively, you might choose to mix breast and formula milk, alternating babies and feeds, and sharing the bottle-feeding with other willing helpers. Although at first breast-feeding twins to any degree might seem overwhelming, it won't be long before your babies

The extra organization required when taking twins out takes some adjusting to.

twin facts

- Fraternal twins (dizygotic) are the result of two eggs fertilized by two sperm, creating two completely separate embryos.
- Identical twins (monozygotic) are the result of one egg fertilized by one sperm. This then splits, and develops as two separate but identical embryos.
- The average twin pregnancy lasts about 37 weeks. The average twin weighs 2.5 kg (5½ lb) at birth.
- The average length of a triplet pregnancy is 34 weeks. The average triplet weighs 1.8 kg (4 lb) at birth.

Q I love my twins dearly, but there are times when I am completely overwhelmed by the amount of care involved – is this feeling normal?

A This is where other women who have had twins can be a great source of support, sharing practical tips but also reassuring you. Ask your midwife or health professional if they know of any other women in your area with twins whom you might be able to contact. It's also worth getting in touch with your local college to see if they offer placements for nursery assistants in their final year of study, who might be able to give you some extra help.

'The day my husband went back to work, it really dawned on me that I wasn't babysitting – these were my babies and I had to get on with it. Most days it was lunchtime by the time I got round to opening the curtains, and afternoon before I could even get showered and dressed.'

Maggie, mother of
Freya and Theo (12 weeks)

shared experience

Coping with twins is more challenging than having a single baby, and at times, the pressure may seem insurmountable.

start to go longer between feeds and eventually you'll find that a routine is evolving. It doesn't matter whether you feed both babies at the same time, or feed one baby on one breast and the other baby later on the other breast.

Initially, feeding your twins will probably be very demanding, regardless of the method you choose. Twins are often born at between 35 and 37 weeks' gestation and may be smaller than an average baby, so they will need to feed more frequently. Following the birth, if your babies are taken to the special care unit because of their early arrival, you may have to express breast milk until they become stronger and are able to feed at the breast. As your twins grow, there will still be challenges, but you will find a way through that suits both you and your babies.

'survival' strategies

- During your pregnancy, join the local twins club. If there isn't one, consider starting one yourself.
- If friends offer to help, you could ask them to cook a meal and bring it over.
- Consider paying for some extra help for the first couple of weeks, particularly if you have undergone a caesarean section and need time to recover.
- If you simply can't make it to the baby clinic, ask your health professional to come to you.
- Sleep when your babies sleep, as when they're awake you will have to be too.
- Keeping supplies of nappies and other changing equipment both upstairs and down is even more important when you have twins.
- Caring for and feeding twins can be demanding. Remember to take care of yourself, by eating and drinking regularly.

Even identical twins may develop very different personalities, interests and skills as they grow older.

identical or non-identical?

During your pregnancy you will have undergone a number of ultrasound scans, and often the sonographer will be able to identify how many amniotic sacs are present. If there is just one sac, then your twins are identical, but if there are two, they could be non-identical or identical! Non-identical twins have separate placentas, but then again so do around 30 per cent of identical twins.

Unfortunately, this information cannot always be determined accurately. However, after the birth your midwife will examine the placenta and sacs, although this still doesn't necessarily provide conclusive evidence. Of course, if your babies are opposite sexes, then they are definitely not identical! For an absolutely definitive result, some parents choose to have a DNA test after the twins have been born, which will usually involve a swab being taken from inside the mouth of each baby.

Q **Everyone refers to our babies as 'the twins'. How can I make sure that they develop as separate individuals?**

A Being aware of this is already a step towards doing something about it. If you refer to your babies by their names rather than as 'the twins', then others will too. You may prefer to dress your babies in different-coloured outfits and keep their clothing in separate drawers, rather than them sharing everything. It's also important to try to have some one-to-one time with each baby, and as they get older, you should encourage any individual interests they may have: don't assume that your children will share each other's hobbies, as if they are given an alternative they may choose it. At birthdays and celebrations, give them separate presents that reflect their own personalities and pastimes. However, despite your efforts to encourage their development as individuals, many twins share a genuinely close bond and often the same interests as well.

adopting a baby

As adoptive parents, you will have many of the same concerns as birth parents, and plenty more besides. The adoption process is usually far more uncertain and stressful than a typical pregnancy and birth, and there is every chance that you will have to wait much longer than 9 months before your baby arrives, whether you are adopting at home or overseas.

The adoption process can be lengthy and your baby may be several weeks old on arrival.

Q **Is it easier to adopt a baby from abroad?**

A Overseas adoption has received a great deal of attention in recent years, thanks to many high-profile celebrity adoptions. As a result, there is an increasing misconception that it is both easy and common. However, prospective parents wishing to adopt from overseas are required to go through the same rigorous assessment and approval process as if they were adopting within their own country. There are other issues to consider too. It is not always possible to get a full health history for an overseas child, so parents cannot always be sure what the future holds for their baby. There can also be issues surrounding adopting a child away from her country, culture and extended family. Consequently, it is far from being the easy option.

preparing for your new baby

Whether you are adopting a newborn or an older baby, it is important to spend this time preparing for your new arrival so that you have all the equipment you need and feel more confident about what to expect.

During pregnancy, most parents-to-be attend antenatal classes that teach them about giving birth and caring for their newborn baby. Just because you're not giving birth there is no need to miss out on parenting classes, which are very useful if you don't have much experience with babies and are worried that you won't know what to do when you bring yours home. You should be able to find suitable classes and workshops in your area that will teach you everything you need to know about caring for your baby. If not, try to spend time with friends or family who have young children, or offer to babysit for a few hours so that you can get some hands-on experience. You may also find it helpful to contact a support group for adoptive parents so that you can discuss your concerns and prepare yourself for what is to come.

There is a good chance that you won't bring your baby home until she is several weeks or months old. It is therefore advisable to read up on her stage of development so that you know exactly what to expect from her and what type of clothing and equipment you will need to buy before she arrives.

bringing your baby home

No matter how eagerly you have been awaiting your baby's arrival, when the big day finally comes it can be a shock to realize that you are now a parent. However, it's important to remember that most birth parents feel exactly the same way. Becoming a parent is a life-changing experience and takes some getting used to.

Many employers now offer adoptive parents the same benefits as birth parents, so you may find that you and your partner are entitled to maternity and/or paternity leave. If so, take advantage of the opportunity to spend as much time with your baby as you can. Bonding occurs as you and your child get to know each other, so keep her close to you, build daily routines, pay close attention to her needs and learn how to soothe and comfort her.

When you are finally able to bring your baby home, most adoptive parents can't wait to show her off to friends and family, but you shouldn't assume that your baby feels the same way. Introducing her to too many new people can be rather overwhelming and upsetting, especially if she hasn't yet had time to adapt to the change in her environment. It is best to keep things calm and quiet for the first few days, until you have had time to get used to each other as a family.

Finally, but most importantly, be sure to refer to your child as 'my baby' and to her 'birth parents' not her 'real parents'. From now on, you and your partner are your baby's parents, and you should make that clear not only to yourself but also to friends and family. It won't take long to bond with each other, and you will soon feel like a proper family.

Q **Is it possible to breast-feed an adopted baby?**

A Perhaps surprisingly, some adoptive mothers are capable of breast-feeding their babies. However, it is only possible if you are adopting a newborn who isn't yet used to bottle-feeding. If you know in advance when your baby will arrive, you can begin stimulating your milk production by using a breast pump for a few weeks beforehand. Your doctor may also prescribe an oxytocin nasal spray, which may stimulate your body to produce prolactin, the hormone essential for milk production. It's important to be realistic and understand that you may not be able to produce milk. Even if you do, you may not produce enough to feed your baby exclusively. In this case, you will need to top her up with formula.

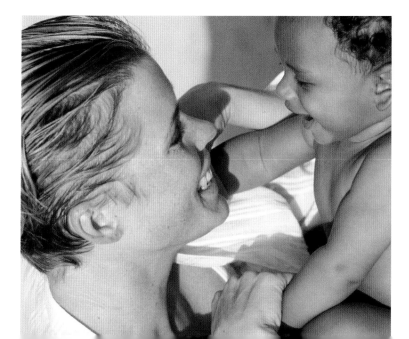

The bonding process is just as important with an adopted baby as with an infant of your own.

introducing a baby to
siblings

Many children are delighted at the thought of having a new baby brother or sister, but once they come face to face with the new arrival, they may become jealous and resentful. Others adjust perfectly well, but it's wise to remember that the transition from only child to older child can be particularly difficult, and sibling rivalry can raise an entirely new set of challenges.

handling the first meeting

Unless you have had a home birth, your child is likely to meet his new sibling for the first time in hospital. If you have to stay in for several days, this could be the first time that you have been apart for more than a few hours, which can be stressful for you both. Do everything you can to prepare him for this, and be sure to make a big fuss of him when he comes to visit. Introduce the new baby by name, if you have chosen one, point out any resemblances between them and take photographs of them together. But don't be disappointed if he seems angry, upset or uninterested – all these are perfectly normal reactions.

bringing your baby home

No matter how tired and busy you are in the early days and weeks, it's important to make sure that your firstborn doesn't feel left out or excluded. Remember, he's had your undivided attention until now, so you will need to make him feel secure and loved.

Many siblings are thrilled to meet a new member of the family and embrace the idea of being the older child.

When the time comes to bring your baby home, it is helpful to involve your child in the preparations. If you're up to it, a small 'birthday' party complete with cakes and decorations can help to increase his sense of excitement. Before the birth, take him shopping to choose a small present for the new baby, and have a surprise gift ready to give to him 'from the baby', as this can often help to break the ice.

It's a good idea to involve your toddler in your baby's care as much as possible, and give him lots of praise and encouragement whenever he tries to help. At this stage, it would be unwise to leave him alone with the baby in case he accidentally hurts her, or deliberately lashes out. But try to come up with ways he can help when you're feeding, changing or bathing the baby, as this should help to prevent him feeling excluded.

You are likely to have lots of visitors in the first few days, but ask them to give your older child lots of attention too. You could also take advantage of visits from close friends and family to spend some time alone with him. It's a good plan to do this daily, perhaps when your baby is sleeping, but you could also ask grandparents to take your new baby for a walk while you read a book or play games with your toddler. Spending time alone together will help to reassure him that he is still very important to you.

coping with two or more children

Initially, your older child (or children) may be unsettled by the new arrival. Her frequent crying may disturb his sleep, and he may struggle to cope with the new demands on your time. Try to keep his routine the same as it was before, and make any major changes before the baby is born. For example, if you plan to move your older child from his cot to a bed, do it during the second half of your pregnancy. If he is ready to be potty trained, aim to accomplish this during your pregnancy so that you don't have to worry about it after the baby is born, when you will be busy with other things.

You may also find that it helps to establish a routine with your new baby as soon as possible, to enable you to manage your time more effectively. At first this will be dictated by regular feeds and naps, but by the time your baby is 6 months old, you should be able to synchronize mealtimes, naps, baths and bedtimes with your older child, which will give you some much-needed time to yourself, particularly in the evenings.

As your children grow, they will inevitably begin to squabble and you will have to act as referee. This often begins when your baby starts crawling or walking and is suddenly able to make a grab for your older child's toys. Minimize problems by making sure your baby is not allowed free access to these, particularly as some may not be safe for younger children to play with. Although you will have your hands full if you have a small age gap between your children, remind yourself that life will become easier when they are able to entertain each other.

Older children revel in showing younger siblings how a favourite toy works.

Q **What is the best age gap between siblings?**

A Generally speaking, the smaller the gap between your children, the more tiring it will be for you at first. On the other hand, a gap of three or more years means that you will have to get used to sleepless nights and dirty nappies all over again. Some parents prefer this, as it gives them more time to spend exclusively with each child, but others like to get this stage over with 'all in one go'. However, unplanned pregnancies or fertility issues mean that some couples do not have the luxury of choice.

chapter 2

you and your changing baby

Your baby's first year is just that – a year of 'firsts':
the first smile, sitting for the first time, first foods,
first words, even first steps. You will find the rate of
change phenomenal, reaching all aspects of your
baby's development, from movement and hand–eye
coordination to language, emotions and social skills.
Your home life will change too, and you can expect
to face various challenges over the coming months,
such as getting back into shape, dealing with stress,
establishing a routine and returning to work.

your baby at
1 day

movement

- Your baby's arms and legs are a little shaky, especially when he cries or becomes distressed.
- He tends to keep his arms and legs bent and very close to his body, as he did in the womb.
- Sometimes he is settled in your arms, at other times he wriggles about.

hand–eye coordination

- Your baby is born with reflexes (automatic reactions) that help him explore.
- If you place your finger along the palm of his open hand, he immediately wraps his fingers around it.
- He may reach out towards you in an uncoordinated way during feeding.

learning

- Your newborn is an active thinker and explorer, although he spends most of his first day asleep.
- His vision is set to focus at around 25 cm (10 in) from his face, enabling him to look at you closely during feeding.

language

- Your newborn cries loudly when he is miserable or hungry.
- His hearing is finely tuned to pick up the sound frequencies of a human voice.
- He makes noises in his sleep, some so loud that he wakes himself up.

social and emotional development

- Your new baby has a basic emotional need to be loved and valued by you.
- Bonding – the formation of a strong, two-way emotional attachment – may or may not begin from the first moment you and he meet.
- He thrives on your attention and snuggles up close when held against your skin.

1 day

physical development

Height
Average length of a newborn is 50 cm (20 in).

Weight
Average weight of a newborn is between 2.812 kg (6 lb 3 oz) and 4.173 kg (9 lb 3 oz).

Head
Large in comparison to his height: about 25 per cent of his total length.

Hair
May have a good head of hair, or be completely bald. Might still have fine hair on his ears, shoulders and back, which rubs off naturally in a few days.

Skin
May be born with vernix, a white coating on his skin that wipes off easily. His skin might also be dry and peeling at first, especially on his hands and feet.

Eyes
May be puffy from the pressure of birth. Nearly always blue-grey, your newborn's eyes don't focus well and he may appear a bit cross-eyed.

Hands
Probably holds his hands tightly closed in a fist, although you can gently prise them open.

Legs
Legs and feet appear skinny and slightly curved, with toes turned in, due to your baby's body position in the womb.

Back
Needs you to support his neck, head and back when you hold him upright, as he has no significant back strength.

your baby at
0–6 weeks

These first few weeks see an amazing transformation in your baby. With every passing day she seems so much more alert and curious about what goes on around her. She puts on weight as well: in the first month, probably around 453–907 g (1–2 lb), although this varies from baby to baby depending on feeding patterns and initial birth size.

Q **Will I hurt my baby's legs by bending and stretching them?**

A As long as you do this gently, without causing any discomfort, her leg muscles will probably benefit from this exercise. However, don't force her legs to move if you detect resistance. Be very gentle so that she thinks this is good fun.

Your newborn will enjoy having lots of close cuddles with you.

growth and appearance

Your baby may look as if she has done a few rounds in a boxing ring when she first arrives, but she will still seem beautiful to you! In the first few days of life, your baby loses up to 10 per cent of her birth weight – this is perfectly normal. But in the subsequent weeks, she gets back to her original weight and then starts to make gains. After a few weeks, she typically puts on 30 g (1 oz) every day. Boys grow by about 2.5 cm (1 in) in length and girls 5 cm (2 in) in total. There is often a growth spurt during the third week, so you may notice that your baby eats much more than usual.

You probably won't notice, but your baby's head circumference increases by about 2.5 cm (1 in). The odd shape her head may have been following the delivery now smoothes out, and by 4 weeks it looks rounder. If she did have hair at birth, it starts to fall out by the end of the first month. The little 'milk spots' that may have been present at birth vanish within a few weeks (see page 15).

A facial rash often appears towards the end of the third or fourth week, and your baby's skin may appear mottled or blotchy at times until her circulation matures. If she was born with fine body hair (lanugo) on her back and shoulders, this usually wears away by 1 month, through normal friction of her body against her clothes.

movement

Every baby is different in her rate of development, but in general your baby's control over her body movements follows two directions:
From the head down She establishes control at the top of her body before lower down. For example, she holds her head up independently before her spine is strong enough for her to sit up on her own, and she sits upright long before she can take steps on her own.
From the chest out Your baby gains control over the middle of her body before the extremities (her hands and feet). For example, she raises her chest off the floor before she can reach out accurately with her hands, and she picks up something with her fingers before she can kick a ball with her toes.

Scientific research suggests that these two directions in movement development match the sequence of development in your baby's brain. In other words, the part of the brain that is responsible for her head and chest control grows faster than the part of the brain that is in charge of her arm and leg movements.

hand—eye coordination

You will probably notice that your baby stares deep into your eyes during feeding – whether she is breast- or bottle-fed – almost as if she is reading the expression on your face. At times, she may even appear to try to reach out and touch your face. She is also interested in other people's faces, but she can distinguish you from all the others. Already you have become a hugely important part of her life.

Your 1-month-old peers closely at any large object in her sight line; she might even try to turn her head sideways to look at something that attracts her attention, although this is very challenging for her. Her eye muscles are still developing, which might give the impression that her eye movements are random rather than controlled. If you bring a new object to her, she stops what she is doing in order to stare at it.

Much of your baby's hand movement is still dominated by her basic grasp reflex, so she instinctively locks her fingers around anything that touches her palm. This is an unintentional act, however, as are many of her hand movements at this time. The earlier jerkiness of her arms and legs has settled, but when she is upset about something, she pulls them tightly to her body.

A newborn baby does not focus well in the first few weeks, but will be able to distinguish simple shapes and colours.

toys

Brightly coloured, musical or noisy toys are best for your baby during this period. She finds it easier to distinguish primary colours (red, yellow, blue) than combined colours (purple, green, orange). She is also drawn to contrasts, such as between black and white. The sights and sounds of rattles are particularly good for grabbing her interest.

sleep facts

- Your firstborn child is more likely than your other children to have sleep difficulties.
- During sleep, your baby's pupils contract, she breathes less air, her heartbeat slows and she produces urine at a slower rate.
- Your baby needs sleep: if she doesn't sleep well, she eventually becomes irritable and loses interest in feeding and playing.

A newborn baby will sleep for the majority of the day (and night) – as much as 18 hours in some cases.

learning

Your baby takes in a lot from all that goes on around her. By peering closely at things, she is able to gain a better understanding of her world. That's why she gives so much attention to the mobile hanging above her cot, just out of her reach but close enough for her to see all the shapes dangling from it.

It's strange to think that your baby is such a sophisticated learner that she can differentiate between colours, but she can. Experiments have found that when a young baby is shown different colours one at a time, she stares for longer at blue and green objects than she does at red ones. Colour preference is present early on, and that's why brightly coloured toys are so useful for this age group.

Your baby's memory isn't just for things that she sees. For example, she also remembers sounds, which explains why she becomes more animated when she hears you speak her name gently. There is also clear evidence that a young baby can distinguish the smell of her mother's milk from the smell of someone else's.

language

By the end of your baby's first 6 weeks, she uses a wider range of cries than before, not just when she is hungry or tired but also when she is bored or just wants some attention. Her facial expressions also convey more meaning: she makes a different face when she tastes sweet, sour and bitter flavours, so she can tell the difference. In addition, her

You will soon tune in to your baby's different facial expressions.

shape discrimination

The length of time for which your baby stares at different shapes confirms that she can discriminate between a circle, a triangle, a cross and a square. Psychologists don't know for sure what she actually sees when looking at them, but she is definitely able to differentiate between those shapes.

expressions are the same as those you probably make in response to these tastes – for example, she smiles at sweet and grimaces at sour.

It's likely that your reassuring words have a calming effect on your baby when she is upset. She has already begun to understand the emotional impact that speech and language can have. Likewise, she makes more sounds herself, not only when she is upset but also when she is happy.

Talking to your baby is important, even though she can't talk back to you. Your use of language is good for her. Because she thinks you are terrific and is fascinated by everything you do, she listens to the wide range of different sounds you produce, and through this she starts to distinguish one from another. Eventually she will begin to imitate them herself.

social and emotional development

You are able to read your baby's facial expressions and body language well enough now to know that she enjoys a good cuddle from you. She snuggles up tight and you can tell that she enjoys the close, loving physical contact. You begin to tune in to her temperament so that you know what pleases her and what upsets her, and how she responds to handling. Her mood is influenced by yours – if you are tense, she is tense too.

Your baby spends a lot of time asleep, on average around 16 hours a day. As this doesn't happen in one chunk, you'll see her drift in and out of naps frequently throughout the day. Try to encourage her early on to learn that night-time is when she should be having her longest period of sleep.

Your baby's cries tell you a lot about her emotional state. You may have started to differentiate between her basic cries and be able to know, for instance, when she cries from hunger, from boredom or from pain. The more you are able to soothe her when she is upset, the safer she feels with you.

Q **When can I expect my baby to show her first smile?**

A A baby's first real smile does not usually appear until around 6 weeks. While many parents are convinced that their baby smiles at a much younger age, these facial expressions are more to do with wind or other physical causes. In a real smile, your baby uses her whole face, not just her mouth.

recovering
from the birth

As well as recovering physically from the birth of your baby, you will need to heal emotionally and adjust to your new role as a parent. If you had a difficult labour, the recovery process may take longer than anticipated, but even a straightforward delivery warrants rest, recuperation and tender loving care – although your demanding newborn may have other ideas!

Q It's a week since I gave birth, but I still feel exhausted, achy and rarely manage to dress before lunch. Is this normal?

A Absolutely! Recovery is a huge challenge because you're also caring for a demanding newborn. Try taking time out to aid your recovery – a relaxing bath, a massage or even an hour watching television will help immensely. Meeting other mothers can also be a pick-me-up.

Support from your partner is invaluable during the first few weeks after the birth.

immediately after the birth

Mild, irregular contractions, known as after-pains, continue sporadically as your womb starts to shrink. After-pains may occur when you breast-feed and may continue, on and off, for the 4–6 weeks it takes for your womb to return to its pre-pregnancy size. You'll also experience lochia (postnatal bleeding), which is a normal loss of pregnancy tissue and blood cells. In addition, you might have haemorrhoids (piles) to contend with. Most new mothers dread their first visit to the toilet, but it's not usually as bad as expected!

Following a vaginal birth, you may experience pelvic pain and your tailbone (coccyx) might be bruised. Stitches are sore, but even without them your perineum and vagina may feel uncomfortable. If you have undergone a caesarean section, you may feel groggy and the incision site can be painful. However you delivered, you'll feel exhilarated yet exhausted, so take advantage of the help you are offered and rest as much as you can.

the first few days

During pregnancy, oestrogen and progesterone levels increase, but drop rapidly to non-pregnant levels in the first 24 hours following the birth. Just as small hormone changes affect your mood before a period, this huge shift can make you feel tired, weepy and depressed. These so-called 'baby blues' should pass after a few days.

Your breasts will feel hard and tender when your milk 'comes in', 48–72 hours after delivery, and minor aches and pains are usual as your body heals. Your pelvic floor stretches during pregnancy and temporary stress incontinence (leaking urine when you laugh, exercise, cough or sneeze) is common. Fatigue also affects new mothers, particularly as you are adjusting to night feeds. Prepare to perspire as you lose the excess fluid accumulated during pregnancy.

the long term

Some mothers feel relatively normal by the end of the first month, while for others it's a longer process. Baby weight is stubborn, stretch

Taking your new baby out for a walk will give you both a boost.

when to seek help

If you experience any of the following symptoms, consult your midwife or your doctor:

- Bleeding through more than one pad an hour or repeatedly passing blood clots.
- Increased pain, swelling, redness or drainage from your episiotomy or caesarean section incision.
- Excessive back pain.
- Nausea or vomiting.
- Smelly vaginal discharge.
- Passing blood or experiencing a burning sensation when you urinate.
- Increasing feeling of tenderness in your abdomen.
- Feeling depressed for over a week.

marks take some getting used to and you may need a new bra. Think of these changes positively: your body did an amazing job and you have the scars to prove it!

Emotionally, you might feel stressed and anxious, particularly if you had a traumatic delivery, and it's normal to feel overwhelmed by the responsibility of looking after your baby. Talk about your feelings and ask your healthcare team for support – it's worth reporting any persistent problems to your doctor. However long your recovery takes, be kind to yourself and ask those around you for their understanding.

getting better

- Go out as soon as you can – even pushing the pram to the local shops can make a difference.
- Boost your iron levels by eating leafy vegetables, eggs and red meat.
- Don't push yourself: family and friends will understand if you're not up to housework or entertaining.
- Ask for help and support. You can repay the favour later.
- Avoid strenuous exercise or heavy lifting, particularly if you have undergone a caesarean section. Even though newborns are tiny, take care when carrying a car seat or using a baby sling.
- Negotiate some time off 'baby duty', even if it's just to have a shower.

Q **My husband read that it's safe to have sex 4 weeks after having a baby – is he being overly optimistic?**

A After a straightforward birth or caesarean section, you can have sex whenever you feel physically and emotionally ready. If you had stitches or an episiotomy, wait until your wound has healed and the stitches have dissolved. Many women prefer to wait until they have had their 6-week check. Talk through reservations with your partner, and a lubricant helps with dryness or sensitivity.

your baby at 7–12 weeks

By now, you and your baby understand each other more. She still sleeps a lot, but the sleep periods are longer. Her head, neck and shoulder muscles begin to strengthen, allowing her to sit upright in your lap leaning against you, as she looks around the room. During this time, her personality begins to emerge as she starts to make her mark on the world.

she's a mover!

For safety reasons, keep a close eye on your baby when she is not in her cot. You'll be amazed at how she can inch her way from one position to another, despite her apparently poor coordination. The combination of her intense inquisitiveness and her determination to explore means that she somehow manages to shift position. From 8 weeks onwards, she may even start to try rolling from her front to her back.

growth and appearance

Your baby looks so much better than she did during the previous 6 weeks, when she was still recovering from the delivery. Her facial skin is smoother, and any earlier rash is likely to have disappeared. If her eyes were blue at birth, they are probably a different colour by the third month. It is possible she has very little head hair, even though she seemed to have plenty at birth.

Bearing in mind that there are variations in growth rates even at this age, by about 8 weeks a baby girl typically weighs around 4.8 kg (10½ lb) and is around 56.5 cm (22 in) long. Her head circumference is now 38.5 cm (15 in). A typical boy weighs around 5.2 kg (11½ lb), with a

It is a good idea to lie your baby on her tummy so that she is encouraged to use her neck muscles to lift her head.

length of around 58 cm (22¾ in) and a head circumference of approximately 39 cm (15½ in).

Your baby is generally more responsive to you as well as to sights and sounds, so she appears more alert and engaging. Her body movements are less jerky and erratic, and you can see that she is slowly gaining control. When people stare at or talk to her, she stares back at them for longer – this is her instinctive way of ensuring she gets the attention she needs.

movement

Your baby still has limited control over her arms and legs, but enough to move them in very general ways when she wants to. When your baby lies comfortably on her back in her cot, smile at her and make a noise to show that you are excited to see her. In response, she kicks her little arms and legs vigorously. You may notice that she kicks in a cycling-type motion, with one leg going up as the other comes down. Her muscles are still weak, so this is great exercise.

Your baby's natural curiosity about her surroundings makes her determined to see what is going on around her. Lying on her tummy, she might push hard and lift her head off the mattress for a few seconds. She is delighted with this achievement – the world looks so much more interesting from this angle! Even so, your infant cannot hold her head up when placed in the sitting position, as her neck and back muscles are not yet sufficiently developed to cope.

Some of the early movement reflexes (see pages 17–19) are not as strong as they were at birth. For instance, the stepping reflex – which has your baby making walking-like movements when the soles of her feet come into contact with a flat surface – has probably disappeared altogether.

hand–eye coordination

Hand control improves noticeably at this age. In the second month, your baby's fingers become more flexible and less tightly gripped. She peers with interest at them and might sometimes manage to put her hand in her mouth. Let her see you place a small object gently in the palm of her hand. Within a few seconds, her little fingers will close tightly around it and she may move her hand as if trying to bring the object to her face. She can't reach out accurately in front of her to an object that attracts her attention, as this is a complex skill, but she tries anyway. Brush a small toy against her hand and then place it a few centimetres from her – you'll see her little hand try to swipe it.

Moving objects grab your baby's attention as she is more alert and more able to focus; for instance, she stares intently at a person or an object close to her, and her eyes follow the person as they move around the room. She can maintain her gaze as long as the movement is not too fast. If she hears a noise, she stops what she is doing, pauses to orientate herself, turns her head to look at the source of the sound and then stares at it, as if waiting to see what happens next.

Your baby will wave and kick with her arms and legs, and may even grab her toes.

Q Why do my baby's leg and arm movements become more agitated when she is upset?

A This is her way of telling you that she's miserable. She can't express her distress through words, so she uses her arms and legs to let you know what she feels. Her tears, accompanied by rapid limb movement, give you an unmistakable message that she is unhappy.

Babies spend much of their day in their cots, so it makes sense to place a few toys within their view.

tracking objects

Your baby can now control her vision more accurately. Take a small cot toy and tie it to one end of a piece of string about 30 cm (12 in) long. Dangle this toy in front of your baby until her attention is attracted, then move it in a sweeping circular motion. Her eyes will stay with the toy as it travels on the circle.

learning

As you now know, your young baby still spends a great deal of her day feeding or sleeping – or crying! But don't let that fool you: there is a huge amount of learning going on. At this stage, she is desperate to acquire new skills and new information, which she soaks up from all around her. She stares at everything she sees, trying to understand it. Better still, she prefers hands-on experience because that's a more effective way for her to learn.

When you wash and change your baby, her eyes roam around, watching your hands, your face and indeed everything you do. She also pays close attention when you speak – she doesn't understand the words, but she gets something out of them.

Colour preference becomes more established, and even at this early age your baby enjoys looking at brightly coloured picture books. Choose sturdy ones made from cloth or card, as she will try to touch the pages of them.

language

Your baby now makes more than one distinctive vowel sound, such as 'ah-ah-ah' and 'ooh, ooh, ooh'. When you listen closely to her vocalizations – known as 'cooing' – you discover that they are not always the same: she makes at least two different sounds. Of course, these are not like words and they are meaningless, but their use reflects a significant change.

Her readiness for speech builds in other ways too. At 2 months, your baby reacts differently to different single consonant sounds. For instance, if the single sound 'p' is repeatedly pronounced to her and then the single sound 'b' is introduced, her heart rate alters at that point, indicating her awareness that there has been a change. And she can also spot the difference between vowel sounds, which can be harder to detect because vowels have greater similarity: for instance, the difference between 'a' and 'e' is not as marked as that between 't' and 'z'.

By now, you have a clearer idea of what your baby's different cries mean, even though they sound the same to a stranger. You just know, for example, when she cries from hunger and when she cries from pain. You might not be able to explain it in words, but you have learned to tell the difference over the last couple of months.

social and emotional development

You are now more tuned in to your baby's temperament and moods. You recognize when she is grumpy and just needs a cuddle to settle her down, or when she is unsettled and it is time for sleep. The more able you are to respond to her changing emotional needs throughout the day, the stronger your emotional connection becomes. Your baby loves it when you talk to her, so although you might feel foolish chatting to a 2-month-old who can't answer back, talk to her anyway.

You can also help her social development by letting other adults hold her. She is used to your handling, warmth and smell, and she likes that, but there is no harm in letting other caring relatives and friends give her a cuddle when they visit. This doesn't threaten the integrity of your attachment to her at all, and gets her used to being with other people from an early age, laying the foundation for future social relationships.

Q **If I go to my baby every time she starts to cry, am I encouraging her to be attention-seeking and spoilt?**

A The danger here is that if you leave your baby unattended at this age while she cries she may feel lonely, isolated and insecure. When she is a bit older, you might decide to wait a moment or two before responding in order to see if she can settle herself, but at this young age she cries because she needs you.

imitation

In one study, each young baby was shown the face of an adult with his mouth open, an adult with his tongue sticking out and an adult with his lower lip protruding. The researchers found that the babies very quickly imitated the adult facial expression, which suggests that they tried to interpret the other person's body language and make a sympathetic response of their own.

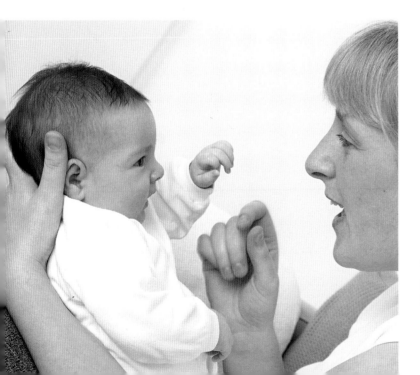

Your baby will watch your face intently as you make different sounds in order for her to try and copy you.

bonding with your baby

Bonding – the strong emotional tie that develops between a baby and his mother and father – is an essential part of parenting. Your baby needs to feel happy and secure, and it is your intense feelings of love and attachment that will motivate you to get out of bed in the middle of the night and change dirty nappies! Once you've bonded, you'll enjoy a love that will last a lifetime.

the mystery of bonding

Many people think bonding is a somewhat 'mysterious' process, but it's just about loving and caring for your baby. You'll know you are bonding when you understand some of his cries and instinctively feed, change, bath and soothe him before bed. There are many myths, but rest assured you don't have to give birth naturally, be a woman, breast-feed, become a stay-at-home mother or fall in love with your baby the second you see him in order to form a bond. Show him how much you care, in whatever way you can, and your bond will go from strength to strength.

natural bonding

For some mothers, bonding is completely natural and takes place immediately or within days of the birth. For others, it develops over time as they adjust to, and start enjoying, around-the-clock care. There are no set guidelines for how long bonding should take, but by showing your baby affection and attention you're on the right track. As your baby changes and grows, your love for him will evolve too. Some mothers don't realize they have bonded, so are surprised and delighted to find that a first smile or giggle fills them with love.

problem bonding

Many parents have mixed emotions following the birth of their baby, particularly if the labour was problematic. Mothers who deliver via caesarean section often say that the disappointment of not giving birth naturally leaves them feeling detached from their baby. Other bonding hiccups could occur if you or your baby spends time in a special care

The first feelings of love you have for your baby will continue to grow.

> 'I don't breast-feed Ophelia, but it doesn't make any difference to our bonding. I give her cuddles and kisses, and communicate how important and loved she is.'
>
> Nicola, mother of Ophelia (8 weeks)
>
> shared experience

unit, if you suffer postnatal depression or if your baby is adopted (see pages 32–33, 119 and 40–41). In these difficult circumstances, keep your feelings in check by talking to your partner, midwife or wider support network. Don't be hard on yourself – a bond may not form immediately, but this doesn't mean you are a bad parent or won't grow to love your baby in time.

encouraging bonding

There is plenty you can do to kick-start the bonding process:

- If you plan to breast-feed, start as soon as possible after the birth.
- Make eye contact with your baby and keep your face close to his so that he can get to know and respond to you.
- Babies love skin-to-skin contact, so leave room in your day for cuddles.
- Bathing (see pages 144–145), baby massage (see pages 158–163) or taking daytime naps together are lovely ways to establish a relationship.
- Your baby may not understand what you are saying just yet, but he loves the sound of your voice. It's never too early to read stories or sing songs.

partner bonding

Fathers need to bond too – which doesn't mean copying everything mothers do! Fathers develop a unique relationship with their babies and spending quality time alone will help them to establish it. Imitating facial gestures, walking with the sling, changing nappies and involvement with feeding are great ways for a father to bond. If you are breast-feeding, your partner can play a role by snuggling up to you or singing lullabies and telling stories while your baby nurses.

If only one partner bonds at first, don't let jealousy take over. Let them lead the way until the other's unique bond develops.

Q I felt depressed after the birth and the cloud hasn't lifted 2 months later. How can I bond when I feel so down?

A Although bonding is essential, your health is also of great importance. Talk to your health professional and doctor about your depression and ask what treatment is available. Family and friends can also offer valuable support. Don't pressure yourself to bond – spending as much time with your baby as you can manage will allow you to enjoy him as you recover.

your baby at
3 months

Many parents feel that this stage is a turning point – you and your baby have adopted a routine that suits you both. She is interested in everything around her and her personality is emerging strongly. As a result, you are able to predict the way she will react to, say, a visitor, game or routine experience. Compared to a new baby, your 3-month-old suddenly seems quite grown up.

growth and appearance

With improved head control, to the extent that she might be able to support her own head when sitting upright, your baby looks more alert and altogether more mature. You notice how curious she is, staring intently at everything that comes into her line of vision and trying to explore anything she gets her hands on.

Of course, she is bigger and taller (although she still drinks only formula or breast milk) – each month since birth she has gained around 0.5–1 kg (1–2 lb) in weight and her height has increased by about 2.5 cm (1 in). Regular checks at the health clinic will confirm that her growth rate is satisfactory.

Your baby's body language is much more expressive. Sometimes she stares so deep into your eyes that you wonder what it is she actually sees in you. Smiles are abundant – as are pouts and tears when she is unhappy. She reacts positively with her entire body when she is excited: hold her under the arms so that she faces you and she will wriggle her hands, arms and legs, and squeal with delight.

movement

Head control is now much better developed, enabling your baby to have a better view of her surroundings. When she lies face up on a comfortable blanket on the floor, hold her hands in yours as though you are about to pull her up and she will start to raise her head firmly in anticipation of being lifted by you, although it still falls back slightly so that it is not in line with her body. When held in a standing position, she begins to bear some of her own weight on her legs and feet.

As well as lying on her back, your baby likes to be placed face down on the mattress or a clean floor. From this position, her natural inquisitiveness makes her want to lift her head up. Her maturing neck muscles allow her to raise her head from the resting position to 45 degrees for more than 10 seconds at a time.

Your baby loves being held so that she sits upright. When left to her own devices, she spends a great deal of time attempting to move herself from a static position. Even with her as yet uncoordinated arm

From about 3 months, you can support your baby so that she can sit upright, to vary her positions.

Choose toys with soft, rounded forms to avoid your baby having a nasty shock when she puts them in her mouth.

choosing toys

Provide your baby with a variety of toys if possible. Although all rattles, for example, might seem the same to you, each one is special to her and she sees different qualities in each of them. Other suitable toys for this age group include a cot mobile, music box, cuddly toy, plastic grab-ring, picture book, pictures of faces and bath toys.

and leg movements, she can shift herself across the floor. You might even see the first signs of crawling, as she tries to pull a leg up towards her tummy.

hand–eye coordination

Your baby's hands now lie open so that she can touch and explore. She watches them intently and likes to put them in her mouth. Your baby's grasp is still involuntary, but she sometimes grasps things using her fist or both hands.

Being an active learner, your baby utilizes her ever-increasing reaching skills to search for toys that are close to her. Propped in a comfortable seat, with a small toy just out of her reach, she stretches out her hand in a somewhat hit-and-miss attempt to grasp it. When a small object such as a rattle is placed in her little hands, she can hold it for more than a couple of seconds.

Your baby loves a gentle tug-of-war over a toy – as long as she wins! Dangle, say, a child's plastic ring above her until she grabs hold of it firmly. Then softly pull at the other side, while smiling at her. Her grip strengthens so much that you can let the ring be rocked back and forwards in this mock tugging.

When given something to hold, your baby's natural tendency is now to put it straight into her mouth. This is why you need to choose her toys very carefully. Combined with her improved sight and her sharper hearing, she likes to use biting, sucking and licking as further methods of investigation.

Q **Should we choose patterned curtains and wallpaper for our baby's room?**

A Yes. You want your baby's bedroom to look attractive, and child-centred patterns (such as brightly coloured cartoon characters set against a white or light background) are great for your baby too. She spends a lot of time looking at her immediate environment, and attractive colours and patterns will encourage her interest.

eye to eye

Make lots of eye contact with your baby. She loves it when you look deep into her eyes, because attention builds her confidence and tells her that she matters to you. It also teaches her the essential social skill of looking other people in the eye when talking to them.

Interacting with your baby becomes more rewarding as she reacts positively to you.

Q Someone told me that watching television will discourage my 6-month-old from speaking. Is that correct?

A It is true that a baby who is left in front of the television for long periods instead of receiving stimulation from her parents may become bored, listless and less likely to vocalize. However, that's a very extreme state that you are unlikely to allow. Sporadic, short episodes of television watching can actually stimulate your baby's language development.

learning

Your baby now sees a link between her behaviour and a particular reaction. When she is lying on her back, grab her attention so that she watches you. Then gently place a clean tissue over her face but keep talking so that she knows you are still there. She will wriggle her body around until the tissue falls off.

Everything your baby sees and does develops her learning skills a little bit further. Playing and talking as you clean and change her, for instance, engages her curiosity. She watches the nappy appear and tries to work out how it arrived there; she feels the sensation of the cleaning cream on her bottom; she gasps in amazement at the way her clothes are put on her. There's so much for her to learn from life's daily routines.

Your baby's improved memory allows her to anticipate events. That's why her hands, arms and legs start to twitch excitedly when she sees you start to prepare her feed. She remembers what comes next and so becomes very animated at the start of the sequence. Similarly, her face lights up on hearing a familiar tune because she remembers from hearing just the first few bars that she likes it.

language

Your baby's listening skills have improved tremendously. Instead of just reacting in a startled fashion when she hears a loud noise, she now seeks out the source. She uses her limited head control to try to turn herself in the direction of the sound. She also goes very quiet when she hears a small noise, as she strains to work out what made it and where it came from.

Your baby now makes a wide range of sounds: these include gurgling noises, perhaps up to two or three different vowel sounds (some of which might be joined together), squealing and giggling, and crying. She really enjoys listening to music and songs, especially if you hold her facing you as you burst into song. These activities stimulate your baby's early enthusiasm for speech, despite her lack of language.

Your speech and hers begin to form a type of synchrony. When you talk to her, her spoken sounds may tail off in volume and intensity or stop altogether, and then start again when you are silent. This is a very early version of 'conversation' that includes the basic component of turn-taking. Your baby realizes that making noises like this is a way of engaging with each other, and as she loves your attention, this is a good incentive for her to develop her speech even further.

social and emotional development

Your baby's social awareness has increased and she smiles when she sees a familiar face, particularly if that person is also smiling. She is a lot more responsive to any adult who shows interest in her, and her need for human attention is obvious. She often cries when left alone, yet stops the moment you come over to see what is the matter. Suddenly she changes from tears to smiles, from sadness to pleasure, as her social and emotional needs are met by your company.

While scientific evidence proves that breast-feeding wins hands down when it comes to protecting your baby from infections during this early period, there is none to suggest that either breast- or bottle-feeding has any particular benefit in helping you and your baby to form a bond. The *style* of feeding does have an effect, however. For instance, if you are tense and hurried when feeding your baby, she'll be tense too; if you are irritable with her, she will sense this and have difficulty taking the feed.

Q **Is it good to let my baby use a dummy at this age?**

A Too much reliance on a dummy can discourage her from making vocalizations, and prevents her from experimenting with putting her hands in her mouth. However, a dummy can help to settle a distressed baby, as the sucking that it induces tends to relax her. More importantly, recent research, validated by The Foundation for the Study of Infant Deaths, has shown that giving a baby a dummy can reduce the risk of Sudden Infant Death Syndrome (cot death).

Your baby readily smiles now, whenever she sees you – and at anyone else who greets her with a smile.

establishing a routine

Well-meaning friends and family members will tell you how easy life will be once you get him into a routine. A routine has many benefits, but when and how you establish one is up to you. Some parents use tried-and-tested methods, others combine their own and their baby's preferences. A routine will provide confidence for the whole family – and, hopefully, a good night's sleep!

Q My partner and I live spontaneously and want our baby to be flexible. Will he be happy without a routine?

A Babies are individuals and yours might thrive on a flexible schedule. However, most babies need at least some sense of routine to make them feel secure, so you may need to compromise a little, tweaking your own lifestyle to accommodate feeding or bedtimes. Even if yours is a completely flexible baby, remember that you cannot avoid routine when he starts nursery and, eventually, school.

Most babies respond favourably to a routine and quickly become accustomed to eating, bathing and sleeping at the same times every day.

making a start

Establishing a routine involves encouraging your baby to eat and sleep at around the same time each day. Most parents concentrate on bedtime, particularly in the first 8 weeks, and then expand the routine to include feeds and daytime naps as their baby grows. Some babies fall into a routine of their own, but most need a little coaching, particularly if you want yours to fit in with your lifestyle. Babies who have a routine tend to feed, sleep and settle well, but this can take time to establish, so don't give up.

bedtime benefits

Introducing a calm and relaxing bedtime routine is a great way to get your baby ready for a restful sleep. Unlike feeding and napping schedules, you can use a bedtime routine any time from birth onwards.

- Aim to put your baby down at the same time each evening. You may need to change your own routine to accommodate this – eating dinner earlier or later, for example.
- A young baby should settle well in the evening after being fed, winded and soothed using quiet play, a bath (see pages 144–145) or baby massage (see pages 158–163).
- Always use a calm, quiet voice when telling bedtime stories.

Feeding on demand can work well for breast-feeding mothers and their babies.

demand versus schedule parenting

Today's parents increasingly turn to scheduled parenting to help them establish a routine. This method involves strict timetables, often from birth, to encourage a baby to sleep and eat well. While this is successful for some babies, it doesn't work for all and some mothers prefer to parent on demand, feeding their baby when he is hungry and putting him to sleep when he is tired. Neither method is right or wrong, but if scheduled parenting doesn't work out, don't think you are a failure – it simply doesn't suit everyone. You don't have to introduce a schedule from birth for it to work either, so it's not too late to change if demand parenting hasn't proved structured enough for you.

- Settling himself is a confidence skill that will eventually help your baby to sleep through the night. Try putting him in the cot while he's still awake, rather than rocking him to sleep or letting him drop off on the breast or bottle.

daytime schedules

Most new mothers feed on demand, but now your baby is over 8 weeks old he will eat at more regular intervals. The same goes for his daytime napping, which shifts as he sleeps for longer stretches at night. A daytime routine can be as structured as you want, but take into account your individual circumstances and remember that your baby is constantly changing and routines must adapt.

- A baby who sleeps for the majority of the day may not settle at night, so keep an eye on his napping habits and encourage him to spend time awake by playing gentle games, reading stories and getting out and about.
- An overtired baby also has trouble settling at night, so make sure he's getting enough sleep during the day.
- Spending routine times each day playing, reading, listening to music or cuddling will help your baby to settle into his new routine and prepare him for meals and naps. It will also help you to plan your day effectively.

However you decide to establish your routine, remember that what works for one family doesn't necessarily work for another, so while it's worth reading books and asking other mothers for tips, don't despair if your baby has other ideas.

'We struggled to establish a routine. I tried three different scheduled systems, but trying to stick to them caused added stress. After 6 weeks, Millie settled and I built on that. Writing down her feeding and nap times, to keep track of the routine she was settling herself into, worked really well.'

Rachel, mother of
Millie (12 weeks)

shared experience

what your baby can do
3 months

movement

- When held in a standing position, your baby is able to take some weight on her legs and feet.
- Lying face down, she can raise her head from the resting position for more than 10 seconds.
- Despite poor arm and leg coordination, she can wriggle across the floor.

hand—eye coordination

- With a toy just out of reach, your baby stretches her hand towards it.
- She holds on for a few seconds to a small object that is placed in her hand.
- She tries to put everything she gets hold of into her mouth – including her feet.

3 months

learning

- Your baby begins to understand cause and effect, and that she can make something happen by moving her arms or her legs.
- Improved memory means that once a familiar routine starts, she can anticipate what is going to happen next.
- She is fascinated by her hands and fingers, wiggling them about, fanning the air or even just chewing them.

language

- Your baby's sounds include gurgling, two or three different speech sounds, squealing and giggling, and crying.
- On hearing a small noise, she strains to work out where it came from.
- Your baby loves listening to you sing or recite a familiar nursery rhyme.

social and emotional development

- Your baby is a lot more responsive to any adult who pays her attention, especially if they smile.
- Her mood often relates to yours – if you are tense and angry, say, she is fractious and uncooperative.
- She can swing from happiness to distress – and back again – quite quickly.

physical development

Height
Average is 61 cm (24 in) for a boy, 59 cm (23¼ in) for a girl.

Weight
Average is 6 kg (13¼ lb) for a boy, 5.5 kg (12 lb) for a girl.

Head
Average circumference is 41.2 cm (16¼ in) for a boy, 39.8 cm (15½ in) for a girl.

Hair
If bald at birth, or early hair soon fell out, it will probably have started to grow back.

Teeth
First teeth may start to appear, although this usually begins at around 6 months.

Eyes
Focus is much better and more controlled. Your baby can track you moving around the room and is able to pay attention to a pea-sized object.

Hands
Can reach towards a small item close to her, grab it and then cling on tightly.

Legs
Leg muscles are stronger and limb movements more coordinated.

Back
Strength improves – your baby is able to hold her head up while sitting upright on your knee.

your baby at
4 months

With his straighter back and better head control, your baby looks far more alert. His head twists and turns all the time, as if he is afraid to miss anything! He is also much more responsive to you, giggling and chuckling when you cuddle or tickle him. Life is very interesting with a dynamic 4-month-old who can't get enough of whatever he's given. His routine may be beginning to match yours.

goodbye reflexes

Some of the reflexes that were present at birth fade and vanish altogether this month. For instance, the grasp reflex – which forced your infant to grab on tight to a finger placed in the palm of his hand – doesn't operate any more, allowing him to choose when to grip and when to release.

Your baby sets about exploring the texture, temperature and softness of a toy by putting it in his mouth.

growth and appearance

Sitting upright in a supported position, your baby surveys all around him. He is filling out and his body is more solid, giving him an altogether less fragile appearance. You'll see that he likes to have fun – for instance, he splashes his hands in the water when he has a bath, although he bursts out crying if the water unexpectedly lands in his eyes.

Your baby is probably around 63 cm (25 in) tall and weighs around 6.6 kg (14½ lb); for girls, these figures are 61.5 cm (24¼ in) and 6.2 kg (13½ lb). He's certainly getting bigger, heavier and more robust. His eyes have now reached their final colour.

Now that he can use his hands and arms more effectively, your baby's natural inquisitiveness comes to the fore. Exploration is the name of the game at this stage as he pulls, pushes, reaches and touches his way through his surroundings. He suddenly seems extremely active, even though he can't really get around yet. His facial expressions are more lively, his eyes have more sparkle and his laughter is more engaging.

movement

Although your baby's back muscles are starting to strengthen and his balance is improving, he is still unable to sit without support. But he will have fun sitting in a bouncy chair or baby seat, or propped up with cushions, as he really likes to look around.

His head control develops further too. You no longer have to support his head, and he can turn it to the side if something interesting attracts his attention or when he doesn't want to eat any more. You'll notice that if his head turns too quickly from one side to the other, it starts to wobble about.

Your baby is now able to lift up his head to 90 degrees when placed on his tummy – he might even be able to raise himself with his arms when he is in this position. When placed on the floor, he may be able to roll over from his front to his back, and possibly back again. When he lies on his back, if you pull him up by his arms he keeps his head in line with his body.

hand–eye coordination

Once he has a rattle in his hand, your baby waves it about vigorously without letting go, delighted with his own ability. He needs to be careful though: sometimes the toy flies out of his hand accidentally, striking him in the face! He is far more confident and accomplished at reaching for objects nearby and he uses both hands for this.

Your baby loves playing when he is in the bath, but he still needs very firm support, as he can easily slip. His hands go in and out of the water, playing with the bubbles, slapping the surface to make a small splash or just letting it trickle through his fingers. He also reaches for bath toys that are floating close to him.

Improved hand–eye coordination means that your baby can spot small objects that are near to him, fix them firmly in his line of vision and then deliberately and meticulously bring them straight to his mouth. With no sense of danger, he tries to swallow everything he can, and you need to make sure he cannot swallow small items – be on the lookout for potential hazards like that and keep them well away from him. Squeaky-squeezy soft toys are very popular because he is fascinated by the sounds he can get them to make just by using his fingers. This gives him an increased sense of control, which results in boosting his self-confidence.

You can play with your baby in the bath, as long as you keep a firm grip on him.

Q **Why does my baby put everything he touches into his mouth?**

A As far as your young baby is concerned, the world is a fascinating place and he wants to explore everything. Each new toy, each new household object, fills him with excitement. One of the best ways for him to discover the qualities of an item is by putting it in his mouth – this is his own way of learning.

Your baby has no idea that the baby he sees in the mirror is actually him.

Q **What sounds can I expect my baby to make at this age?**

A A month ago your baby could make a few vowel sounds, but now he starts to make consonant sounds as well. He may also be able to put these together in single combinations, such as 'ba', 'ga' and 'da'. He tends to repeat the same ones because he likes what he hears; this is also his way of practising his language skills.

notice me

Your baby tries to engage your attention whenever he can. Sometimes he uses sounds, in the way that someone might call for a waiter's attention in a restaurant. At other times he cries loudly so that you will notice him. More and more, however, he uses a smiling facial expression when he sees you – aside from expressing his genuine happiness at your arrival, he knows that you respond positively to this.

learning

Your baby's memory increases to the extent that he recalls how to play with a particular toy in a particular way. For instance, take an activity toy with several different moving parts and show him how to operate one of them. After letting him play with this for a couple of minutes, remove the toy for a few days. When you give him the toy again, he knows immediately what to do.

Mirrors start to fascinate your baby now, and he likes looking at his own reflection, even though he doesn't yet realize that it is his image in the glass. He also enjoys it when you put your face beside his and they both appear in the mirror. But it will be some time and quite a jump in his learning before he understands that the mirror reflects what is actually outside it.

Your baby is not only awake for longer during the day – he now sleeps for only 13 or 14 hours, most of which is at night – he is also more alert. He notices so much more, including the small details that used to slip by his attention. He looks closely at what you are wearing and stares unashamedly at anyone who comes near.

language

Your baby now becomes a more active participant when you talk to him – he even gives you the impression that he wants to join in the discussion, despite still only making random sounds that don't resemble clear words. That's why you should pause when talking to him, just as you do with an adult – you may be surprised when he starts to gabble at you the moment you pause in your speech.

Smiles and laughter play a larger part in your baby's life now. He chuckles gleefully at anything that amuses him. For instance, tickling him brings squeals of delight, and your smile receives a huge smile from him in return. He can't get enough of interactive games that make him laugh.

The range of sounds your baby makes becomes clearer. His babbling is more varied and distinct, and he makes both vowel and consonant sounds. Sometimes you think he might be trying to imitate the sounds in your speech and he probably is, because that's another way he naturally improves his language skills.

social and emotional development

You now understand your baby's personality much more clearly. He starts to show his likes and dislikes consistently – for instance, he has his favourite toys that he happily plays with to the exclusion of all others. There are some games you know he just doesn't like, while he will join in with others time after time. He cries when he realizes he can't get his own way.

Familiar faces create great excitement. You can tell by your baby's facial expression and arm and leg movements that he is delighted to see you walk through the door, and the same goes for any other familiar adult. But he has also reached the stage where the sight of an unfamiliar face – previously welcomed without complaint – can send him into a flood of tears. You can't predict which strangers will upset him, because sometimes he copes very well with unfamiliar people.

Your baby is now more able to relax and enjoy himself. Any activity that involves you giving him attention is easy for him to manage. Unexpected bouts of tears during familiar routines such as bathing are infrequent, because he knows what to expect and has more confidence in himself. His contented manner helps you to relax when you are together, heightening his enjoyment.

peek-a-boo

One of the most popular games for babies of this age is peek-a-boo. Let your baby see you hide your face behind your hands, and then suddenly pull them apart so that he sees the huge grin on your face. He knows you are there behind your hands, but he still moves back slightly when you appear, and then he bursts out laughing. If you do this too quickly, though, he may get a fright and start crying.

Peek-a-boo is a game you can play with your baby for months to come.

balancing relationships

Welcoming a baby into your home brings a time of change, as existing relationships adapt to suit your role as a parent. As well as altering the way you relate to your partner and close family members, becoming a parent also affects your interaction with colleagues, friends and the new people you will meet. You may well find that parenthood fills you with a newfound confidence.

Q **Having a baby has changed the way I feel about my husband – he just doesn't seem as important to me any more. Will I always feel this way?**

A You are going through a period of adjustment and it is unlikely to last forever. Invest some time in your relationship so that the way you feel now doesn't affect it in the long term. You've fallen in love with another person, but don't abandon your partner. Think about the chemistry you shared when you first met, appreciate how well he's doing in his role as a father and, when you gaze adoringly at your little bundle, remind yourself that she's here because you and your husband love each other.

baby love

Meeting your new baby was an exciting and wonderful time. At first, your relationship seemed one-sided: you gave her all your attention while she ate, slept and filled her nappies. Now she's growing, and when she smiles, babbles and prefers you above all others, you know your relationship is moving forward.

all change

Having a baby changes the relationship you have with your partner, but not necessarily for the worse. Pregnancy and birth can strengthen the bond between you, as can experiencing the journey of parenthood and loving your baby together. As your lifestyle adapts, your relationship shifts. The demands of a young baby can limit your quality time, and when you are alone you may be too tired to take full

Two become three: having a baby can enhance and strengthen your relationship.

advantage. Your partner may feel that the baby is monopolizing your attention and sleepless nights can also put a strain on your relationship, particularly as they continue into the third and fourth months. You won't be the first couple to argue over whose turn it is to feed or settle your baby in the early hours!

Although this is a stressful and sometimes testing time, there are strategies you can employ to keep your relationship healthy:

- Think about leaving your baby with family or a babysitter so that you can go out together (see pages 104–105).
- Reserve time on a regular basis just to chat. As well as discussing the wonderful things your baby is doing, it's also important to talk about other subjects so that babycare doesn't absorb your relationship.
- Don't struggle to cope alone: by letting your partner pitch in and solve problems, you will increase your respect for each other.
- Add spice to your sex life by making love in the afternoon, when your baby is napping. If she sleeps in your bedroom, turn another area of the house into a love-den!
- Avoid telling each other how to parent, instead praising each other's strengths and boosting confidence.
- Talk to each other. Don't let minor niggles become huge problems.

Find time for each other – remember that you're a couple, as well as parents.

sibling rivalry

Older children may be delighted or disgruntled about a new member of the family, but either way there are simple things you can do to foster their relationship. Involve them in preparations for the baby's arrival, encourage them to help with babycare and reassure them that you love them as much as ever, spending time together on a regular basis.

outside the home

It's healthy to get back in touch with colleagues and old friends following the birth of your baby, but many new mothers prefer the company of other parents who can offer practical help, moral support and advice, especially in the first few months. If they are occasionally competitive or patronizing, don't take it to heart. Some old friends may drift away after struggling to accept the changes in your social life, but friendships with people who already have children are often rekindled. You can use the internet as a lifeline by emailing colleagues, and join an online parents' community to build new relationships.

single success

If you're a single parent, the relationship you build with your baby may be closer and more intense than in a two-parent family. Finding the time to manage relationships with friends and extended family can be even more of a challenge than for mothers who have a partner on hand to help, but if anything, you need support and reassurance even more. Make sure you ask friends and family for help, join mother-and-baby groups to make new friends and visit online forums specifically for single parents where you can let off some steam.

‘ Before Faye was born I worried whether I'd love another child as much as Oliver – but the instant she arrived, it was the same. Oliver adores Faye and I love the way her birth has changed our relationship. We're both getting to know her and sharing the experience of having a new little person in our lives. ’

Clare, mother of
Oliver (2 years) and Faye (14 weeks)

shared experience

your baby at
5 months

Your baby's energy level now appears to soar. His continued physical development means he can control his arms and hands, legs and feet much better, and his learning skills are more advanced, so he is more adventurous. He has high expectations of himself, and if he can't achieve his target, he may become cross and frustrated.

safety first

You need to take account of your baby's increasing ability to move and explore places that previously were inaccessible. For instance, those dark little holes in the electric sockets fascinate him and he can't wait to stick a finger in them. Prevent this by blocking the sockets with plastic safety covers.

Although your baby cannot crawl yet, he has sufficient strength to stretch for a toy.

growth and appearance

Your baby smiles a lot more now, partly because he is genuinely pleased with everything that goes on around him and delighted when you are with him, but also because he has learned that smiling is a powerful tool for ensuring attention. One study found that the most frequent emotion conveyed non-verbally by babies aged 5 months is happiness. The next most frequent emotion is displeasure, and the next is interest.

Eye movements become part of your baby's body language repertoire, especially now that he has more control over them. You know exactly what he means when he grabs a toy and bangs it loudly against the side of his cot. He could just be playing, but his furrowed expression and fiery eyes let you know that on this occasion he is driven by temper not playfulness.

His height increases to 65 cm (25½ in) and weight to 7.3 kg (16 lb) – slightly shorter and lighter for a girl. He likes you to hold him under his arms so that he can take his weight on his feet.

nothing is safe

Your baby is uninhibited in the way he grasps everything within range. Your spectacles in particular provide a considerable source of interest, and he has them twisted in his hands before you realize this game is no longer funny. He does the same with any fragile jewellery, especially dangly earrings and necklaces.

Your baby will not be able to keep hold of his bottle without your support.

movement

With better back strength, the moment when your baby can sit on his own without support is fast approaching. But it's not here yet: as soon as you let him go, he starts to tilt slowly to the side – more quickly if he loses his concentration. Surrounded by cushions, your baby can play with his toys in a sitting position.

His stronger arms and legs mean that he has more power in his limb movements. When lying in his cot, he turns himself around and pushes his feet firmly against the sides. When you hold him upright with his feet touching the floor, he keeps his knees locked together – he doesn't understand that he needs to relax and bend them.

When lying on his tummy, your baby gathers all his strength and pushes up his chest, shoulders and head, taking his upper body weight on his hands. Once he's up there, his head bobs from side to side as he takes in his surroundings. When he tries to reach something, he manoeuvres his trunk and often ends up pivoting in a circle.

hand–eye coordination

Your baby's reaching skills become his main means of exploring during any activity, including feeding. He is more successful at grabbing things that interest him – he grasps the bottle while having his feed (but don't let go of it yourself). His grasp is more effective than previously because he uses his palm and outer three fingers. He reaches for everything in the bath, so you need to keep a very firm grip on him.

Visual searching and hand–eye coordination improve. Reach out to give your baby a small toy, then just as his hands touch the item, let it drop to the floor. Ask him, 'Where is the toy?' He will probably look down for it, and when he spots it, will stare and may try to reach for it.

Q **Why does my baby now keep his legs off the cot mattress whereas before he used to rest them on it?**

A This is just the effect of the growth in his leg muscles, and the fact that he is no longer as passive. Keeping his legs in the air like this is more comfortable for him, and he enjoys watching his toes and playing with them. Also, in that position his legs can move around more freely without bashing against anything.

A baby of this age will stare intently at a new toy, assessing its form.

Q **What educational toys should I choose for a baby of this age?**

A Although many toys are sold as 'educational', at this stage every toy is educational in that your baby learns from everything with which he plays. That's why the cardboard box which contained the expensive toy you bought for him may be of more interest to your child than the toy itself! Its bright colours, smooth surface and cardboard lid teach him about shape, texture, colour and movement.

learning

Your baby's increased confidence in his ability to explore makes him an active learner whenever he has the opportunity. If you place a wide array of small toys in front of him, he reaches for each of them in turn and plays with it until he loses interest and goes on to the next. He drops one object absent-mindedly when another attracts his interest.

Your baby's understanding of cause and effect has improved. He deliberately pushes a toy in a certain way because he knows what happens: pushing his feet against the building blocks on the floor causes them to move away from him.

Increased attention span and concentration allow your baby to play with the same toy for a few minutes before searching for something else. While playing in this way, he is often very quiet – he sees more details in toys when he stares at them, including colours, shapes and texture. His depth perception matures during this month, giving him a better sense of visual perspective.

language

Your baby's range of sounds increases, due partly to the development of the muscles and vocal chords associated with speech and partly to his general maturation. He uses perhaps three or four different babbling sounds – such as 'b', 'm' or 'w' – consistently, although not always in the same order. He may combine them to form longer strings, such as 'baba', sometimes with three or four syllables. He seems very pleased with these sounds, although on occasions he uses babbling just to get your attention.

Your baby may be sensitive to the sound of his own name. Talk to your friend while your baby sits comfortably, playing with a toy. When he's engrossed, insert his name into one of your sentences. Don't pause artificially or make a special emphasis when you say it. You may find he pauses, smiles and looks at you, although many infants don't fully recognize their name until some months later.

Your baby loves language games that combine words and movement. Reciting a poem that includes actions makes the experience much more vivid for him and heightens his awareness of movement as part of communication. A rhyme that ends up with a tickle delights your infant.

social and emotional development

Sleep comes more easily when your baby has his favourite cuddly toy beside him. An attachment to a comforter – whether a soft toy or blanket – may begin at this age. Snuggling up close to it at night seems to help him settle down to sleep. He might even reach for it during the day when he feels the need to relax.

Your baby begins to learn the social skill of reciprocation, if given a good example to copy. When he smiles at you or makes sounds to grab your attention, speak back to him, go over to him and play with him. Reciprocate his gestures: if he smiles, smile back, if he passes you a toy, pass him a toy, and so on. This reinforces his social skills.

Your baby is increasingly able to keep himself amused when he wakes up earlier than everyone else in the family. Instead of crying for attention or shouting loudly, he plays quietly with his toys in the cot. Make sure he has plenty available to him for first thing in the morning: if he is bored, he'll wake up everybody else.

Q **Is it true that baby boys tend to be more difficult to manage than girls?**

A There is very little evidence to support this idea. It all comes down to each child's individual personality and sociability. However, it is generally true that boys of this age tend to be more adventurous than girls. This could be because parents allow boys to behave in this way but discourage girls from displaying such high spirits, rather than being anything to do with differences between the genders themselves.

It is quite common for a baby to single out one toy above all others for comfort.

ask questions

You can encourage your baby's speech, language and thinking skills by posing questions to him. Of course, he can't give a coherent reply to the sorts of questions you ask, such as 'Do you feel more comfortable now that I've changed your nappy?' or 'Was that good fun, did you enjoy it?' Yet there is no harm in looking as though you expect him to answer you. Through this interaction, he learns about the significance of accent and tone.

relaxing
with your baby

If you've got a feisty 5-month-old, the idea of relaxing together may sound impossible, but now you are getting to know each other better, it's important to have some shared 'down time'. For some parents, relaxation with a baby comes easily, for others it takes a little practice and some inspirational ideas are needed. When you get there, relaxation is hugely beneficial to both of you.

Q Whenever my baby sleeps or my boyfriend looks after her, I'm cleaning, ironing or catching up on correspondence. How can I find time to relax?

A It's hard to find time for yourself when you have a baby, but unwinding is crucial to your health and well-being. Try relaxing with your baby, and when you're not on baby duty, prioritize your chores so that you have time left for you. Only iron clothes when they absolutely need it, tidy as you go so that cleaning doesn't mount up and keep in touch with friends by setting up a blog or emailing people in groups. If it's impossible to relax at home, organize some childcare and enjoy time out at a spa, shopping or the cinema.

relaxation and bonding

Relaxation time is perfect for bonding, as it's just about the two of you (or three if your partner can join in). You can enjoy skin-to-skin contact, tickle your baby and let her explore your face and fingers. It's a good time to use baby massage (see pages 158–63) and stimulate her senses with beautiful music, reading stories and gentle play. Even just lying together in a quiet room, sharing precious relaxation time, will strengthen your bond.

family time

If you have older children, relaxing in a busy and noisy home is a little more challenging. Involve older children in 'quiet time' by encouraging them to cuddle up with the baby while you sing or play games. They may enjoy reading a book to their little sibling or learning baby massage techniques. If you can't get older children to settle, take advantage of their nursery or nap time to relax with your baby.

It's important to rest on your own when your partner is around to care for the baby, but it's also a great idea to spend time relaxing together. It's lovely to hand your baby over whenever help is available, but occasionally sharing the experience of relaxation will help you to recharge your batteries and bond as a family.

Your baby can sense how you are feeling and will respond favourably if you take time to slow down and relax.

Make sure your baby spends time relaxing with siblings and other children.

right from the start

Life with a newborn is filled with so much worry that most parents find relaxing incredibly difficult. You are so busy trying to work out if she is the right temperature and breathing properly that it seems impossible to stop, even for a second. Relaxing with your baby is, however, a key factor in helping her to feel secure and comfortable. She's been learning to read your moods and emotions from the moment she was born, and watching you relax will show her how important quiet time is.

out and about

Learning to relax with your baby in social situations is important, particularly now she is getting older and you can travel more regularly:

- If you get flustered when your baby cries in public, carry her to a quiet place and attend to her in private.
- If you don't like other people holding her, be honest about your feelings – people do understand.
- If you're staying in a hotel or with friends or family, spend time alone when you arrive to acclimatize your baby to her new surroundings. Half an hour playing or resting on the bed will help you both to settle in.
- Carry a bag containing spare nappies, wipes and muslin, a change of clothes for both of you, essential medicines (such as baby paracetamol and travel-size nappy rash cream), a light blanket, bottles and milk, if you use them, and a snack or two for you, particularly if you are breast-feeding. Having these items to hand will help you to relax.

the keys to relaxation

Try these simple relaxation tips:

- Revisit the breathing exercises you used to keep calm during the early stages of labour.
- Reserve a space in your home – a sofa, spare bed or beanbags, for instance – for relaxation.
- Eliminate distractions by turning off the television, switching off your phone and turning off kitchen appliances.
- Don't feel pressured to use gimmicks such as relaxation tapes – your favourite CD, a comfortable spot and your baby's favourite toy are all you need.
- If your baby starts crying, carry her away from your relaxation area, meet her needs, calm her down and then try again.

'Lee is very curious and always wants to be on the move. I bought him a huge, soft play mat with mirrors, toys and rattles attached and he loves rolling around on it, exploring. I lie with him, catching up on my book. It helps us both to relax and has become a very special activity.'

Debbie, mother of
Lee (4 months)

shared experience

your baby at
6 months

Two major changes take place this month: first, your baby may manage to sit up on his own without support, which is a huge boost to his self-confidence; and second, he may start to master the early stages of crawling. Combined with his increased enthusiasm for communication, these surges in independence mean that life with him is hectic as he craves constant stimulation!

growth and appearance

Your baby now reaches double his birth weight, and it's hard to imagine he was so small and fragile only a few months ago. When you think back to his shaky, uncoordinated early arm and leg movements, you realize how much he has developed. Now, when you hold him under his arms with his feet touching the floor, he begins to make bouncing moves, bending his knees a little and then straightening them. Starting on solids at this age, he begins to fill out more.

Your baby may have a good head of hair by now, although there are plenty of bald infants aged 6 months. There is a good chance that you can see his first tooth, usually at the centre of his lower front gum, but this often doesn't make an appearance for another month.

movement

Your baby will now be able to support the weight of his torso on outstretched arms.

Your baby may be sitting comfortably without needing your support. He may even use his hands to balance himself in that position. Do

Many babies of this age are already able to sit unsupported and will enjoy the new perspective this brings.

Q Would a baby walker be good for my 6-month-old?

A He'd love one because he would be able to cruise easily all over the place. However, babycare professionals usually advise against them because they can impede the development of walking skills. Baby walkers develop the lower leg muscles, but the upper leg muscles weaken, and these are needed for walking. Baby walkers are also associated with a higher level of domestic accidents.

what you can to keep his toys close to him – if he has to over-reach, he loses his balance and falls over, which can dent his confidence. When held upright, he is much happier to take more responsibility for bearing his weight on his feet. He often makes little bounces up and down because he loves to see the world moving.

Your baby is much more mobile all round. For instance, when lying on the floor he can easily roll from his front to his back, and then from his back to his front – or he might just keep rolling in one direction until he reaches the other side of the room. He might even start to make serious efforts to crawl. When he is face down on the floor, watch him try to pull his knees towards his tummy with his arms stretched out in front – with enough determination, he slowly inches forward.

hand–eye coordination

Hand movements are less erratic than before and more coordinated. Whereas before your baby could only hold a toy in one hand at a time, there are probably moments when he holds one in each hand simultaneously and several seconds pass before he drops one. When a toy does slips from his grasp, he usually searches for it – it's certainly not a case of 'out of sight, out of mind' any more.

Your baby also makes deliberate one-handed movements. For example, he picks up an object, shakes it while peering closely, hits it against the wall or on the floor and then throws it away when he loses interest. All these hand–eye movements are intentional. He also tries to use his cupped hand in order to rake in small toys towards himself so that he can then lift them up.

Increasingly fascinated by his own body, your baby never tires of exploring all those little holes – don't be surprised to find his finger in his ear, up his nose, in his mouth... or elsewhere! Since he can reach his toes, he likes to play with them too. Sometimes he twists his body into strange positions as part of his manual explorations.

setting limits

Your baby is still quite young, but nevertheless you need to establish rules about touching. Decide what objects you don't want him to explore (for example, your china ornaments, electrical items, the fire) and tell him not to touch these. Of course, he forgets and touches them anyway, so you will need to keep reminding him.

television

Television can be a rich source of stimulation for your growing child, as long as you only let him watch educational programmes that are aimed specifically at his age group and television viewing is only one small part of his total daily activities. Use your judgement to decide which programmes are best for him and how much time he should spend watching them.

You can start to introduce more complex toys now, like stacking cups and rings.

Q **Why does my baby often startle when I appear in front of his cot, even though I have been speaking to him in the process of approaching him?**

A He relies on a number of cues to prepare for someone who is about to enter his line of vision: the sound of that person's footsteps and their voice are good indicators of an impending arrival. Perhaps your baby doesn't hear these sounds very clearly and hence his surprise when you appear in front of him. Arrange to have his hearing checked.

learning

Your baby is now more creative in his play so that he actually looks smarter. For instance, he bangs two small wooden blocks together or tries to hit the large, soft button on the cause–effect toy. It's almost as if he studies his toys, and then thinks about new ways he can play with them.

Since the ability to concentrate is fundamental to learning – even the brightest child won't learn unless he focuses long enough to absorb new information – it's good that your baby is now able to concentrate better. He is also able to search for objects that are not directly in front of him. Let him watch you put his teddy on a chair in another part of the room that he can see. Play with him for a few minutes, then ask, 'Where's teddy?' He will actively scan for the object.

Now when you give your baby a non-glass child-safe mirror, he explores the image more intensively. He tries to stare straight into it. Although he still doesn't fully understand that he is looking at himself, he has a sense that what he sees in the mirror is connected with him in some way. After peering at himself for long enough, he may give a big smile because he likes what he sees.

Your baby may already understand which objects you are referring to when you say the names of basic household items – you can tell because he looks at them when you say the words. He also follows your line of pointing so that he knows which item you are indicating, and he sometimes points himself.

language

Your baby loves listening to music and his arms and legs move excitedly when his favourite tune is played. Sometimes gentle soothing music can help him to fall asleep.

Although he is still babbling, you begin to get the impression that he is actually trying to take part in a conversation with you. It's as if there is some underlying meaning behind his babbling sounds. In particular, he is more tuned in to the social nature of language: he babbles, then pauses while you reply, then babbles. This pattern is similar to the turn-taking that takes place in a mature conversation.

The range of your baby's babbles has once again increased – he makes at least four or five different babbling sounds, such as 'aa', 'goo', 'da' and so on. They include vowels and consonants, and will be combined in strings of up to three or four syllables. When playing happily by himself, he uses contented gurgling noises more than coherent babbling sounds.

Your baby now begins to understand both the meaning of the word 'no' and the tone of voice that you use to accompany it. He doesn't like it when you block his wishes in this way, but he is aware of your intention. His growing understanding of context and the ways in which words are used, rather than just the meanings of the words themselves, signifies maturation in his language skills.

social and emotional development

Not only does your baby identify your voice instantly but his ability to differentiate it from others he hears talking at the same time also improves. This is one of the many signs that the emotional bond between you is intensifying.

As his ambition to explore and have bigger adventures increases around this time, so too does his frustration when things don't go according to plan. Instead of simply giving up at the first hurdle, your baby persists until he achieves his target – and if he doesn't make his goal, his temper may flare. He needs you to help him calm down.

If you haven't already introduced a bedtime routine, you'll find that at this age your baby definitely benefits from having a structured, consistent pre-sleeping pattern. For example, you might change him, bath him, dress him, cuddle him, read him a story and then sing a lullaby to him before he falls asleep. He very quickly gets used to the routine and starts to relax as soon as it starts, so that by the time he is in bed, he is ready to sleep (see pages 64–65).

pushchair games

Don't be surprised if your baby loves to throw toys out of his pushchair. However, resist the temptation to tie them on to a piece of ribbon. Although this would solve the problem of the toys falling to the ground, there is a danger that your baby could wrap the ribbon around his neck, so you would have to keep it shorter than 15 cm (6 in). A better idea is to give him back the toy a couple of times and then put it away in your pocket.

Your baby still does not recognize himself in a mirror, but may try to engage with the reflection that he sees.

getting back in shape

You were warned not to pack your pre-pregnancy jeans in your hospital bag, but nevertheless were probably not prepared for the reality of your post-baby body – even 6 months down the line. Although a lucky few new mothers spring back to their pre-pregnancy shape, the vast majority have to put in time and effort. Getting fit is a positive goal, and it's a journey you can share with your baby.

the feel-good factor

A healthy diet and exercise regime can make you feel positive. Physical activity alters your brain chemistry, leading to feelings of well-being. Exercise can also be an effective treatment for anxiety, easing the symptoms of postnatal depression.

your post-pregnancy body

During pregnancy, your body goes through its biggest change since puberty. You have gained weight, and following the birth your breasts may be bigger or smaller, your stomach loose and/or saggy, your feet bigger and your body shape different.

Many women are shocked to find that their body does not resemble its pre-pregnancy state, and partners, family, friends and media images can all add to the pressure. A pre-pregnancy figure is tough to achieve for most women, but breast-feeding and rushing around after your newborn will help, and with the right combination of diet, exercise and time, you can actually look and feel better than ever.

getting started

- However you delivered, walking and very gentle pelvic floor or abdominal exercises can help you to recover. Start when you feel ready and always talk to your doctor first if you have any questions or concerns.
- Following a caesarean section, you should allow a minimum of 6 weeks for your incision to heal before you begin an exercise programme. Even if you had a straightforward labour, it's advisable to wait until the gap in your abdominal muscles has closed, which again usually takes 6 weeks.
- Eat a balanced diet of vegetables, fruit, lean meats, wholegrains, eggs, low-fat dairy products and beans/pulses, avoiding sugary foods such as chocolate and pastries.

above Walking with a pram is a great way to get in shape if you're pushed for time.

right A healthy, balanced diet is essential, particularly for breast-feeding mothers.

Although gentle exercise is beneficial, you must not overdo it at this stage, particularly if you had a caesarean or a difficult birth.

- Don't attempt to lose weight yet, particularly if you are breast-feeding.
- Start slowly – 5 minutes a day can be beneficial at first. Your body is still recovering, so give yourself time.
- Walking is a great way to get in shape. If you're pushing a pushchair or wearing a sling, watch your posture so that you don't damage your back muscles within 6 months to 2 years of giving birth.
- Find out if your hospital runs postnatal exercise classes or check out the crèche facilities at your local leisure centre.
- Postnatal yoga and pilates classes can make perfect workouts.
- Be realistic. You might not run a marathon or squeeze back into your skinny jeans any time soon, but most women who exercise and eat well report getting back into shape within 6 months to 2 years of giving birth.

get physical

For the first 6 weeks, try these gentle exercises:

- Tone your pelvic floor by lying down, breathing in and, as you exhale, gently squeezing your pelvic floor, as though you're trying to stop urinating. Hold for 5 seconds and release slowly, breathing normally. When you can, increase the hold to 10 seconds. Start with four or five squeezes, gradually building up to ten.
- Tone your stomach muscles by pulling them in as you breathe out, then holding for a few seconds. Relax, and repeat as often as possible.

After 6 weeks, gradually build up to a simple workout:

- Lie on your back with your knees bent and feet flat. Contract your abdominal muscles and slowly slide your feet away, aiming to straighten both legs. When your back arches, stop and slide your feet back towards your bottom. Repeat ten times.
- Involve your baby by lying down as before and placing him on your tummy. Inhale and lift him up, squeezing your abdominals like a sponge. Exhale and lower your baby back down. Repeat as many times as you can, but be warned: he may not want you to stop!

If you feel uncomfortable or dizzy at any time, stop exercising and contact your doctor. Take extra care if you have a history of back, pelvic or abdominal problems.

'Breast-feeding has definitely helped me lose baby weight. I have a huge appetite but fill up on fruit and raw vegetables instead of cake and biscuits. It's hard to resist sugary food, especially when I'm tired, but the cupboard is always stocked up with healthy snacks.'

Mel, mother of
Jack (6 months)

shared experience

Q **I'm thinking about my next baby – when will my body be ready for another pregnancy?**

A Most medical studies indicate that the safest gap between pregnancies is 18–23 months, giving your body ample chance to recover. It's a personal decision and many women take the leap much sooner. Consider the physical, emotional and practical aspects, and be aware that if you had a caesarean section the first time, it's best to wait over a year.

what your baby can do
6 months

movement

- When held in a standing position, he bears some weight and bends his knees slightly to make the beginnings of bouncing movements.
- Lying on the floor, he rolls easily from his tummy on to his back, and back again.
- Lying face down, he pushes his head, neck, shoulders and chest firmly off the floor to look around.

hand—eye coordination

- Your baby holds one toy in each hand for a couple of seconds, before letting one drop.
- He tries to lift a small toy from the floor to look at it.
- He begins to use pointing, although you can't tell if he is asking for that item or just showing it to you.

6 months

learning

- Your baby's concentration improves and he is able to play with the same toy for several minutes.
- He is excited when he looks in a mirror, although he doesn't understand that he is looking at himself.
- He learns the names of some household objects.

language

- Your baby loves music, sometimes becoming excited, sometimes relaxing so much that he falls asleep.
- His range of babbling sounds increases to five, including vowels and consonants.
- He synchronizes his babbling with your speech, as if having a real conversation.

social and emotional development

- Your baby enjoys company, especially if he is the centre of attention.
- He can show frustration, especially when he is not able to do what he wants.
- He chooses which toys to play with and definitely has his favourites.

physical development

Height
Average for a boy is 67 cm (26½ in), for a girl 65 cm (25½ in).

Weight
Average for a boy is 7.8 kg (17 lb 3 oz), for a girl 7.2 kg (15 lb 13 oz).

Head
Average circumference for a boy is 43.7 cm (17¼ in), for a girl 42.4 cm (16¾ in).

Hair
Probably has a reasonable head of hair, although many this age are still bald.

Teeth
One tooth may have erupted, usually at the centre of the bottom gum.

Eyes
Chooses where to look, concentrates more effectively and switches his attention at will. Can now see as well as an adult.

Hands
Reaches for a toy and grabs it, lifts it up, shakes it, bangs it against the table and then drops it.

Legs
Makes early crawling movements with his arms and legs, which move him around, though not necessarily where he wanted.

Back
Sits upright on the floor with your support and leans on his hands occasionally in order to steady himself.

your baby at
7 months

Your baby has now begun the second half of her first year, and she is really on the go. She sits upright, reaches and grabs hold, rolls all over the place when lying on the floor and is making good progress with crawling. With her newfound self-belief comes occasional frustration when things don't go according to plan, and at these times she turns to you for emotional support.

Q **My baby sometimes leans against the side of the cot and bangs her head against it. Why does she do this?**

A Nobody knows for sure why some babies like to do this. Perhaps it's a form of self-soothing – your baby's way of relaxing herself. However, this habit holds no danger and is nothing to worry about, as long as the banging isn't carried out at a furious pace. Your baby will grow out of it.

growth and appearance

Your baby now appears so much older. This is partly because she is continuing to put on weight and height, but also because she reacts more to her surroundings. She wants to do more, preferring to try things for herself rather than sit passively while you do everything for her. Of course, there are times when her aspirations outstrip her ability, but most of the time her sheer determination carries her towards her goal.

Then there is her sense of humour – she now laughs a lot. Sometimes she giggles at something that you think is totally unfunny, and yet within seconds the sound of her laughter sets you off. Sharing a joke together, laughing with each other, makes both you and your baby happier. She looks as if she enjoys life more than ever before.

movement

In addition to pulling herself from lying to sitting – although not every baby of this age can manage it on their own – she starts to show consistent early crawling ability. For example, already when your baby lies face down at the bottom of the cot with a toy at the top end, she reaches out for the item. Now, however, she tries to move her whole body towards it by bringing her knees up to her tummy. Sometimes she creeps by raising herself up off her tummy on to her hands and knees.

Many babies show signs of crawling by 7 months, even though it is still a number of weeks before they actually achieve it.

When held under the arms in a standing position, the increased power in your baby's legs and back allow her to take her own weight on her feet, and she does this happily. As well as bouncing while held vertically, she starts to make little steps on the spot. It's as if she already imagines herself walking. Her excellent neck and back strength means that while upright she can hold up her head for long periods without tiring. She likes looking at the world from that position.

hand—eye coordination

Mealtimes are much more interesting. Your baby wants to have a go at feeding herself, and she sometimes manages to pick up a small piece of food from the tray of her high chair and bring it to her mouth. Initially she does this by gripping it in her closed fist, although she soon moves on to using her thumb and index finger. More often than not, however, the food slips from her grasp before she manages to eat it. Undeterred, your baby tries again. Be very careful to keep anything unsuitable out of her reach.

Your baby's improved hand—eye coordination results in more advanced explorations. When given a toy, she examines it fully. You'll notice that she pulls at it, pushes it, shakes it, tastes it and turns it round in her hands. She wants to know all about this object. And if you don't give her what she wants, she grabs for it. Objects pass from one hand to the other without dropping, and if she has something in each hand at the same time, she likes to bang them together.

Your baby may try to feed herself with a spoon, but will have some difficulty keeping the food on the spoon.

crawling by degree

There are several stages in the development of crawling – your baby doesn't go from having no crawling skills one day to confidently crawling the next. In fact, one study confirmed that there are up to 14 different progressions your baby goes through before she can crawl competently.

Your baby will love to hear nursery rhymes and songs, and will anticipate the actions or animal noises involved.

baby talk

Opinion is divided over whether or not parents should use 'baby words' when talking to their babies instead of the ordinary words. Some people argue that it is better, for example, to use the term 'bow wow' than the word 'dog' because that term is more akin to the speech a baby of this age uses and will therefore catch her attention quickly. Others argue that the danger with this strategy is the child learns the 'baby word' first and will then have to relearn the proper word later on when speech skills are more mature.

Q **When my baby son babbles, he uses sounds that aren't part of our language. Why is this?**

A Investigations have found that babies from different countries, with different languages, tend to have the same range of babbling sounds (including some speech sounds they haven't heard before). Your baby will eventually focus on those sounds that are relevant to your language.

learning

Your baby's memory has greatly improved and lasts longer. For instance, you can tell that she recognizes someone, even though she has not seen that person for several days. Her eyes light up when the visitor appears, she might even give a broad grin and there is no sign at all of the anxiety you expect when she sees a stranger.

Object permanence – that is, your baby's awareness that an object continues to exist even though she can't actually see it – starts to emerge this month. If she sees a toy that is partly hidden behind a cushion, she makes an attempt to lift the cushion in order to get hold of the toy because she knows it is under there. A few months ago, she would have stopped looking the moment part of it was concealed. In addition, her increased attention span means that she can keep looking until the task is complete, without her attention wandering.

Anticipatory skills also progress. If your baby sees a ball bounce along in front of her, she follows the line of movement with her eyes, anticipating where the next bounce will come. This confirms that she is able to think ahead using current information.

language

Your baby has a better understanding of spoken language, and now responds to very basic instructions. Hold a small toy and move it towards her. As you do this, say clearly, 'Take the toy'. She will probably reach out her hands to grab hold of it. Not only does she understand your command but she is able to recognize that it refers to her and that she needs to act on it.

Vowel and consonant strings become longer, and she can say up to four or five vowels or consonants in a row – for example, 'gagagagaga' or 'bebebebebe'. When she hears you speak to her, she often tries to imitate you to the best of her ability. In many ways, her speech sounds like adult speech – except that it makes no sense whatsoever. She especially likes songs and poems that have clear rhyming sounds at the end of each line – words with the same end sound seem to engage her attention in particular. Her gurgles and chuckles confirm her enjoyment of these word games. A new game emerges at this age: she has great fun blowing saliva bubbles, accompanying them with lots of different sounds.

social and emotional development

Your baby is more outgoing socially and makes active attempts to respond to other people. Although as yet she has no meaningful speech, she babbles loudly when someone talks to her – this is her form of sociable conversation. She also enjoys it when you and she play clapping games together.

Your baby has no difficulty letting you know when she is in a bad mood. If things don't go according to plan, she can become very upset. All it takes is for a toy to fall from her grasp, or for you to remove her food before she has finished eating, and tears quickly follow.

She doesn't like being separated from you, even temporarily. When she senses that you are about to leave, or sees that you have actually left, she bursts into tears. Your baby just wants you to stay with her at all times. Your return, however, is greeted with delight and she makes a miraculous recovery! Many parents going back to work and using childcare at this stage find the separation each day very difficult, precisely because of their baby's tearful behaviour in response. However, most babies soon learn to adapt to new childcare arrangements eventually, and they gradually settle down into a comfortable routine (see pages 92–93).

into everything

If your baby has started crawling or creeping, she can extend her sphere of learning and discovery to new territories. That's why you'll suddenly find that she has thrust her hand deep into the DVD player: she's not being naughty, just keen to find out what goes on inside the mysterious gap that takes the disc. Now she can press the button to open and close it by herself.

All babies are drawn to gadgets with buttons – telephones, remote controls – and more so if they beep when pressed.

finding the right
childcare

Leaving your baby with a childcarer can be a wrench – and a blessing! You will probably have mixed feelings, and making your choice of childcare is one of the most important decisions you will ever take. Lots of options are available to working mothers, and even if you are not going back to work, you may occasionally need 'emergency' help or some time to yourself.

Q If I take on a nanny, will my baby grow to love her more than me?

A This is a common concern – but if your baby loves and trusts his nanny, that's a good thing. Nothing can replace the bond you share: your nanny is doing his or her job, but you love your baby unconditionally. Eventually your nanny will leave, but you will always be there. If you feel jealous or anxious, talk this through with your nanny, and when you do spend time with your baby, make it special with games, cuddles, stories and shared activities.

childcare benefits

Using childcare can be beneficial for both you and your baby. You can focus on work and your own well-being, while your baby boosts his independence and learns to be looked after by other responsible adults. It's impossible to say exactly how he will respond.

choosing childcare

Finding the right childcare can be a long process, so if you are returning to work, start looking at your options as early as possible. Childcare can be expensive, so think about your finances. Also consider your individual requirements: for example, some mothers would rather leave their baby in a nursery with lots of children than in a one-to-one situation with a nanny, but if you work long or flexible hours, or need additional help in the evenings, a nursery may not meet your needs.

day nursery

Many nurseries accept babies and generally take between 25 and 40 children. Contact each nursery to ask about their waiting list, costs, opening hours and policies on safety, education, routine and ratio of

It is normal for a day nursery to operate on one staff member to every two or three children. Babies enjoy being with other children in a nursery setting.

Nurseries usually have quite structured day-to-day routines with fixed times for playing, eating and reading.

staff to children. Happy, calm and engaged children are the best indicator of a good nursery. Nurseries are run by professionals, but your child may be looked after by several different people. They can be expensive and won't be able to look after your child if he is sick.

nanny

A nanny cares for a baby in his home. Some live in, while others work on a daily basis or participate in a nanny-share with another family. A nanny provides hours to suit you and follows your routines. You become the nanny's employer, forming a contract, paying salary and tax and providing suitable working conditions. You also need an adequate insurance policy to cover domestic staff in the event of injury. You will need to get on well with a nanny, particularly if they are living in. If your nanny is young, make sure they have experience with babies.

childminder

Self-employed childminders are usually experienced and offer flexible hours. Your baby is cared for within a small group of children in a home environment. A childminder will usually ask you to sign a contract to cover hours, holidays and overtime. They agree their own fees, and usually won't look after your child if he is ill.

Whichever professional childcare you choose, ask about a trial period, and request references, a copy of qualifications and/or registration with an appropriate agency or professional body. If possible, talk to other parents who use the same childcare provider. You will want to spend the first few sessions with your baby so that you can watch the childminder interact with him.

family members

Relatives are the cheapest and least unsettling childcare option, but before asking grandparents, consider whether they are healthy enough. Relatives may struggle to switch off from their childcaring role and may have inflexible ideas about discipline, routine or diet. Informal arrangements do go wrong and can damage family relationships.

when childcare doesn't work out

Childcare isn't always successful. Your baby might not settle at nursery, or you could experience a personality clash with your nanny, disagree with your mother-in-law's methods or decide you are unhappy back at work. If your baby is having problems, talk to his carer and try to help. Your childcarer should keep you abreast of his progress. If you are unhappy with the service provided, the action you can take depends on the type of childcare and the contract you agreed. You may need to observe a notice period or follow a complaints procedure at a nursery.

> ' I worked part-time after 9 months and my sister-in-law, who has a toddler, offered to childmind. She fell pregnant again after a month and couldn't cope. A neighbour was looking to nanny-share and my employers let me change my days to fit in with her schedule, which worked out perfectly. '
>
> Katherine, mother of Eloise (12 months)

shared experience

your baby at
8 months

Your inquisitive baby's desire to learn is now influenced very strongly by two factors. On the one hand, she's starting to increase her mobility, which allows her to extend her boundaries. On the other, her social awareness increases, making her vulnerable when she meets new people – suddenly her curiosity gives way to fear and she bursts into tears.

Q **My friend's baby is energetic and on the go the whole time, but mine is much more passive. I am worried she may have a problem.**

A Every child is different. Your baby's lower level of discovery and exploration probably has more to do with her personality than with any lack of ability. She is most likely just very laid-back. What matters is that she is curious about toys and looks responsive when you chat to her. It sounds as though she is simply one of those babies who isn't particularly motivated to move around all the time.

growth and appearance

The typical weight and height for a girl is around 8.1 kg (17 lb 13 oz) and 68.5 cm (27 in); for a boy around 8.8 kg (19½ lb) and 70 cm (27½ in). Your baby's appearance is also changed by the emergence of more teeth. She probably has between six and eight, upper and lower, which makes her look very grown up!

Your baby loves to make good eye contact with you as much as possible. She uses other body language positively to engage you,

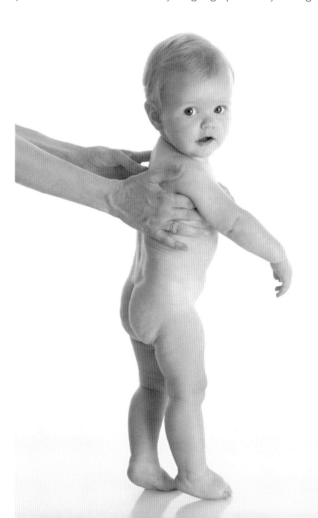

Your baby may take a cautious first step if supported by you, but she is unable to walk independently as yet.

including plenty of smiles and putting her hands and arms out towards you when she sees you. Both of these draw you to her.

Physically, your baby is becoming much more mature. She sits up confidently while playing with her toys, and the way she manipulates them in her hands is quite impressive. She is able to crawl more readily whenever the mood takes her, and is also much more actively involved at mealtimes, as she makes a good effort to feed herself. It's these dynamic qualities that really shine through.

movement

Now that your baby's leg muscles are stronger, she likes to spend more time in an upright position. Although she still can't stand independently, if you hold her under the arms so that she is vertical, she stretches out her legs to touch the floor. Now she goes beyond just weight bearing or bouncing and actually begins to try to push off the floor with her feet, as if in the early stages of taking her first step forward.

One of the downsides of this upward mobility is that your baby falls a lot. Her hand grip on the furniture, which supports her while standing, can slip or she may move her upper body too far ahead of her feet. Another problem is that she is unable to swivel herself at the waist, so she regularly topples over on to the floor.

If your baby is crawling, she'll continue to improve, although she discovers that she sometimes crawls backwards by mistake. She still hasn't mastered the synchrony of arm, leg and body movement needed for forward motion, although she can sometimes move in this direction; as part of the learning process, she may unintentionally put herself into reverse gear.

hand—eye coordination

Combining her thumb and index finger in a grip like pliers, your baby holds a small toy firmly. Her grip is so secure that she lifts the toy without letting it slip from her fingers. Banging toys against a hard surface becomes one of her favourite games, although this can end in tears if she accidentally swings her hand so far back that the toy hits her on the head. She particularly enjoys picking up different shapes, such as blocks, triangles and spheres.

Your baby can now pass a small object from one hand to the other and back again. She does this almost absent-mindedly, as if it requires no thought or concentration. She still cannot always let go at will. She also makes an amazing effort in order to reach a toy that isn't immediately to hand: she leans as far as she can towards it, and if that doesn't solve her problem, she moves her whole body.

Visual skills are sharper too. Your baby turns firmly in the direction of a voice that she hears, at first turning her head and then moving herself into a new position if necessary. She makes a thorough and accurate visual search until she is satisfied that she has identified the source of the sound.

A baby of this age will have no trouble crawling towards a favourite toy.

left- or right-handed?

Around this time your baby may start to show hand preference, appearing to favour using one hand rather than the other. Let her make her own choice in this matter. Certainly you shouldn't put her under any pressure to use her right hand if you think she tends towards left-handedness. However, hand preference won't be fully formed for several months yet.

Stacking cups and rings present less of a problem for your baby now, and she begins to understand how they work.

luring her in

Your baby often finds objects more interesting when they are further away from her – that's why you find her straining hard to reach an ornament situated on a raised shelf. She cannot resist the lure of the unknown. If she sees you hold up an interesting object and then place it a few metres away from her, she'll make an effort to pull herself towards the item, grab hold of it and then inspect it closely.

Q Why does my baby cry so easily? How can I encourage her to be more resilient?

A It might be that she cries so much because she has learned that this is a good way to keep you glued to her side! Start to ignore her for at least a couple of seconds when the tears flow, unless you are sure there is something wrong. Her crying might decrease when she sees that her tears don't bring you rushing to her.

learning

Your baby understands two new concepts that previously eluded her. First, she sees the connection between two toys that are related in some way. For instance, when you give her a plastic cup and saucer to play with, she holds one in each hand and then tries to balance the cup on the saucer. This is very difficult for her because the coordination skills required are beyond her, but it demonstrates that she understands their connection. Hand movements during play are therefore more purposeful.

A second concept she now understands fully is that of object permanence – she now realizes that an object still exists even though it is totally concealed from sight, and she tries to look for it. For example, let your baby watch as you deliberately cover a small toy with an upturned cup. Do this right in front of her. Then ask her, 'Where is the toy?' As soon as you have finished the question, she puts her hand out to lift up the cup. She smiles at the success of her search and shows no surprise that she found it there. Her face also lights up when she catches sight of a toy that she hasn't played with for a few weeks.

language

Your baby tries to imitate words or sounds that she hears. If you regularly sing a song to her so that she is totally familiar with the tune, you'll find that without any prompting she suddenly tries to join in. Of course, she can't say the words properly, but you know she is trying to sing with you. The more you show your enjoyment of her actions when she does this, the harder she tries to say the words.

Mouth and lip movements are an essential part of spoken language. Your baby tries out new oral movements, as if in preparation for the spoken-word stage of language development: she opens and closes her mouth as she watches you eat, blows bubbles with any liquid in her mouth and often repeats the same sound over and over again.

By this stage, your baby knows the names of an increasing number of family members and also those of many everyday household objects and toys, and she looks more confidently at an item when you say its name. She may on certain occasions shout just to capture your attention, which is another clear sign that she understands the purpose of speech.

social and emotional development

Your baby's confidence with strangers gets both stronger and more fragile. On the one hand, she is more confident in the company of adults she does not know very well and she no longer bursts into tears the moment a stranger talks to her. She is more likely to give a neutral response, and she might even smile at this unfamiliar person in reaction to their smile. In fact, your baby goes even further than this – her social enthusiasm allows her to initiate social contact with other adults, even those she doesn't know particularly well. On the other hand, this apparent self-confidence can crash in a second, and your baby suddenly clings tightly to you in the presence of a stranger when you thought she was at ease.

Your baby plays happily on her own, but becomes very anxious if she thinks you are about to leave the room or if you actually go out of sight, although she does not become quite as upset as she did previously. Even so, she wants you with her at all times, even when you are doing something else and are not totally preoccupied with her alone. She dislikes any form of temporary separation from you. Once you come back into the room, she very quickly stops crying and is happy once again.

frustration

Lack of spoken language at this age can lead to a build-up of frustration, because your baby can't tell you exactly what she wants. Instead of expressing herself through words, she ends up doing so through rage. When you see her frustration building, try to defuse her temper before it reaches explosion point. It may help to distract her attention on to something else.

Your baby is likely to become increasingly frustrated at his inability to articulate what he needs and wants.

returning to work

For many mothers, going back to work isn't as much a choice as a financial necessity. Even though your baby is approaching 9 months, making the decision to go back can be fraught with worry and feelings of guilt and frustration. Whether you're dreading your return or feeling excited about refocusing on your career, working post-baby won't be quite the same as it was before.

Q **I'm exclusively breast-feeding my baby but want to go back to work next month – can I continue to breast-feed?**

A Within the EU, employment law supports breast-feeding mothers, so if your baby can be brought to you, you may be able to breast-feed during working hours. (In the USA, the law varies by state.) You could also express milk, but get into the habit now, expressing two or three times a week, and feeding with a bottle so that your baby gets used to it. He could have formula milk while you're at work and be breast-fed the rest of the time – combination feeding works well for some mothers and even one breast-feed a day is beneficial.

making the decision

Your decision will probably be influenced by feelings, finances and your maternity rights. Statutory laws are in place, but talk to your employer to confirm your position and benefits, and ask for new hours in writing. If you are unclear about your rights, seek professional advice. If your employer operates a crèche, find out if your baby can have a place and how the crèche operates.

how you might feel

If you found the last 8 months of childcare unfulfilling or you are very focused on your career, you will probably appreciate going back to work. If you fell hopelessly in love with motherhood and relished life at home, it may take longer to adjust. If your baby is happy and thriving with his carer (see pages 92–93), it will be easier for you. Some mothers find the first few days very upsetting, but a photo on your desk and bringing your baby in to meet your colleagues – so they know what you are missing – can help. If you feel guilty, remind

Going back to work for the first time is a milestone moment that may unsettle everyone involved.

Working from home may be an option, but you may find it hard to give your baby all the attention she will need.

new ways of working

Going back to work doesn't necessarily mean spending 5 days a week away from home. You can tailor your job to suit your new life as a parent:

- Part-time working combines your job with childcare.
- If a colleague also wants a flexible work/life balance, you may be able to job-share.
- As a freelancer, you choose when you work, who you work for and how much you take on, which means you may be able to juggle work and childcare.
- Flexi-working involves working whenever your partner isn't. This does limit the time you can spend as a family, and may involve working evenings and weekends. However, it also saves you money and means both of you can spend plenty of time with your baby.
- Telecommuting cuts out your commute, but you may still need some childcare.
- You may be able to take a career break, returning to your job when your children are older. Discuss this possibility with your employer.

yourself that you are working for your family and that being with other carers and children will help your baby to hone his language, social and emotional development.

potential problems

If you don't want to return to work but need the money, consider alternative working options such as flexi-working or freelancing. Talk to your employer about telecommuting (home-working) or going part-time. Depending on the childcare you have arranged, you may need time off if your baby is unwell, so discuss this with your employer. If it doesn't work out, talk to your human resources department and check out the benefits to which you will be entitled. If you experience discrimination or difficulties getting time off, seek independent professional advice.

work/life balance

Whenever you go back, it is important to get the work/life balance right. Make time spent with your baby special, but don't over-compensate by showering him with gifts. Avoid bringing work home and keep a healthy flow of communication going with your employer. Most importantly, keep abreast of employment laws for working mothers – they are always changing and new legislation may benefit your individual circumstances.

your baby at
9 months

For many babies, this is a period of consolidating the skills they already have, almost as if they are taking stock of their own development. Your baby can do a lot for herself now, such as pulling up to stand, crawling to wherever she wants, reaching for any item that grabs her interest, smiling and babbling to gain your attention and even feeding herself with finger food.

A baby is just as happy with a saucepan and a wooden spoon as with a toy drum.

growth and appearance

Your baby has a good head of hair, plenty of first teeth clearly showing through and her weight and height have continued to increase. All in all, her appearance is markedly different from that of a baby who is only a few months younger.

Your baby's ability to make controlled body, arm and leg movements means that she can make greater use of gestures to convey her ideas. Her ability to communicate her underlying feelings non-verbally – through the use of more sophisticated movements such as touching, pointing, throwing and pushing – creates a stronger relationship with you. The more she feels you understand her, the stronger her emotional attachment to you becomes.

Your baby appears most comfortable when following a structured routine. For example, she perks up with the familiarity of her pre-bath and pre-bedtime routines because these actions signal what is about to come. She starts to smile when she sees you bring her own bath towel from the cupboard or when she catches sight of you tidying her cot toys. Of course, you need to be flexible; in general, though, your baby appears most content when following a routine.

movement

Sitting will probably pose no challenge whatsoever. Your baby sits with legs forward, pointing outwards, and uses her hands to keep balance while she leans to one side and then the other. It's the same with her crawling movements, which are probably more coordinated, and she moves her entire body. While on the floor face down, she makes very vigorous attempts to move ahead. She draws both knees up towards her tummy and her arms stretch out. Bear in mind, however, that some babies prefer to bottom-shuffle rather than crawl – and they can go straight to walking without ever even attempting creeping or crawling.

Your baby's ambition again outstrips her ability, and she is none too pleased to discover that she can't manoeuvre herself around the table that is in her way. Tears of frustration flow freely at this age. She needs to find a balance between her desire to explore new territories and

Shape-sorters appeal to babies of this age, as long as the shapes are very basic and easily posted through the slots.

filling and emptying

Once your baby has watched you put a small toy or wooden block into an open cup and then turn the cup upside down so that the block falls out again, she wants to try this herself. Of course, this game looks easier to her than it is, but with your prompts and support, the block eventually finds its way into the cup. You might have to show her the action a few more times before she masters it for herself.

causing herself too much frustration. The same applies to climbing stairs: this is now something that interests her, but she struggles to get past the first step.

hand–eye coordination

Hand movements are now more within your baby's control and she can coordinate them much more efficiently. Take a piece of cloth and tie one end around a small toy. Attract your baby's attention to it, demonstrate how you can get the toy to come towards you by pulling the cloth and then put the end of the cloth in her hand. She will probably copy you and tug at the item until she is able to pick it up using her thumb and index finger. This gives her a huge sense of achievement. She also uses her index finger to prod, poke and point, and is now able to let go of objects at will.

You and your baby have great fun playing 'musical instruments' together. She likes nothing better than to make a loud noise by banging two or more objects together. Find a couple of old pots and pans and add in a wooden spoon or two, then pass this fine orchestral array to your enthusiastic baby. Before you know it, she bangs the spoon against the pot, the pot against the pan and the lid against the spoon. The bigger the noise, the broader the smile on her face. She is even able to clap both hands in approval at her own performance.

Q **I'm worried my baby will hurt herself badly one of these days when she falls over. How can I keep her safe?**

A The only way your baby can learn new movement skills is by tackling new challenges, and there is always a minor risk of injury in that situation. Instead of restricting her movements, stay close to her when she manoeuvres herself around the furniture – that way you are better placed to prevent a potential accident.

the feel-good factor

Even at this young age, your baby responds positively to success – it boosts her 'feel-good factor' and increases her self-confidence. It really doesn't matter where her achievements occur: simply reaching the target makes her happier with herself. Hitting a small toy, grabbing hold of an item she has reached or completing a simple puzzle toy are some of the ways your baby achieves success. The positive effect is even more powerful when you acknowledge her achievement with a big hug or words of praise and a smile.

Your baby will examine scraps of paper and fabric for different textures and sounds.

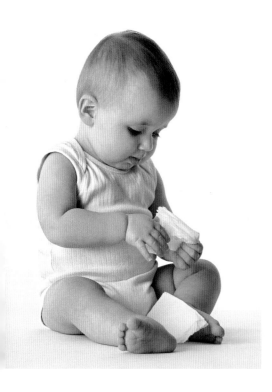

learning

Bits of paper and fabric fascinate your baby. She instantly picks up a section of any material lying beside her and rubs it against her face. If she gets hold of paper, her little fingers start to crumple it into a ball – she may even bite off a piece. You may also see her comparing objects in each hand.

Your baby also learns through water play while having a bath. She often stares intently as she fills a plastic beaker, empties it, then fills it again. This is the first stage in learning about volume and the way that liquids 'change shape' depending on the containers that hold them. This is another example of the way free play enhances your baby's thinking skills.

Remember too that your baby still learns from playing with familiar toys. Perhaps she has had a large ball for a couple of months. At 9 months, however, she still learns something new – for instance, that it bounces if dropped from a height, and that unless the surface is perfectly flat, the ball doesn't sit still when placed there. In other words, she learns new things from old toys.

language

Your baby begins to use the same vowel string to apply to the same object and you might think that you have heard her first word. She also uses a lot of pointing and speaking at the same time in order to convey meaning to you, and most of the time you know what she is trying to tell you. Babbling contains new sounds, including some of the consonants that you haven't heard her use before. She understands the meaning of dozens of spoken words.

Hearing is still not yet fully developed, but she is good at discriminating and locating a sound source as long as it is not directly above or below her. Sit your baby in her cot, facing towards the door. When she no longer pays attention to you, move to a corner of the room behind her and switch on a music CD. She immediately turns to look at the music in the right place.

Research suggests that boys typically develop language at a slower rate than girls at every stage. This is a trend, however, and doesn't necessarily mean that every boy develops at a slower rate. Nevertheless, this could explain why your daughter learned to speak much faster than your son.

social and emotional development

At parent-and-toddler group, your baby stares curiously at the other children; she watches them closely, studying their every move. She becomes curious about other babies her own age, even though she can't talk to them or even play with them. She may reach out to touch, poke or pull at the child nearest to her, until the focus of her interest bursts out crying at this unwanted attention.

By now, you should have begun to form clear ideas on discipline to use with your baby. Remember that discipline is not about controlling

Babies of this age interact with each other, but will not yet play together.

her but about encouraging her awareness of others and her understanding that other people have feelings just like her. Rules about behaviour enhance her social awareness and help her to establish self-control. However, this doesn't mean she happily does as you ask!

Your baby now knows exactly what you mean when you say 'no', even though she can't say the word herself – and she doesn't like it. She may even erupt with rage at you for preventing her doing what she wants. That's a typical reaction at this age. Stay calm and try not to give in to her. She'll gradually learn to control her own temper and to consider other people, not just herself.

exploring with food
There is no harm in sometimes letting your baby make a mess when feeding. Food fascinates her not just because it is tasty and satisfies her hunger but also because it can be moulded and smeared into all sorts of shapes. Of course, you want mealtimes to go smoothly, quickly and neatly because you have a family routine to follow. But when there is time, you can consider allowing her to play with her food if she wants to, instead of expecting her to eat it straight away.

Q Is praise good for my baby? Can I give her too much?

A Praise is one of the greatest boosts to your baby's self-esteem. She loves to know that you value her and approve of her behaviour, and she never tires of your words of encouragement and admiration. Praise is most effective, though, when it marks an actual achievement; if used too often without real justification, it loses impact for your baby.

organizing babysitters

When your baby was newborn, you probably didn't think you'd have a night out ever again! Now he is getting closer to his first birthday and is easier to look after, you can re-invest in your social life. Going out is a lifeline, particularly if you do the majority of the childcare. A night out provides a much-needed break and all you need to enjoy it is a trusted, responsible and affordable babysitter.

Q **I am desperate for a night out with my husband. Is my baby too young for a babysitter?**

A It really depends on how confident you feel about leaving your baby. If you are the only person who can feed or comfort him, it may be too early. On the other hand, if your baby enjoys being cared for by other people, or is unlikely to wake up while you are out, give it a try!

Once you feel ready to let a babysitter take charge, you will welcome a night out.

babysitter bonuses

If you are struggling to spend time with your partner, evenings out can re-ignite your relationship. Accepting social invitations from friends and colleagues is liberating, and socializing outside your parental duties boosts your sense of 'self'. If you're a full-time parent, learning to trust a babysitter is a positive step forward, as you will have to entrust your child's care to others at some stage.

when to start

The right time to get a babysitter is when you feel ready – it's no fun going out if you can't relax. Some parents feel the best time is when they have a routine established and their baby goes to bed at the same time each evening. Knowing when he is likely to wake for a feed or cuddle will help you to plan your evening. If you are very nervous, book your babysitter for just an hour or two at first and stay close to home.

finding a babysitter

Many parents begin by asking family members. This works well, particularly if your relative has a close relationship with your baby. However, if they are sitting for free, you may feel indebted, and older relatives may not want to stay up late. If you'd rather, pay a professional, ask friends for recommendations or look online for a local babysitting service. Interview potential sitters and ask about experience, qualifications and references. Rates vary, so ask what they charge. If you are using an agency, find out if their employees have had recent background checks. Make sure you introduce your baby to the sitter before you go out or at an earlier meeting – watching how well they interact will help you to make a final decision. Even if your baby is asleep when you leave, you don't want him to be alarmed by a stranger if he wakes up.

first night

The first time you leave your baby with a sitter, make sure they are clear on your ground rules. Be assertive, telling the sitter exactly what you

If you have no willing relatives to hand, consider using an agency for babysitters.

babysitter checklist

This checklist will save your babysitter from having to ring you repeatedly:

- Mobile and emergency telephone numbers.
- Any allergies your baby may have.
- How to settle your baby if he wakes.
- Preferred feeding and bedtimes.
- Favourite toys or soothers.
- Where you keep first-aid essentials, nappies, spare clothes and milk/bottles.
- Any ointments or medicines your baby needs or that you are happy for the babysitter to administer.
- Who is permitted to visit while you are out.
- Circumstances under which you want to be contacted.

want them to do if your baby wakes up, and explaining your baby's bedtime routine thoroughly if they are putting him to bed. If you don't want the babysitter to use amenities such as your phone or computer, tell them. It is better to be honest than create misunderstandings, and you'll enjoy your evening more if you have made your wishes clear. It's a nice gesture to leave refreshments for your babysitter to enjoy, and to call or text once during the evening to make sure everything is fine.

problem babysitters

By choosing a reputable agency, qualified professional or trusted friend or family member, you shouldn't encounter problems. Teenage neighbours may provide a cheap and cheerful babysitting option, but always choose someone responsible and trustworthy over the age of 16. If you do encounter problems, such as your babysitter being late or repeatedly cancelling, deal with it straight away. Casual babysitters don't need a notice period, but agencies may have their own conditions with regards to cancellation, particularly at short notice. When you find a new sitter, go through the approval process again and introduce your baby to them as before.

'My mother-in-law used to babysit but wouldn't stay overnight, driving home by herself in the early hours. I felt uncomfortable with the arrangement and asked a friend if I could call her professional babysitter. We pay Linda to stay as late as we like, so there's no guilt involved, and she gets on brilliantly with Esme.'

Leigh, mother of Esme (9 months)

shared experience

what your baby can do
9 months

social and emotional development

- Your baby watches other children closely, studying their every move.
- She responds positively to praise and even claps with delight.
- She may have a cuddly toy or other comforter, which she adores.

movement

- Lying face down, your baby draws her knees up to her tummy and stretches out her arms as she tries to move forwards.
- She is easily frustrated when unable to climb up the stairs or move herself around the object blocking her way.
- She sits with legs forward, pointing outwards, and uses her hands to balance while she leans sideways.

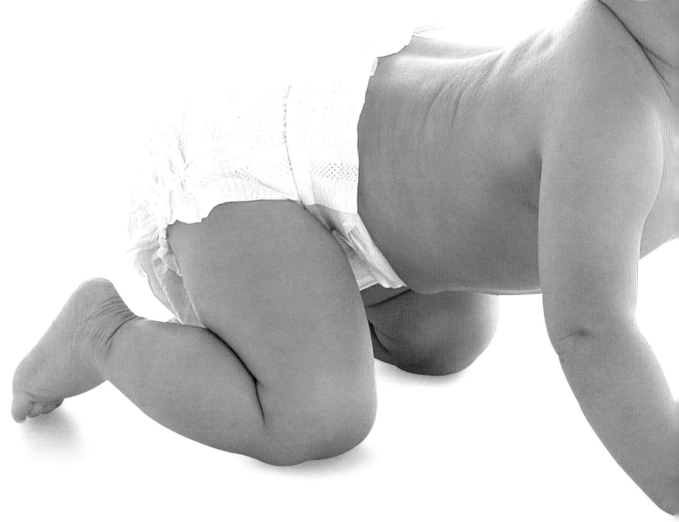

learning

- Your baby is fascinated by the textures of paper and fabric.
- She enjoys filling and emptying a plastic beaker while in the bath.
- She still learns new things from toys she has played with for several months.

language

- Your baby begins to apply the same vowel string repeatedly to the same object.
- By pointing and babbling at the same time, she tries to convey meaning to you, often successfully.
- Her hearing is sharp but not fully developed – she has difficulty locating the source of sounds from directly above or below her.

hand–eye coordination

- Your baby can pull on one end of a piece of string in order to get the toy attached to the other.
- She can use her thumb and index finger to pick up small items of food.
- She coordinates her hands, to hit a spoon against a plate or bash two wooden blocks together.

9 months

physical development

Height
Average for a boy is 72 cm (28½ in), for a girl 70 cm (27½ in).

Weight
Average for a boy is 9.2 kg (20¼ lb), for a girl 8.5 kg (18¾ lb).

Head
Average circumference for a boy is 45.2 cm (17¾ in), for a girl 44 cm (17¼ in).

Hair
Most likely has plenty of hair, perhaps even some curls.

Teeth
At least two upper and two lower teeth are through, and maybe several more.

Eyes
Eye contact is strong and your baby scans her surroundings more methodically for what she is seeking.

Hands
Mature pincer grip enables her to pick up smaller items and hold on to them for longer periods.

Legs
Can pull her legs up to her tummy when face down, to begin crawling.

Back
Can sit upright on the floor, as well as twist, turn and reach out without falling over.

your baby at
10 months

With enough skills to play, explore and connect with you and others around him, your baby is having a great time. More new skills start to emerge: progress in movement and understanding of language are especially noticeable, and he is altogether more confident socially. He knows what he likes and dislikes, and you may have a hard time trying to encourage him to expand his preferences.

growth and appearance

Your baby's toothy grin, shiny hair and the look-at-me-I-can-crawl-upstairs expression on his face dominate his appearance. He has his moments of temper and frustration, but most of the time he is happy and a delight to be with. He giggles a lot too, which helps to generate a very positive atmosphere around him. His humour is developing and he now understands simple jokes.

Once your baby is pulling herself up to a standing position and cruising around the furniture, it will not be long before she starts to walk independently.

When he is awake, your baby's preferred position is probably trying to stand. That's where he finds life most interesting, and he is curious about things that you simply take for granted, like the cushion resting at the back of the chair or the spoon that's slightly out of his reach on the table. The sitting position is used more for quiet playing, when he surrounds himself with his favourite toys. Overall, he looks more organized than before.

Your baby also seems a lot more solid now. The combination of his natural development tendencies coupled with a good eating regimen – he eats a range of solid foods now as well as milk at each meal – has enabled him to grow bigger and stronger. He can still hurt himself if he falls, but his strong muscles and body growth mean that he looks (and is) is less fragile than before.

movement

Your baby may now be cruising around the furniture, standing upright and holding on to it with his hands as he slowly edges his way along. His confidence grows steadily and you notice that he tries to take slightly bigger side-steps. Any fall sets him back, but he is usually willing to get back up on his feet after a few minutes. If you think he can cope with the challenge, steadily increase the spaces between the pieces of furniture so that he has almost to lunge at the next one. If he is not ready for this, he will stop at the first gap.

Your baby may now crawl up stairs, at least past the first step, and may even try to get back downstairs by himself. However, he needs you to supervise him on the stairs at all times, as he can easily roll off a step at this stage. When he gets stuck – perhaps because his confidence runs out and he suddenly feels overwhelmed by the position he is in – lift him up, cuddle him and put him back into a sitting position on the floor at the bottom of the stairs. He learns from experience that going up stairs is easier than coming down them.

hand–eye coordination

Your baby loves playing with toys that can move across the floor, even though he still cannot walk independently. Small balls are a particular source of amusement. He happily sits on the floor with his legs splayed out in front of him, facing you a few metres away. When you take a small, soft ball and roll it gently but accurately towards him, he stops it with his hand and picks it up. He may even try to roll it back towards you.

Boxes with lids on fascinate your baby. Take a small cardboard box with a reasonably tight-fitting lid, place a small object inside it, then put the lid back on. Bring the box over to your baby and shake it so that the object rattles around noisily inside. After a couple of seconds, hand the box to him without saying a word. He immediately tries to remove the lid in order to discover what's in it. Having achieved that, he is content to spend a few minutes attempting to fit the lid back on to the box.

Introduce toys that challenge your baby both physically and mentally.

Q My baby loves putting shapes into the holes in a shape-sorter toy, but he often can't achieve this. Should I show him the solution?

A He likes to push the plastic shapes into the holes by himself. However, if you see that he is stuck because a particular shape is too awkward for him to twist and turn into the right orientation, by all means show him what to do. Once he has seen you do it, make sure he tries it by himself.

Cuddling your baby becomes more rewarding around this time, with him reciprocating from time to time.

say it!

Your baby wants to speak as much as you want him to. In your desire to hear him say his first word, you may slip into the situation where you refuse to give him what he wants unless he says a word that sounds like the desired object. But he doesn't respond well to that. He simply becomes frustrated when you won't give him what he wants, which doesn't help his speech and language development.

learning

Your baby grasps the concept of imitation more fully. With his increased understanding and better sense of self, he realizes that he can observe an action by you and then make an attempt to copy it himself. If he sees you smile at him and you then gently clap your hands together repeatedly (but not so loud that he blinks), he tries to clap his own hands together in imitation.

Your baby begins to look at objects or pages in a book in a more methodical way. Previously, his glance would have shifted from one item to the next in a random pattern, taking in a very quick visual impression for a few seconds and then moving on to the next. Now he looks more purposefully, scanning the object from top to bottom, gathering as much information as he can about it, before moving on to another one.

Your baby understands simple commands and is able to follow them through to completion. For example, if he holds a cup and you put your hand out towards him, saying softly, 'Give me the cup, please', he reaches forward to do exactly as you ask (assuming he is in a cooperative mood!)

language

Your baby loves chatting to you in his own way, using various consonant–vowel babbling sounds that are combined into longer strings, which may be repeated. He also spends more time looking at you when he talks, as his awareness of the social dimensions of communication develops. Your baby's attention improves so that he now watches more closely when you point out various people and objects to him. Sometimes he gazes at an object long after you have referred to it, as though trying to absorb more information about it.

You might hear that elusive first word at this stage. However, you cannot be sure because your baby probably doesn't say the whole word, just the first part, and he doesn't use it all the time. Nevertheless, you can tell that he is close to this milestone.

Your baby uses body language more deliberately and creatively. It's almost as if his frustration at realizing he can almost speak boosts his need to use non-verbal communication. Facial expressions are clearer and more intense, pointing with his finger is more frequent, eye contact is used to express both positive and negative feelings and he shakes his head for 'no'.

social and emotional development

You may find that your baby is easily frightened by routine domestic experience. The noise of a door banging, for example, or of the washing machine suddenly starting the spin cycle makes him agitated. This is normal behaviour and a sign of his increasing sensitivity to his surroundings. He responds best to a calm, reassuring approach. When he sees you smile and feels you soothe him reassuringly during his anxious moments, he feels a lot better. If you react to his fear with anxiety of your own, he will simply become more afraid. With your support, these minor fears will pass.

Your growing baby is more aware of the emotional significance of cuddles and hugs, now that he can give them as well as receive them. His improved hand and arm control, coupled with increased understanding of the impact he has on you, means that he now reciprocates the loving action. Hugs are two-way and he no longer perceives himself as a passive recipient. When you read him a story or sit beside each other, he likes to cuddle up against you.

Q My baby gets upset when we leave him with a babysitter. Will he ever manage to settle with another carer?

A Yes, he will adapt. You can help him by using a familiar routine when leaving him with the babysitter. When you go out without him, follow the same format of saying goodbye, kissing him, then waving goodbye to him. Encourage him to do the same actions, directed towards you, and then leave. The consistency of this approach helps him to cope with the temporary separation. For more information on babysitting, see pages 104–105.

fun at mealtimes

A mealtime is no longer a time for just eating or exploring – it's an experience that brings your baby a great deal of pleasure. He has fun chewing with his new teeth (sometimes this has more to do with play than with eating), and he likes to hold a spoon and try to feed himself (sometimes the food ends up everywhere except in his mouth). It is also a time when he can interact closely with you, especially when you sit beside him. Your presence makes mealtimes more enjoyable and helps the experience to go smoothly.

Your baby is better at holding a spoon now, but still manages to lose most of her food.

involving the grandparents

If your baby is lucky enough to have grandparents, she will probably have a life filled with extra helpings of love – and fantastic birthday presents! However, it may take time for this new relationship to blossom. Just as you are still adjusting to motherhood, your parents are coming to terms with their new roles too. It's a change that can strengthen relationships, but there may be ups and downs.

Q **My mother-in-law won't stop interfering. Should I tell her to stop coming round?**

A Banning her visits is a drastic move that could inflame the situation, and it's important for your baby to develop a bond with her grandmother. You need to sit down and have a chat or, if you feel too uncomfortable, ask your partner to play diplomat. Your mother-in-law's actions may be well intentioned, but she needs to know that she is upsetting you. If you handle the situation sensitively, it's likely to boost her respect for you and nip the problem in the bud.

what is a grandparent?

There's no definitive role for a grandparent and most families find theirs according to existing relationships and proximity. Some grandparents can't wait to get involved, changing nappies, buying gifts and babysitting. Others are reluctant to interfere and feel unsure about their new role in your lives.

Grandparents can be a godsend, providing free childcare, helping around the house and offering love and moral support. By encouraging your baby to bond with them, you are offering her the chance to get to know another generation of her family and enjoy even more unconditional love.

all change

Your parents were your closest relations until now and such a huge shift is bound to have an impact. Understanding the love a parent feels for a child can bring you closer, but if they like being in control, you may be on the receiving end of unwanted advice and be pushed to do everything their way. Although it's annoying, try to be patient. Assure them that you appreciate their concern and experience, but assert yourself as the parent. There's nothing wrong with making your own mistakes.

Having grandparents living nearby can give your baby a valuable new dimension to forming close relationships.

Leaving your baby with a grandparent for a while will give you time to recharge.

getting it right with grandparents

- Encourage grandparents to help you rather than looking after your baby – cleaning, for example.
- If grandparents are causing tensions between you and your partner, ask them for some space to spend time within your own family unit.
- If grandparents are spoiling your baby, raise the issue gently. Suggest they put money into an account rather than buying countless toys.
- If grandparents aren't seeing your baby as much as you'd like, offer to visit them, as they may feel more comfortable in their own home.

Q **Since I had my baby, I really need help and support from my parents. Should we move closer to them?**

A Many parents want to be closer to their relatives after starting a family and it can certainly be handy for babysitting, company and shared family activities. It's a huge and personal decision, so weigh up the pros and cons. Ask your parents how enthusiastic they are about babysitting, think about the friends and facilities you'll have and carefully consider the financial and career implications.

becoming a grandparent

Your parents may feel unsettled by their new role: it could make them feel old or rejected because you don't need them in the same way any more. They have fallen in love with your baby, just as they fell in love with you, and taking a back seat can be very difficult for them. Your new relationship dynamic may take a while to sink in, but give your parents plenty of reassurance and keep talking to them.

coping without grandparents

If your baby's grandparents live far away, put photographs in her room and play family videos to her. You could also invest in a webcam. They'll soon become familiar faces and she'll love it when they do visit. If your baby doesn't have grandparents, or circumstances make a relationship impossible, she can still experience the benefits of an extended family if you maintain close ties with living relatives, neighbours, friends and other mothers.

your baby at
11 months

On the verge of walking – perhaps he has already taken his first step – your baby is almost a toddler. He needs less help from you with moving, playing and eating, loves to be on his feet and is able to amuse himself quietly for several minutes at a time. Yet you also thrive in each other's company: he actively tries to include you in his play, and is thrilled if you sing him a song or read a story.

You can encourage your baby to walk by placing small objects in positions in which he needs to pull himself up in order to reach them properly.

encouragement to walk

At this stage, your baby might benefit from some gentle encouragement to take his first step. One way is to pull him up to a standing position and hold his hands firmly in yours so that he can't fall. As you deliberately and slowly edge away from him, he might try to take a small step forward. Give him lots of verbal encouragement – you can even pull gently at his hands.

growth and appearance

Despite his obvious enjoyment, your baby often has a very serious look about him. It's his intense concentration when trying to solve puzzle toys, his strong determination to take that first (or second) step on his own and the close attention he pays to the story book that gives the impression he is a serious scholar of life. The fact that he now drinks from a cup rather than a bottle adds to his more mature appearance.

Your baby's muscles are stronger and thicker, giving him more power in his limb movements. With longer, stronger bones in his arms and legs, his body is getting ready for walking. When he stands, his legs appear bowed, but his feet are firmly flat on the floor. He appears quite stable when sitting or standing.

Now that he has a good sleeping routine, with one nap less during the day, your baby looks more alert during waking hours. Those moments of tiredness that cause his fractious behaviour are less frequent. However, he may be so determined to stay upright that he nods off while holding on to the furniture!

movement

Your baby is probably ready to take his first step. However, remember that every child develops at his own pace and he will walk when he is ready. So if he hasn't done so yet, don't worry. In the meantime, your infant likes to have lots of standing and stepping practice. You can make things interesting for him by giving him small challenges – his confidence is boosted when he beats them. For instance, you could place him at one end of a long sofa or row of small chairs and wait at the other end for him.

Crawling is free, active and directional – he knows where he wants to go and he gets there by the fastest, most direct route. He may crawl on his hands and knees or sit upright and shuffle his way across. Each baby has his own distinctive style of pre-walking movement. Whatever the method, he moves himself successfully across the floor. When sitting, he is very competent at leaning without toppling; in fact, he can even reach behind himself without too much difficulty.

hand–eye coordination

Your baby's advanced hand–eye coordination means that he attempts more complex manipulative toys and games, such as ordering shapes of different sizes. He enjoys tackling the demands of nesting cubes – a series of boxes of diminishing size that fit inside one another. He finds this hard to complete, but rises to the challenge and is pleased to show you that he has managed to get at least two or three boxes to fit. Likewise, he focuses hard when placing rings of different size on a stacking toy, although he doesn't fit them all in the correct order.

Your baby enjoys letting a small toy drop from his grip and then looks to see if it falls where he intended. He also turns pages in a book, and can hold two small items in one hand without dropping either. He enjoys action rhymes involving hand movements.

keep watching

Although your baby is steady when sitting in the bath and able to keep himself amused by playing with the bath toys floating around him, it is never safe to leave him alone. He could easily slip under the water if he over-reaches or twists his body and slides on his bottom. Keep an eye on him throughout bathtime.

Q **Would it be wrong to let go of my baby's hands suddenly when I am holding him upright so that he is left standing alone and is forced to take his first step on his own?**

A That could possibly work, but it does seem rather harsh. The chances are he would simply sit down on his bottom the moment he realized he didn't have you to support him. By all means try to coax him if you want, but don't overdo it or you risk denting his confidence – or he might hurt himself by falling over.

By this age, most babies can work with the more difficult pieces in a shape-sorter.

115

Q **Can sucking a dummy at this age interfere with my baby's speech and language progress?**

A Many professionals worry that sucking a dummy can restrict the range of movements a baby of this age makes with his lips, tongue and throat muscles. When the dummy is in his mouth, he can't babble or speak. However, it's a question of balance. A moderate use of a dummy at this age is not a problem, as long as you ensure that it isn't in his mouth too much of the time.

Your baby is fascinated by the actions of others and will readily imitate a wave, a nod or a smile.

learning

Your baby's concentration has matured to the point where he keeps going until the task is complete, perhaps for 10 minutes or more. When you sit him on your knee to read him a story, he is no longer restless and wriggly but perches there, watching the pages of the book as you turn them over and staring intently at the pictures without losing interest. He is also better able to associate two events: for example, when he sees a picture of a bird in a book, he points roughly in the direction of the sky.

Your baby's increased attention means he is able to try out new ideas and practise existing learning skills in new situations – he is at the stage where he can adapt old strategies to novel problems. For example, he is able to fit toy nesting boxes into each other properly. If given other items that fit this way too, such as plastic cups or small plastic barrels, at first he hesitates but then soon applies his existing knowledge to solve the puzzle. Experiences like this build his confidence as a learner, making him a motivated problem-solver who adapts and applies his learning concepts.

language

This could well be the time when your baby says 'mama' and 'dada', specifically referring to his parents. He may even have a couple of

Take more care when saying 'no' to your baby, as she is easily upset if she thinks you are displeased with her.

other words as well, such as the name of his older sibling or the family pet. He also realizes that words refer to something that may not actually be in front on him, so when you make meowing sounds, for example, he turns and points to the cat's basket, even though the cat isn't there.

Your baby follows basic instructions without a visual prompt. For instance, as you move towards the door on your way out of the room, turn around, wave to him and say 'Bye bye'. Put your hands down and ask him to wave goodbye to you – he knows what you want him to do, and he remembers how to make the action.

Your baby soaks up everything he hears. He reacts positively whether you speak to him, sing songs, read stories or even ask him questions. Perhaps because he can now say a word or two of his own, he has a renewed awareness of the importance of language. He loves jabbering away on the toy telephone, although you probably can't understand a words he utters.

social and emotional development

Temper control becomes variable now. Whenever your baby's wishes are blocked, his threshold for frustration is quickly crossed and he loses his temper quite easily. When he plays with a puzzle toy, or you tell him that he isn't allowed to do something, he transforms quickly from a contented child into an outraged one. The intensity of his feelings may catch even him by surprise, so he needs you to wipe away his tears and help him to settle.

Your baby recognizes that the word 'no' doesn't just mean that you want him to stop what he's doing – it also means you disapprove of his actions. This adds to his consternation, because he prefers to please you.

His fascination with other babies increases. Whereas before he would simply stare unashamedly at them, totally unaware that his piercing gaze might make them feel uncomfortable, or try to touch them if he was near enough, now he actually moves up so that he is right beside them. Lacking all social inhibition, he then peers closely at their every move! He learns a great deal from these observations.

he said 'dada' not 'mama'

Don't be upset if your baby's first word refers to your partner rather than you – it doesn't mean that he has more love for one than the other, just that this word is easier for him to say. Instead, be pleased with the amazing achievement of his first word, irrespective of its nature. You can be sure that his vocabulary will only increase from now on and that he will soon be saying your name too.

dealing with
stress

Caring for a baby is a stressful time. You were thrust into the unknown world of parenting 11 months ago, and although you're getting used to motherhood, new problems arise with every stage of your baby's development. Dealing with stress can prove challenging because you're so busy, but it's worth tackling the issue for the sake of your health and those around you.

Q **Sometimes I get frustrated with my baby's behaviour and feel like lashing out at her. How can I control my feelings?**

A Take a deep breath, put her in a safe place and leave the room for a couple of minutes. Babies and young children can be very trying, but control yourself before doing anything you will regret. A few minutes to get your head together makes all the difference, even if she's upset. Once you feel calmer, go back and give her a cuddle. She's too young to enter into a discussion about her behaviour, but she'll get the message that you are feeling upset as a consequence of her actions.

causes and symptoms

Stress is no stranger to parents. Sleepless nights, breast-feeding issues, recovering physically and emotionally from a caesarean section or difficult delivery, responsibility and lifestyle changes all add to the strain. Beyond the first weeks, worries about work, childcare, overbearing grandparents and tantrums can stress you out. Stress carries many symptoms, but you may have trouble sleeping, suffer from headaches or high blood pressure, feel dizzy, experience a shortness of breath or regularly feel anxious and uptight.

stress-busting strategies

- Avoid alcohol, nicotine and caffeine, as they exaggerate symptoms.
- Manage your time effectively, keeping on top of housework and tidying away toys and games when your baby finishes with them.
- Make sure there is a safe area, such as a play pen, for your baby so that you can catch up on domestic chores. Having a little time to play alone also helps her development.
- Take time out to relax, meeting friends and enjoying time with your partner if possible.
- Be realistic – taking on too much will add to your stress.
- Exercise and a healthy diet are great stress-busters, as is a good night's rest. Ask your partner to manage the night shift occasionally so that you can catch up on some sleep.
- Look at your problems from a new perspective. If you're fed up with disturbed nights, remind yourself that they won't last forever and try new ways to encourage your baby to sleep through.

the truth about stress

As a relatively new parent, occasional bouts of stress are very normal. It doesn't mean you're a bad parent or can't cope. If your feelings are overwhelming, you can't stop crying or you feel constantly low and depressed, you may be suffering from postnatal depression and need to talk to someone about available help and therapies. If your partner is stressed, encourage him to talk and share his feelings. Keep working as a team and consider seeing a relationship counsellor if you're always bickering or ignoring each other. Some fathers report the same symptoms as postnatal depression, so professional advice may be needed. Remember that stressed parents are not happy parents. Your baby wants you to be calm and relaxed, so take positive steps to deal with stress for her sake too.

dealing with postnatal depression (PND)

PND is an illness that most commonly appears at 10–14 weeks and again at 8–12 months, but symptoms can appear up to a year later and perhaps take many months to resolve. It is a temporary condition treated through counselling and/or antidepressant medication. If you feel depressed, try talking to your doctor or health visitor, as well as family and friends, so that you can be diagnosed. Talking about your feelings can be difficult, but getting help will initiate your recovery. If you're suffering from PND and experience severe symptoms, such as wanting to harm yourself or your baby, seek medical help immediately. Professionals will understand and can always help.

Q **Ever since the birth of my baby I've worried about her health. I still go into her room at night to check her breathing. Is this normal?**

A Most parents spend a lifetime worrying about their children, but if it gets too much, ask your GP or health visitor for advice. If your anxiety was triggered by a difficult birth, you may be experiencing post-traumatic shock disorder (PTSD) – your doctor can help.

' Having young children can be very stressful, and I felt constantly anxious after the difficult birth of my second child. I spoke to my doctor and he referred me for counselling, which really helped. After that, when things got too much I'd ring my friend and we'd go for a walk, shop or sit in a café with our children. Being in a different environment with a good friend immediately released the tension. '

Leanne, mother of
Ezra (2 years) and Seth (1 year)

shared experience

Parenting can be rewarding but stressful – reach out for help when you need it.

your baby at
12 months

What a difference a year makes! Your toddler seems a completely different person to that little baby you brought home from the hospital a year ago. And he is. No longer so dependent on you to fetch and carry for him, he actively creates his day around what he wants. Of course, he still relies on you for structure and routine, but he thinks for himself and has his own personality.

Q **Should I give my baby a toy to pull along with him when he walks, even though he is still unsteady on his feet?**

A This usually makes walking more fun, but it also makes it more challenging because he needs to concentrate on walking and pulling at the same time. Don't be surprised if he falls over while trying to manage both tasks simultaneously. You need to keep a watchful eye on him. Most times, however, your baby delights in having the power to make a wheeled toy follow him.

growth and appearance

Your baby has gradually transformed into a thinking, feeling, sensitive infant who is completely fascinated by all that happens around him. His birth weight has tripled and his height has increased by around 50 per cent. The bones in his head have begun to fuse together and that vulnerable soft spot right at the back has closed.

Your baby's jaw looks stronger and more pronounced because more teeth are through. This helps him to chew his food more effectively,

Many babies are walking independently by now – or are very close to doing so.

which in turn develops his mouth and jaw muscles. He has a full head of hair, no longer with a bald patch at the back, because now he spends the bulk of his time sitting or standing.

Your baby's pride in his achievements shows through. He beams as he takes those hesitant steps across the room, looking to you for your approval. His back is straighter and his posture is good. Being able to say at least a couple of words reduces all the frustration that goes with pre-speech communication. Your 1 year-old is altogether a more confident individual, with strong self-belief and a determination to reach his goals.

movement

The moment when your baby surges forward on his own two feet without any support – usually around his first birthday – signals a new stage of independence in his development. As he progresses, his toes start to point towards the front rather than out to the side, enabling him to move more quickly. He also begins to keep his feet closer to the ground instead of lifting them up high. These small changes gradually improve his stability and control.

Despite this, your baby's crawling skills remain important and you should continue to encourage them in new ways. For example, you can put him in one corner of the room and then attract his attention when you are in the opposite corner. This is good exercise for him and he likes the experience of moving over relatively longer distances. You can also build mini obstacle courses for him to negotiate – a thick cushion placed strategically between you and him means he has to climb over it to reach you. Within the next few months, crawling disappears in favour of walking. Your baby now moves from sitting to standing easily, without any help.

Baby strollers are a great way to encourage your baby to spend more time on two legs rather than crawling.

hand–eye coordination

Your baby is good at using toys constructively together in play. When he plays with a plastic cup, saucer and spoon, he handles them appropriately, perhaps putting the cup on top of the saucer or the spoon into the cup. He also has no problem using pointing to let you know what he wants – by now, you know clearly what that rigid index finger is indicating! A noticeable change is that he no longer automatically puts everything straight into his mouth, as he prefers to discover and investigate through his hands.

Your baby is especially fascinated by puzzles that draw on his improved hand–eye coordination. He loves tackling a small wooden inset board, the type that has just one or two pieces cut out in a circle or other simple shape. During mealtimes, he insists on trying to feed himself, although less food reaches his mouth than you would like. Drawing interests him now, especially if you model the actions for him. He grips a crayon tightly in his hand as he tries to make a mark on the paper, but it is faint – more often than not, he accidentally tears the paper with the crayon.

first shoes

The time to buy your baby his first shoes is when he has started to walk by himself, not before. Putting shoes on the feet of a non-walking infant does not make him more likely to take his first step. In fact, until he walks independently, he is best off without socks or shoes on when standing on a carpet because he learns how to use his toes, soles and heels more effectively.

Your baby becomes more interested in games that involve copying everyday activities in the home.

understanding body parts

Your baby's vocabulary for describing parts of his body builds in stages. He learns these words from you – for instance, when you tickle his hand and tell him, 'This is your hand', or stroke the sole of his foot and explain, 'This is your foot'. Stick to the obvious parts such as hair, head, eyes, feet, hands, mouth and ears. Simple activities like this help your baby to learn the names of these body parts easily. Soon he is able to point them out to you on a doll.

Q What can I do to stimulate my baby's creativity?

A Try setting up a small tray with a thick mixture of sand and water. Make the texture solid enough to stick together, roll up your baby's sleeves and let him immerse his hands in the substance. At first, he just picks up the mud and then lets it drop, but after a while he starts to use his memory and background knowledge to create shapes and patterns.

learning

Imagination starts to play a role in your baby's life, which represents a major shift in his learning capacity. Before, he could only think in terms of what he saw directly in front of him. Around now, however, he starts to use symbolic thought. For example, a small shape can become a spoon in his mind and he then pretends to eat with it.

This ability to use his imagination opens up a whole array of learning opportunities. Your baby enjoys playing 'pretend' games with you – for instance, pretending to organize a tea party for his cuddly toys. Reading him stories with an animated expression is another way to enhance his imagination.

Your baby's learning skills are promoted by a wide range of toys, such as play dough, a sand and water tray, plastic shapes, an action toy, a plastic tea set and construction blocks. He learns new ideas and increases his understanding more when he is actively involved in playing with these items. Encourage hands-on play so that he engages with his toys, using them in whatever way he wants.

language

Your baby's first word is probably a 'holophrase' – a unit of sound that is a substitute for an entire sentence. For instance, 'mama' might just refer to his mother or it might mean 'My mother is in the kitchen'. Once the first word has been spoken, the rate at which your baby develops new words will be slower than you expect and he might add only six or seven new words in the next few months. Don't worry: although his slow rate of vocabulary development contrasts sharply with the wide range of sounds he uses in his babbling, the reduction in pace is a universal phenomenon.

Your baby focuses better when you use his name while talking to him. For instance, if you want him to play with a toy, instead of saying, 'Here's a toy for you', start the sentence with his name and then wait until he turns towards you before completing the sentence. Your baby likes you to do this because otherwise he doesn't tune in to your instruction until you are halfway through it. Saying his name at the start gets his attention, and gives him time to concentrate on what you have to say.

social and emotional development

Although your baby still relies totally on you to meet his needs each day, his inborn desire to become independent shows through in small ways. For example, when you are dressing or changing him, he puts out his hands as you bring the jumper towards him; he might even try to pull off some of his clothes. He just wants to play his part.

One-year-olds are notoriously challenging and determined, and can be remarkably confident with others. Yet this is also the time when small fears can develop. In fact, research confirms that most children have a least one fear – of cats, dogs, insects and so on – from 12 months on. If your baby shows fear of something, don't make a fuss. Stay calm, reassure him that he will be fine and then carry on with his normal routine.

Your baby's sense of humour shows through more strongly now. He is relaxed enough in your company to recognize that humour adds to your enjoyment. Unusual situations make him laugh. For instance, if you put his favourite soft toy up your jumper so that only the head pokes out through the top, and then ask, 'Where's...?', he gets the joke and giggles loudly. Bear in mind that every child's sense of humour is different, and some babies are, by nature, less likely to laugh than others. You'll gradually get to know what is guaranteed to set him off in peals of laughter – that's part of the bonding process.

becoming sociable

Your baby needs you to teach him social skills. People fascinate him and he loves watching them. If someone arouses his curiosity, he toddles over to them and sticks his face as close to theirs as he can – he is as likely to do this in the supermarket as he is at parent-and-toddler group! On these occasions, bring him back to your side and tell him not to stare. Even though he doesn't fully understand what you mean, he gradually learns that his actions are not appropriate.

Tickling your baby will make her giggle out loud and probably come back for more.

managing your time

By the end of her first year, your baby will be scrambling about the house, close to walking unaided and more confident about tackling the stairs. She needs less sleep and may now be awake for up to 11 hours a day. She will be into everything and probably getting pretty grubby in the process! At times it will feel as if you have your hands full just coping with her and her needs.

It makes good sense to set up a routine for mealtimes, and this will establish a pattern that can continue for life.

basic ground rules

Although it is impossible to plan every minute of your day and stick to it, you can certainly try a few simple strategies to make your life easier.

Get organized This is the key to successful time management. If you think ahead and have a number of set routines, you will be amazed at how once-impossible day-to-day living can become manageable and enjoyable. You can save yourself a lot of time and energy if you plan your day or week well: know what you should be doing, how you will do it and when. Learn to prioritize your tasks, deciding which need to be sorted urgently, but also those that are important to you. And once you have started something, be sure to finish it before moving on to anything else.

Keep your house tidy This may seem daunting with a growing family, particularly if you work, but there are ways of managing. Toddler-proof your home if you have not already done so (see pages 224–227). This will limit the number of cupboards your baby can empty while your back is turned! Tidy a different room thoroughly once a week and spend 10 minutes a day putting things straight.

Establish routines Now that your child is 12 months old, you will find she responds well to the routines you have in place for meals and bedtime, and these should be cornerstones in your day. You can fit additional activities such as playing and tidying around them. Establish routines for yourself as well to help you keep on top of domestic tasks such as cleaning, washing and ironing, whether this involves the order in which you do things or using systems to make you more efficient.

useful strategies

- Keep a diary – not just of your own appointments but also those of your partner and children – and make a note of everything from library-book due dates to nursery holidays and events.
- Write 'to do' lists and spend a little time each day updating them, adding new items and crossing off those you've completed.
- Keep a pinboard in the hallway or kitchen so that upcoming events and useful phone numbers are easy to locate.

Although your baby loves to feed himself, there will be times when you do not have the time to indulge him.

two-in-one

Find tasks that you can carry out easily as part of another activity: when playing with your child, build in time at the end and make tidying up part of the fun; when preparing food for your baby, cook enough for two or three meals and freeze portions individually; exercise or do the ironing while you watch television.

- Set up routines for everyday household chores.
- Focus on doing one thing at a time and aim to do it as thoroughly as you can.
- Choose one day of the week, or the same time each day, to deal with phone calls, emails, correspondence and bills.
- Rid your home of superfluous clutter – your baby will certainly generate quite a lot, so try to avoid accumulating things you don't really need.
- Tidy up as you go, putting things in their proper place after use so that you don't waste time looking for them next time you need them.
- Take up offers of help wherever possible.
- Allocate one day every week or fortnight on which a grandparent or your partner takes care of your baby.
- Make some time each day for yourself. You need this 'me time' and should make the most of it.
- Learn to relax when your child is asleep.
- Make a conscious effort to spend time playing with your baby.
- Make use of online shopping facilities.
- Keep your storecupboard stocked with all the basics.

know your limits

No parent can be superhuman, and you will wear yourself out if you try to follow routines and organizational plans all the time. Things are bound to go wrong once in a while and the slightest change in plans can have a knock-on effect. Above all, be flexible. Take care of what you can when you can. Have a plan B for things that might not go according to schedule and be prepared to juggle your priorities once in a while.

Never be afraid to ask for help in managing your time, whether you hire a weekly cleaner, have someone collect your baby from childcare or get a friend to do the shopping once in a while. You are seeking to eliminate the stress in your life, and to make sure that the time you spend with your child is quality time. It doesn't matter how many people it takes to achieve this.

Don't lose track of why you have a child, and remember to spend quality time with her when you can.

what your baby can do
12 months

social and emotional development

- Your baby likes to get involved in dressing and undressing.
- He becomes afraid quite easily, usually of small insects or animals.
- His developing sense of humour allows you to enjoy a joke together.

movement

- Around his first birthday, your baby may take his first steps.
- He still crawls, although walking is soon his preferred option.
- He is able to move from sitting to standing with ease.

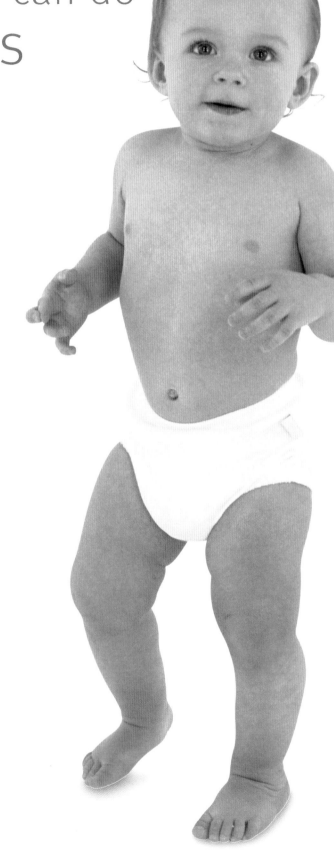

12 months

learning

- Your baby begins to engage in forms of pretend play.
- He can complete some inset-board puzzles, as he sees the link between the shape and the hole.
- He searches accurately for toys played with some time before, as he can now remember where to find them.

language

- Your baby may say his first words, but then his vocabulary growth rate is slow for a number of weeks.
- His concentration and listening is better when you say his name at the start of a conversation to get his attention.
- He is easily discouraged if you correct his speech mistakes, so instead give him a good speech example to copy.

hand–eye coordination

- Your baby no longer puts everything straight into his mouth, preferring to investigate through his hands.
- He can grip a crayon to try to make a faint mark on paper.
- He plays constructively with related toys, such as a plastic cup and saucer.

physical development

Height
Average for a boy is 75.5 cm (29¾ in), for a girl 74 cm (29¼ in).

Weight
Average for a boy is 10.3 kg (22¾ lb), for a girl 9.5 kg (21 lb).

Head
Average circumference for a boy is 46.4 cm (18¼ in), for a girl 45 cm (17¾ in).

Hair
With a full head of hair, the little bald patch at the back of your baby's head has disappeared.

Teeth
More teeth means more powerful chewing, with his jaw more prominent and mouth muscles strengthened.

Eyes
Your baby's strong eye contact helps to intensify your relationship.

Hands
More precise hand control and pincer grip mean he can hold his feeding spoon, and pick things up and drop them where he wants.

Legs
Takes his first independent steps, although he still crawls, especially when negotiating stairs.

Back
Spine posture is very good, keeping him stable when upright, and he no longer tires so easily from physical exertion.

chapter 3
handling your baby

Constant contact with your baby is essential for the bonding process, and you will quickly learn how to hold and carry your baby the best way. Also, by following the step-by-step instructions, it will not be long before you are expert at changing nappies, topping and tailing, massaging and dressing your baby. Establishing a daily care routine means you will always be in close contact with your baby, enabling you to cope with minor skin irritations and the emergence of first teeth, as well as maintaining your baby's hair and nail condition.

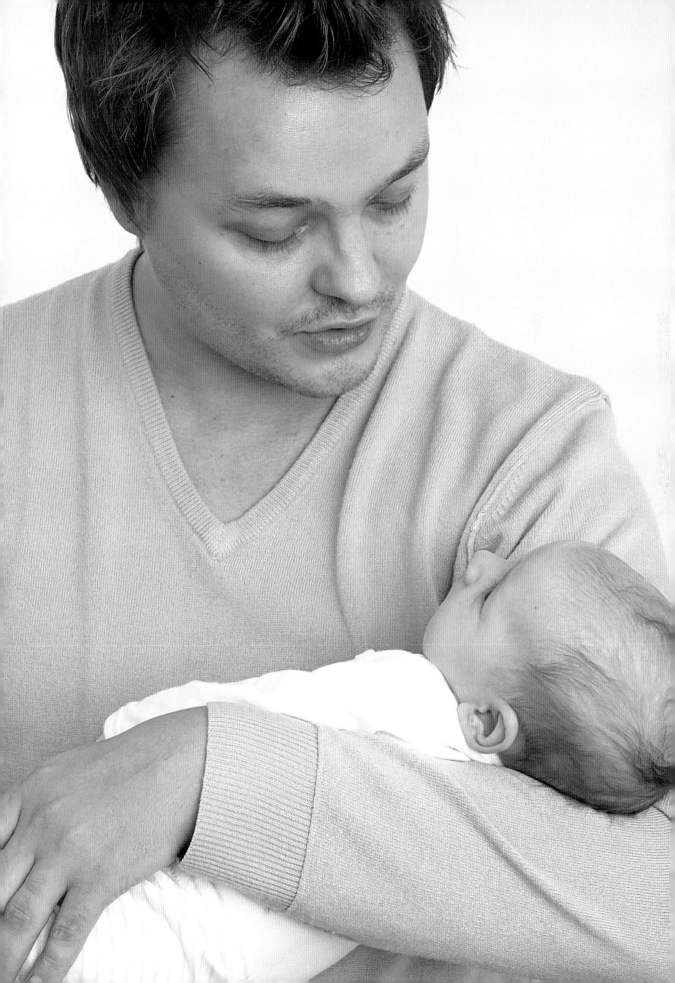

swaddling your baby

Swaddling a baby means wrapping him tightly in a sheet to help him feel safe, secure and cosy. It's an ancient childcare technique, and parents who do it with their babies claim it has all sorts of benefits, from soothing colic to improving a baby's sleep.

sleep benefits

You may have noticed that as he sleeps, from time to time your baby seems to 'startle', throwing his arms and legs backwards. This is the Moro reflex (see page 19), and it can cause babies to wake frequently or have difficulty settling. Swaddling can suppress this reflex, as your baby's arms and legs are firmly wrapped, so it may mean that your baby sleeps for longer periods.

a womb-like environment

Being swaddled can help your baby feel safe in the same way as being held in your arms does. This is because the feeling of being contained that it creates is similar to being tucked tightly inside you, as he was during the last months of pregnancy – although your baby could wriggle and roll, he couldn't wave his arms and legs freely, as there just wasn't enough space.

As your baby gets older and more active, you can progress to a half-swaddle, leaving his arms free but wrapping his body and legs.

what to use

Depending on the time of year, you can use a soft sheet or a shawl for swaddling – make sure it is 100 per cent

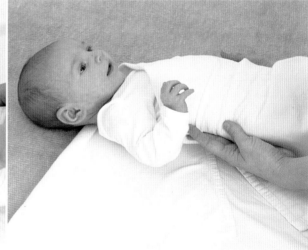

1 Lay out a square cotton sheet with one of the corners at the top so that it forms a diamond shape, then fold down that corner by about 15 cm (6 in).

2 Lie your baby on the sheet so that his neck is level with the fold. Pull the sheet taut, then fold the right-hand corner down over your baby's shoulder and tuck it firmly under his body.

Q When should I stop swaddling my baby?

A Expert opinion varies from 1 month to 6 months. One reason for stopping early is so that swaddling doesn't interfere with your baby's mobility and muscle development. However, as long as you make sure he has plenty of time to kick and wriggle around during his waking hours, there's no need to worry about him being wrapped while he's asleep. If he wriggles and tries to get free, try a half-swaddle or leaving him unwrapped, but if he settles and seems content when swaddled, keep doing it.

cotton so that your baby's skin can breathe. It's also a good idea to use fabric that is a little stretchy so that you can pull it taut and get a really firm swaddle.

Don't double up the sheet or shawl, as this creates too many layers and your baby could overheat. The swaddle sheet counts as a layer of bedding, so adjust the rest of your baby's bedding accordingly (see page 169).

'I swaddled both my babies from birth, and they loved it. My second baby was particularly colicky in the evenings, and we would wrap him up tightly and carry him around, which really calmed his crying. During the night, I'd unwrap and feed him from one breast, then re-swaddle him and offer him the other before putting him back in his cot. He soon realized that this was the signal for him to get sleepy again, and would grow calm and start to breathe more deeply as soon as he was wrapped.'

Edie Martin, mother of
Estelle (2 years) and Thomas (8 months)

shared experience

3 Lift the bottom corner up over your baby's legs.

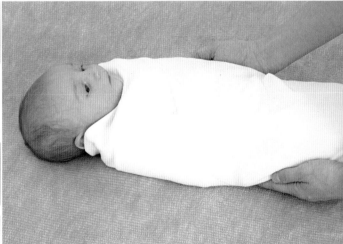

4 Pull the other side taut and fold the left-hand corner down over your baby's other shoulder, again tucking it under his body to hold it firm. The idea is for your baby to feel held, not squashed, so make sure he's swaddled firmly but not too tightly.

holding
your baby

All new parents worry that they aren't holding their baby properly, or that they might hurt or drop her. Fathers in particular can often feel clumsy and uncoordinated when faced with such a tiny and delicate little person. But other than crying, touch is the only way your baby can communicate with you, and close physical contact is what makes her feel safe and comforted.

close to you

Your baby has spent the last 9 months cushioned and protected by the warm surroundings of the womb, and during that time she's grown used to the muffled sounds of voices – particularly those of her parents, the thud of her mother's heartbeat and the gently rocking sensation of her movements. The transition into the outside world can be a shocking one, so it's a good idea to try to make your baby's surroundings as safe and comforting as you can.

There is no better way to hold a newborn baby – for you just as much as for her – than close to your body, with skin on skin.

By holding your baby close to your body, you're providing the warmth and security she's accustomed to, and she'll also be able to

feel and hear your soothing heartbeat. If you hold her while you walk and move around, either in your arms or in a sling or papoose, she will also enjoy the sensation of motion.

how you feel

Your baby cannot understand your words yet, but she will use her other senses to pick up on your emotions, to help her make sense of the world around her. She'll quickly learn how the intonation of your voice communicates whether you're happy, sad, excited or worried, and she'll be able to sense these feelings when you touch her too. If you are feeling anxious when you pick her up, because you don't know why she's crying or aren't confident in your ability to soothe or care for her, she'll become anxious too.

You may be new to this, but the most experienced midwife or childcare expert in the world doesn't share the special bond with your baby that you do, so there's no need to let your inexperience make you feel unsure. Each time you go to pick up your baby, remind yourself of how precious she is to you, how much she needs you and how comforting it is for her to be close to you. She might not stop crying straight away, but the more calmly and confidently you handle her, the more soothed she will feel. Think about the tone of voice you use when you hold her too. You may not be talking to her directly, but she doesn't know that, so don't argue with others over her head or hold difficult telephone conversations while you cuddle her.

constant contact

In some cultures, mothers carry their babies with them at all times, and they sleep, feed and watch the world from the security of their mothers' back or front. In our society, it's a bit more difficult to have your baby with you constantly, but if you choose to, you can have your baby close to you as often as you want.

There's often pressure on you as a new mother to have 'time to yourself', usually from well-meaning friends and relatives who know how exhausting it can be caring for a newborn. But sometimes new mothers are happiest when they are close to their babies, no matter how tired they feel, as only then can they be sure that their child has everything she needs. Don't feel that you have to put your baby in a chair, bouncer, pram or even another person's arms if you don't want to. There's nothing strange or abnormal about wanting to be physically bonded with your baby, and as the weeks and months go by, both of you will gradually feel happier to become more separate from each other, at your own pace.

On the other hand, when you do feel the need for your own time and space, don't fear that your baby will be unhappy to be separated from you. It's healthy and natural for a child to develop a bond with a wider family and social group, and if you have people close to you who want to help and get to know your baby better, take advantage of their offers of assistance when you feel you need a break.

At this early stage, you can stay close to your baby for as much time as you want.

'When my son was 2 weeks old, he developed colic and would cry for hours. The only way to soothe him was to hold him close and walk with him. When he was 5 weeks old, we stayed with my mother-in-law and one evening she said, 'You sit and relax, I can walk with him'. It was like a weight being lifted from me. I realized that although my baby needed to be held, it didn't always have to be me that did it.'

Siobhan, mother of
Conor (4 years) and Aaron (1 year)

shared experience

how to
hold your baby

Holding and carrying your baby is something that will soon be second nature to you. The vital thing is that your baby's head is well supported, as her neck isn't yet strong enough to support her own head. Try these positions to find out which is best suited to you and your baby.

When you pick up your baby, start by putting one hand behind her head and neck, and the other underneath her bottom. Lift her towards you gently, keeping your hands behind her head, neck and bottom for support, and cuddle her head close to your chest.

Some babies like to be held on your arm, facing downwards. Lay her across one forearm, with your other hand underneath her for extra support.

'My second baby wanted to be held all the time, and was really only happy and settled when she was in my arms, or my husband's. Some people called her 'clingy', but we liked to describe it as 'cuddly'! I quickly learned that fighting her nature was pointless, so we decided to go with it and I carried her around in a sling, with her face cuddled into my body. I could wash up, make sandwiches, sweep the floor, and she was happy and contented. It was actually nice for me to have her close, and she's grown into a happy, contented toddler – not clingy at all!'

Erin, mother of
Nathan (3 years) and Evie (1 year)

shared experience

Holding your baby on your arm facing you means she can see your face, which some babies find comforting. Cradle her head in the crook of your arm, supporting her bottom with your other hand.

You can also hold your baby on your shoulder, which is particularly good after she's had a feed, as it will help her to burp. Support her head with one hand, and put the other underneath her bottom.

changing
your baby's nappy

In the early days with your baby, you may need to change his nappy as often as ten times a day. It is therefore a good idea to get everything you need at the start, which means you will have to decide what nappies and changing equipment you want to use.

'Evie had awful nappy rash for weeks, starting at 3 weeks old. I tried antifungal cream from the doctor and strong nappy cream, but nothing worked. The thing that did the trick was lying her on her mat with no nappy to kick around for ages – I put towels underneath her just in case! Luckily, it was summer so I could do that without her getting cold.'

Jane, mother of
Evie (8 months)

shared experience

what's in his nappy?

Your newborn's faeces will be almost liquid, but even at this early stage they will be hugely affected by what kind of milk he receives. If you are breast-feeding, you will notice a difference if your baby has even small amounts of formula, as the faeces will be a different colour and a little more solid. Once you introduce your baby to solid foods, the contents of his nappies will seem much more 'adult', and can change in colour and frequency depending on what he has eaten. At this stage he may even suffer from constipation: if this happens, consider increasing his fluid intake.

A baby may have runny nappies for a few days as one of the after-effects of an immunization, a change in diet or even having eaten some dirt in the garden. If your baby seems well in every other way, don't worry, but if the runny faeces are accompanied by other symptoms such as loss of appetite, a temperature or appearing generally unwell, contact your doctor.

To avoid unnecessary irritation, always make sure your baby's bottom is dry as well as clean before putting on another nappy.

If you can afford the space in the nursery, a changing table can make nappy changing quicker and more efficient, as everything you need is always in the same place.

wet nappies

The only indication you'll have as to how often your baby is urinating is the weight of his nappy. You'll soon learn what a nappy feels like when it's very wet and how often your baby needs to be changed. If your baby goes off feeding due to any illness, it usually does no harm for a few days as long as he doesn't become dehydrated. However, if his nappies seem quite dry, try to encourage him to take more fluids and contact your doctor if you are concerned.

nappy rash

If your baby wears a dirty or wet nappy for a long time it can quickly lead to a sore, red rash (see page 254), so make sure you change it promptly, especially after a bowel movement. Nappy rash can also be caused by a fungal infection (thrush). Preventative measures include cleaning your baby's bottom thoroughly at every change, using a nappy cream, changing nappies regularly and leaving his bottom bare when possible to allow it to air. Treat nappy rash with a thick layer of nappy cream to soothe and heal, and contact your doctor if it doesn't clear up within a couple of days.

changing equipment

Changing mat or table Mats vary hugely in price, but really cheap ones tend to crack and split quickly. A changing table has a mat on top plus useful drawers and shelves, but you can lie your changing mat on the floor or bed instead.

Wipes There are many types available, including eco-friendly ones. The perfume and other chemicals in wipes can cause some babies' skin to become sore. If this happens, switch brands, try unscented ones or use cotton wool and water, which is cheaper and just as effective.

Nappy cream A barrier cream will protect your baby's skin from urine and faeces, and will also help his skin to heal if he has a rash.

Nappy sacks Scented bags in which to seal up smelly nappies can be a good idea if you are out and about. These are not biodegradable, so if you're at home, consider just putting dirty nappies straight into an outside bin to stop your house getting smelly. There are eco-friendly bags available too, which are unscented but still seal off the smells.

the eco-friendly option

Modern reusable nappies come in a huge variety of styles with a range of fastenings, so no pins are required. As well as potentially being better for the environment than disposables, reusable nappies can save you money:

- After the initial outlay, all you'll be spending is a little extra on your fuel bills for washing. Alternatively, you can use a nappy laundry service that picks up and delivers to your door, which is more expensive but very convenient.
- If you have more children, you can use the same nappies again.
- If you don't, your nappies will have a good resale value.
- Consider buying your nappies second-hand to begin with, as this is often very good value. Some local authorities have incentive schemes where you can buy cloth nappies at a discount or borrow sample packs to see if you like them.

Although disposable eco-nappies are available, some of which use unbleached materials, as yet none is 100 per cent biodegradable.

how to
change a nappy

Although the thought of a dirty nappy may seem unpleasant, you'll find that newborn faeces aren't particularly smelly and before long you'll be so used to it all that you won't think twice. The key is having everything close to hand before you start, including your changing mat, wipes or cotton wool and water, nappy cream and a clean nappy.

a time for fun

Changing a nappy may seem like a mundane, everyday task, but that doesn't mean that you can't try and make it more enjoyable for you and your baby. After all, it's one time of the day when you are completely focused on your baby and can't be distracted by any other tasks!

Try singing some songs and rhymes while you change him – these can be anything from traditional nursery rhymes such as 'incy wincy spider', where you can use your fingers to be the spider and tickle your baby's tummy, or your own little songs that you make up about what you're doing.

Lots of babies don't seem to like having their nappies changed, so the more enjoyable you can make the experience, the better. Remember to include lots of kisses, smiles and encouragement while you are

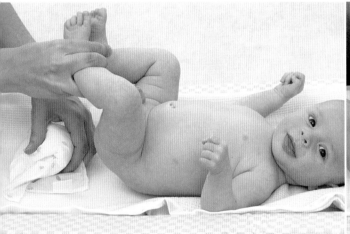
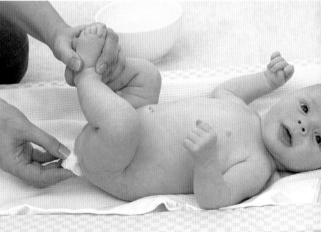

1 Lie your baby on the changing mat and undo the tabs on the nappy he is wearing. Gently lift him by his ankles and pull the old nappy from under him. If it is soiled, use the clean portion at the front to wipe the worst of the mess off your baby's skin before you clean him.

2 Clean your baby by gently wiping his skin with cotton wool soaked in lukewarm water or a baby wipe. With a boy, hold his testicles out of the way and clean under them, then wipe over them and under his penis. Don't try to push his foreskin back to clean under it. With a girl, wipe from front to back and don't try to clean inside the vagina. Now dry your baby if you used water, and apply nappy cream if you wish.

> 'Changing a newborn's nappy is easy compared to what comes later – the real challenge starts when your baby is older, and can roll over and crawl away when you're halfway through!'

Theresa, mother of
Frankie (8 months)

shared experience

nappy-free from birth

If changing so many nappies sounds daunting, you could consider going without. Some mothers practise a technique called Elimination Communication (EC), where you learn to identify the signals your baby makes to show that he needs to urinate or open his bowels. In some cultures, babies are carried around strapped to their mothers' bodies all day and are simply taken out of the papoose when needed. Anthropologists studying this method discovered that the babies tend to twitch or clench their thighs when they are about to go, and because their mothers are in such close physical contact, they can feel this signal in plenty of time. EC works on the same principle: spend time close to your baby and you will learn to spot the particular grunts or wriggles he makes when he needs to go, so you'll be able to hold him on the potty in time.

changing the nappy. If you have time, allow your baby to have a little kick around on his mat without a nappy on, as he'll enjoy being able to move his legs about freely, and it's also good for his skin to get some fresh air. Make sure that the room is a comfortable temperature, and it's a good idea to place a couple of towels underneath him just in case he urinates.

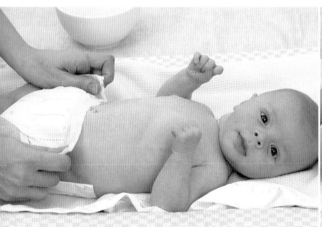
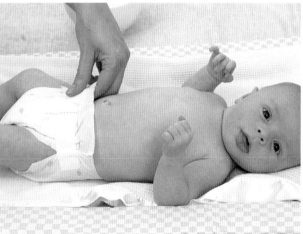

3 Lift your baby gently by his ankles again and slip a clean nappy underneath him. The side with the tabs goes under his bottom. Make sure the nappy is straight, then pull the front of it up between his legs, tuck in the waistband and fasten the tabs. With a boy, make sure his penis is tucked down so that the urine doesn't go up towards his tummy.

4 Check that the nappy isn't too tight by ensuring you can slide one finger between your baby's skin and the waistband. Dispose of solid nappy contents in the lavatory pan. Never throw disposable nappies in the toilet – put them in your rubbish bin.

topping and tailing

Your newborn baby doesn't need a bath every day. She is not doing very much at the moment and therefore doesn't get particularly dirty, and her skin is still adjusting to the conditions of the outside world, so may be too delicate to be washed all over too often.

priorities

The main parts of your baby's body that are important to keep clean are her face and neck, which may get milk and occasional bits of vomit on them, and her bottom, in order to avoid nappy rash (see page 137). The best way to do this is to top and tail your baby, which literally means to wash just her 'top' and her 'tail'. You will need a changing mat with a towel spread on it, a bowl of lukewarm water and some cotton wool. You should also get your baby's clean nappy and clothes ready for when she is clean.

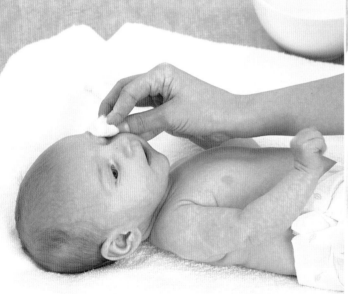

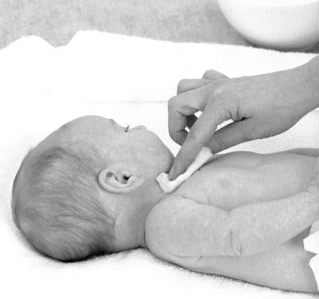

1 Lay your baby on her changing mat, with a towel underneath her. Dampen some cotton wool with the water and wipe one eye from the inside corner outwards. Use a clean piece of cotton wool for the other eye to avoid any transfer of germs if your baby has a sticky eye or eye infection (see page 244).

2 Use another piece of cotton wool to wipe your baby's face and neck, paying special attention to the creases. Then wipe her ears, including behind them (but not inside), again using a new piece of cotton wool for each ear. If you want to clean your baby's hair, simply wipe it over with a flannel and water or another piece of cotton wool – but there's no need to wash her hair every day.

3 Wash her hands with damp cotton wool, uncurling her fingers, then clean her feet and in between her toes, and under her arms. Pat her dry with the towel.

Q The shops are full of toiletries made specially for babies, and I'm unsure if I need to buy them or not?

A Plain water is perfectly adequate for washing your baby's skin and hair, particularly when she is tiny, as the chemicals in soaps could dry her skin. But if you do choose to use bubble bath, soap or shampoo, it's a good idea to buy those specially formulated for babies, as they are kinder to the skin and safer if they get into your baby's eyes. There are lots of natural ranges available now, as well as the better known mainstream brands, so shop around to find something you like.

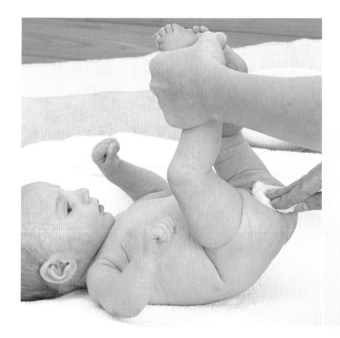

4 Last of all, clean your baby's bottom and genitals. For a girl, wipe with damp cotton wool from front to back, and never inside her vagina. For a boy, wipe his penis, testicles and underneath, but don't pull back his foreskin.

5 When you have finished, wrap your baby in the towel and gently pat her dry. Then put on her clean nappy and clothes, and give her lots of cuddles.

caring for
your baby's cord

At birth, your baby's umbilical cord is about 30 cm (12 in) long and is attached to his tummy button. It was the route by which food and oxygen passed from the placenta to your baby, but now he can breathe for himself, the cord can be cut and stops functioning immediately.

cutting the cord

When your baby is delivered, your midwife will put a little plastic clamp on the umbilical cord about 2 cm (¾ in) from his navel before cutting it.

Within a day or two, this remaining piece of cord will dry up and become hard, still with the clamp on it. The clamp may be removed by the midwife who visits you at home, but it is more likely that this will be left on until the cord drops off completely.

Take care when putting on nappies in the first few days, as they may catch on your baby's cord, causing it to bleed.

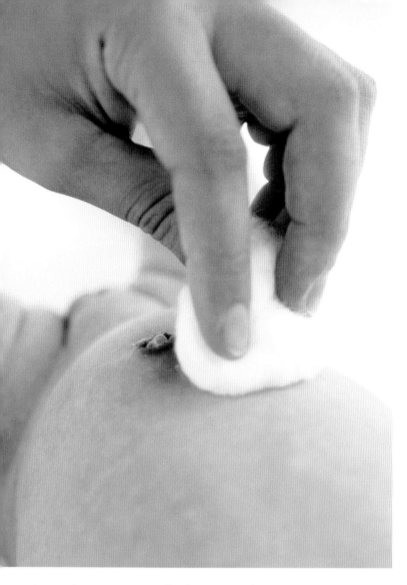

You can keep your baby's cord clean simply by wiping it with cotton wool dipped in fresh warm water.

warning signs

Look out for any unpleasant smell or more than a few spots of blood or discharge around your baby's cord. If you spot either of these things, let your midwife know, as it could be sign of infection.

Q We are about to have our baby son circumcised – how should I keep the area clean and healthy afterwards?

cleaning around the cord

You don't have to do anything different with the area around your baby's cord – just keep it clean and dry, like the rest of his skin. Don't be frightened to touch the cord – it doesn't have any nerves in it, so it won't hurt your baby. Clean the cord with a baby sponge or a piece of clean, damp cotton wool, while you top and tail or bath your baby (see pages 140–141 and 144–145).

Make sure the skin around the cord is completely dry, by patting it with a soft towel or dry cotton wool, before putting on your baby's nappy and clothes.

When you put your baby's nappy on, you can fold the front part of the nappy down a little so that it doesn't catch on the cord. If it does catch, this can sometimes cause a tiny amount of bleeding, but this doesn't hurt your baby and is nothing to worry about.

Around days 7–8, you may notice tiny spots of dried blood or a yellowish discharge on the front of your baby's nappy or vest at navel level. This is a sign that the cord is separating and will probably drop off in a day or two. Once the cord drops off, your baby's navel may look a bit raw, but it's usually not sore and should heal within a few days.

A Once your baby boy has been circumcised, you just need to keep his penis clean using plain water, at the same time as you bath or top and tail him. For the first few days following a circumcision the penis may look a little inflamed, and you may notice a yellowish discharge. These are both signs that the area is healing normally, so are nothing to worry about. Circumcision sites are unlikely to get infected, but if the redness doesn't disappear after a few days, your baby's penis is swollen at the tip or there are yellow sores with fluid in them, contact your doctor straight away.

bathing your newborn

For the first few weeks of your baby's life she will not be getting particularly dirty, so a 'top and a tail' once or twice a day is fine (see pages 140–141), with a full bath a couple of times a week. If bathing upsets your baby, give her a sponge bath on your lap instead or take her into the bath with you (be sure to adjust the temperature).

a full bath

It is a good idea to use a plastic baby bath for the first few weeks, as the size of a regular bathtub may intimidate your baby. Alternatively, you could use the kitchen sink, where the draining board can be useful for hair washing. Before starting, make sure you have everything you need to hand, as you won't be able to leave your baby once you have begun. Gather together at least one clean towel, nappy changing equipment, baby shampoo, a mild soap, cotton wool and clean, dry clothes.

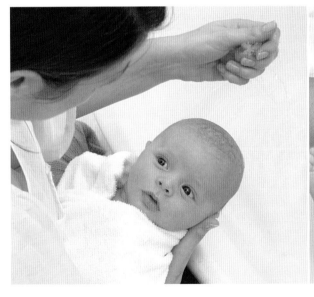

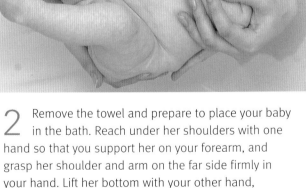

1 Fill the bath to a depth of around 10 cm (4 in), with warm water at body temperature (see box opposite). Undress your baby, remove her nappy and clean the nappy area with cotton wool and water or a wipe, if her nappy was soiled. To prevent her getting too cold during bathtime, wrap her in a towel and wash her hair over the edge of the bath (see page 152). Hold her with her legs under one arm, with your forearm supporting her back and your hand holding her head.

2 Remove the towel and prepare to place your baby in the bath. Reach under her shoulders with one hand so that you support her on your forearm, and grasp her shoulder and arm on the far side firmly in your hand. Lift her bottom with your other hand, holding one thigh firmly, and lower her slowly into the water.

safety first

- Always fill the bath with cold water first, then add the hot, to avoid burns.
- By dipping your elbow in the bath water you can tell whether or not the water is approximately body temperature (29.4°C/85°F). Your hands are generally cooler than the rest of you, so are not a reliable gauge.
- If you use the sink or an adult bath, keep your baby away from the taps, as she may kick against them or be scalded by a hot drip.
- Never leave your baby unattended in the bath.
- Keep hold of your baby at all times so that she doesn't slip.

For more information on bathroom safety, see pages 224–226.

' My newborn baby really took to bathing and splashed about happily right up to the moment when I started to wash his hair. He simply hated having water poured over his head and would scream and thrash about. I got round the problem by using a flannel to sponge his head when it came to rinsing – it made bathtime a much happier experience for both of us. '

Julie, mother of
Simon (8 weeks)

shared experience

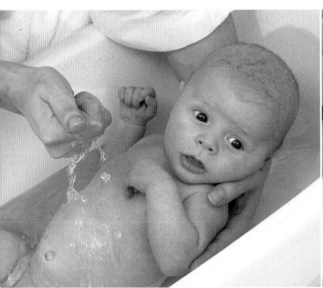
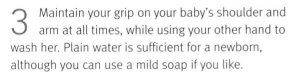

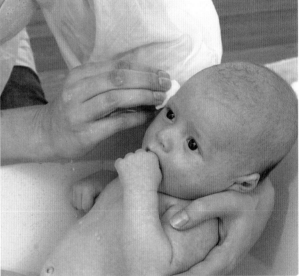

3 Maintain your grip on your baby's shoulder and arm at all times, while using your other hand to wash her. Plain water is sufficient for a newborn, although you can use a mild soap if you like.

4 Clean your baby's face using cotton wool – a separate piece for each eye – then around but not in her ears, and the rest of her face, including any creases (see page 140). When she is clean and rinsed, lift your baby out of the water on to a large dry towel and wrap her quickly. Pat her dry, taking particular care in the creases, and again use cotton wool to dry her delicate areas.

your baby's
first teeth

Your baby's first set of teeth are called 'milk teeth' and usually start to come through the gums any time from around 4 months old – although some babies are actually born with teeth, while others don't get their first tooth until well after their first birthday. If you are very lucky, the first sign you'll notice is the tip of a tiny white tooth peeking through your baby's gum, but many parents find that the arrival of each tooth is preceded by days of crying, sleepless nights and flushed cheeks.

making an appearance

Milk teeth appear gradually, usually one at a time, although your baby may sometimes seem to be getting two at once. This is the order in which they usually appear:

1 First incisors (bottom) 6–8 months
2 First incisors (top) 6–8 months
3 Second incisors (top) 8–10 months
4 Second incisors (bottom) 8–10 months
5 First molars (top) 12–16 months
6 First molars (bottom) 12–16 months
7 Canine teeth (top) 16–20 months
8 Canine teeth (bottom) 16–20 months
9 Second molars (bottom) 2–3 years
10 Second molars (top) 2–3 years

This is the most common order, but if your child's teeth come through slightly differently, this is nothing to worry about. The teeth often come through crooked and then straighten up.

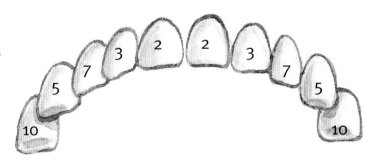

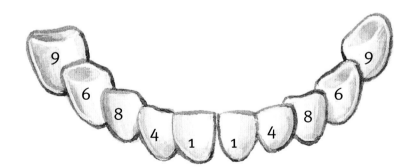

Babies often distract themselves from the pain of teething by chewing on something close to hand. A chilled teething ring can be very soothing.

' If Cleo was grizzly, all I had to do was give her some teething powders. They worked instantly and Cleo seemed to like the sensation of having them on her tongue. I recommended them to my friends, who were sceptical, but couldn't believe the difference in their babies once they tried them. '

Jenni, mother of
Cleo (20 months)

shared experience

coping with teething

The discomfort of teething is usually worse with the first few teeth, although the molars can cause some soreness. Try these tips to help your baby cope with teething discomfort.

Give your baby something to bite on – teething babies seem to want to chew anything they can get their hands on. He may enjoy a chilled carrot stick or piece of apple, but beware of the danger of choking. Alternatively, give him a teething ring – the type you can chill in the fridge is very soothing. Also try rubbing his gums with your finger or a baby gum massager, which are available from pharmacists.

A teething gel, which you rub on to your baby's gums to ease pain and inflammation, can be very effective. The gel works for about 20 minutes, so it can be helpful in allowing your baby to get back to sleep during the night.

If your baby is really suffering, from the age of 3 months, you can try a dose of infant paracetamol to relieve the pain.

A teething baby who is weaned may go off solids for a while, and may need more milk as a result. This should only last a few days, so if your baby loses his appetite for a longer period, he may be unwell, and it's best to check with your GP or health visitor.

teething symptoms

Doctors and dentists will usually tell you that teething doesn't cause any symptoms other than sore gums, but many parents notice a range of other problems such as a temperature, nappy rash and diarrhoea. If your baby has any of these symptoms, don't assume it's just teething, as he may be unwell. Seek medical advice if you are concerned.

toothcare tips

- Look for alternatives to sweets and biscuits as snacks: try dried fruit, chopped fresh fruit, dry cereal or vegetable sticks.
- If you must give sweet treats, chocolate is a better option than sweets. Lollipops are the worst, as they bathe the teeth in sugar for a long time. With a young baby, beware of the danger of choking.
- Make sure anyone else who looks after your baby – whether it's grandparents, a childminder or a nursery – sticks to your rules about what he can and can't have.

'I thought that baby toothpaste was a waste of money, until I found out that the levels of fluoride in the adult kind could cause my child's teeth to discolour.'

Sandra, mother of
Toby (9 months)

shared experience

caring for your baby's teeth

Just because your child's first teeth will fall out a few years down the line doesn't mean you shouldn't take care of them. It's important to get into a regime of cleaning your baby's teeth as soon as they begin to show through the gums, not only to prevent decay but also to get your baby used to the sensation so that it becomes a part of his routine before he is old enough to protest about it.

The health of your baby's first teeth can have an effect on what his adult teeth look like too. If your child has teeth removed due to decay, the gaps in his mouth can cause the adult teeth below the gums to shift so that they're not as straight as they should be when they come through.

a good diet

The key to avoiding tooth decay is diet. It is vital to avoid sugary foods: this doesn't just mean sweets and chocolate, but also sugary cereals, cakes and biscuits. Even savoury foods such as crisps can stick to the teeth for a long period of time and cause decay. Check the labels of everything you give your baby, and look out for 'hidden' sugars such as sucrose, glucose or lactose. Processed foods are often higher in sugar than you might expect, so it's best to give your baby as much home-prepared food as possible to be sure what he's eating.

What you do let your baby eat is just as important as what you don't. Making sure you provide lots of calcium will help him to build strong, healthy teeth that will be better able to resist decay. Milk, cheese and yoghurt, plus sardines and other oily fish, are all rich in calcium. It's also worth ensuring you eat plenty of calcium yourself during pregnancy, as your baby's milk teeth and adult teeth are all formed while he is still in the womb.

what's in his drinks?

You may think your baby is safe if he's not on solids yet, but you also have to be extremely careful about what he drinks. While sugar in drinks is harmful, 'reduced sugar' or 'no added sugar' juice drinks and squashes can also contain acids that erode the enamel of the teeth over time, making them more vulnerable to decay.

When babies suck on a bottle or beaker, the liquid swills around their teeth, so stick to plain water or, if you really want to give juice, then water it down. A sippy cup is better for the teeth than a baby bottle, as your baby will tend to suck only when he's thirsty, not for comfort. Never let your baby fall asleep with a bottle of juice, squash or even milk (which contains a sugar called lactose) – you should brush your baby's teeth after his last bedtime drink.

visit the dentist

Problems with your baby's teeth, such as areas of decay, are much easier to deal with if they are caught early, so it's important to pay regular visits to the dentist from the time your baby's first teeth appear. If he gets used to this early on, it will be much less frightening for him.

how to brush

Choose a small-headed brush with soft bristles. You will be brushing your child's teeth for him until he's around 7 years old, so a brush with a long handle for you to grip can be useful. Fluoride in toothpaste strengthens the tooth enamel, which helps to protect the teeth against decay. Use one formulated specially for children, as adult ones contain too much fluoride for babies.

1 Hold your baby in your arms while you brush, as you would if you were were giving him a bottle.

2 Brush in small circular movements, concentrating on one section of the mouth at a time. Don't forget to brush behind the teeth as well.

caring for
your baby's skin

Nothing feels softer than a new baby's skin. It's like silk, or velvet, and it can seem incredibly delicate too, when you think of all the things it will have to face in the outside world. Heat and cold, the rubbing of nappies and clothes, water and soap can all be damaging, but at the same time your baby's skin is tougher than it looks, and will soon adjust to its new surroundings.

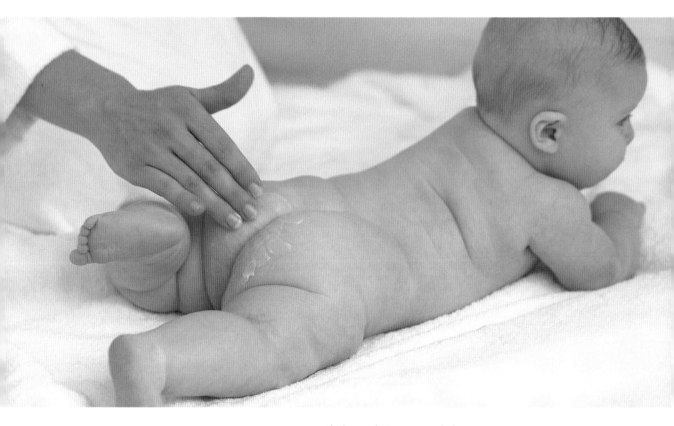

Many minor skin problems will clear up on their own or with routine care, but consult your doctor if they persist.

possible skin problems

There are lots of minor skin niggles that you might encounter in the early weeks and months with your baby, but most of these are easily treated, and many will go away on their own.

Dry skin In the womb your baby's skin was protected by a waxy layer, but now she is out in the world, her skin can easily become dry. This will resolve itself with time, but in the meantime you can massage a natural plant-based oil – such as olive or grapeseed – into her body (see pages 160–163). You can also talk to your doctor or pharmacist about using aqueous cream.

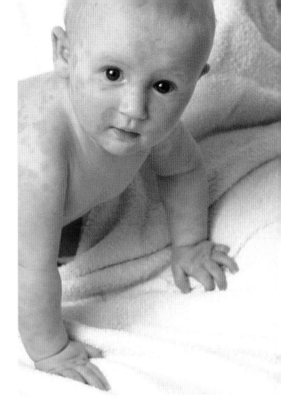

Milia (milk spots) These little white spots are very common in the first few weeks of life and are nothing to worry about. They feel smooth, and babies get them most often on their noses and chins. They are caused by blocked sweat and oil glands, and should vanish of their own accord.

Heat rash It doesn't have to be particularly hot for a small baby to develop heat rash, as her tiny pores will clog easily when they sweat. The rash, which is bright red and pimply, is most common where the skin rubs together – under the arms, between the thighs – but is sometimes all over.

Dress your baby in cotton clothes to let her skin breathe, keep her in the shade and let her kick about on her mat with no clothes on. Cool her skin with cool flannels or a tepid bath, and dab calamine lotion on the rash.

Eczema There are different kinds of eczema, but the symptoms are the same: red, cracked and itching skin. Atopic eczema, part of a family of conditions that also includes asthma and hayfever, often runs in families, while contact eczema is caused by sensitivity to clothing, washing powder, toiletries or other triggers. Some children with contact eczema develop atopic eczema as well.

Use cotton clothes and bedding to let the skin breathe, and avoid perfumed bath products or washing powder. Your doctor or pharmacist will be able to recommend a good emollient cream, or may prescribe a mild steroid (hydrocortisone) cream. Keep your baby's nails short so that the skin doesn't get broken with her scratching and become infected. You could also consider dietary triggers: talk to your health professional about how to identify foods to which your baby might be sensitive.

rashes

Babies can get a rash for all sorts of reasons. Most are completely harmless, such as a heat rash or milia (see above). A rash can also be a reaction to a soap, bubble bath or washing powder, so if your baby's skin seems irritated, it is worth trying products designed for sensitive skin. You could also think about using soap nuts – a natural, environmentally friendly laundry product that is much kinder to skin than detergent.

However, a rash can also be a symptom of something more serious, such as rubella (German measles), measles or meningitis. For more information on the rash associated with meningitis, see page 247. If you are concerned, contact your doctor immediately.

safety in the sun

The skin of children and babies is much more sensitive to the sun than that of adults. Research shows that early exposure to the sun can increase the chances of developing skin cancer in later life, so it's vital that you protect your baby's skin now, using suncream, hats and sensible clothing. See page 229 for details.

It is rare for a rash to be a symptom of something harmful, but check with a doctor.

Q My mother wants me to get my baby girl's ears pierced. She's only a few weeks old. Is it safe?

A Piercing involves damaging the skin and is best avoided for young babies. Anything that breaks the skin can potentially allow infection in. If you do decide to go ahead, it's essential that you get the piercing done at a reputable establishment, that only pure metal such as gold is used and that you care properly for the ear lobes afterwards. If your daughter's ears show any sign of infection, such as redness, swelling, pus or an unpleasant smell, contact your doctor immediately.

caring for your baby's
hair and nails

The amount of hair your baby has can vary enormously: some babies are born with a thick, bushy headful, while others remain almost hairless until well after their first birthday. It doesn't matter either way, although there will certainly be less washing and brushing involved if your baby's hair is at the thinner end of the spectrum.

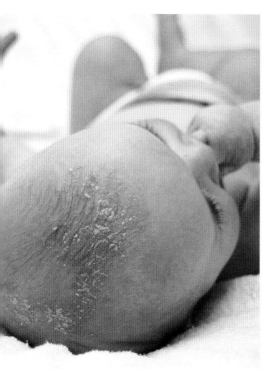

Babies rarely seem bothered by cradle cap, and it usually disappears of its own accord over a period of time.

washing your baby's hair

There is no need to wash your baby's hair every day, nor do you need to use shampoo if he has just a light covering of hair – plain water is fine. If his hair is very thick, you may want to use shampoo. Choose a gentle variety formulated for babies, which is less likely to irritate his eyes if he gets splashed.

It is best to be as quick and efficient as possible, leaning your baby's head back over your arm (see page 144), shampooing once only and rinsing with clean, warm water. You can buy a shampoo shield to fit around your baby's head, which will prevent water and soap getting on his face, but some babies find this even more frightening. If your baby really doesn't like hair washing, keep it to a minimum – certainly no more than once a week and perhaps even less frequently, as a baby's hair doesn't get very dirty.

Gently use your hand to wet your baby's hair. If you are using soap or baby shampoo, take just a tiny amount and lather it by gently stroking your baby's hair. Then use your hand again to scoop a little water over his hair, rinsing out the soap. You can also use the bubbles from the bath, if you've used bubble bath.

It's not necessary to use conditioner on your baby's hair, as it is already soft – not like thicker, coarser adult hair. As he gets older and his hair gets longer it may become tangly, in which case you can use a detangling spray. This is a conditioner that you leave on, which makes combing out the tangles easier and less painful.

Cradle cap consists of scaly patches of often yellowish skin on your baby's head. It's caused by his skin producing excess oil (sebum), is very common and is not serious. Sometimes, however, cradle cap can be a sign of a skin condition called seborrhoeic dermatitis (see page 254), so get it checked if you are worried.

You can buy cradle cap shampoos, or rub olive oil into the scales and gently loosen them with a soft toothbrush, but it's best to leave it to clear up on its own with time. Don't pick at it, or it could become infected and sore.

cutting your baby's hair and nails

It's quite unusual for a baby's hair to grow really long before the age of 12 months, so the most you should need to do is give the front an occasional snip if it's falling in his eyes. Try to get your partner to do this while your baby is having a feed, or even while he's sleeping, to cause the least stress. There's really no need to go to the hairdresser until your child is a toddler, as this will be expensive and potentially upsetting for your baby. Stick to trimming his hair gently at home for the time being, or just leave it to grow.

Cutting your baby's fingernails will need to be done much more regularly, as they grow at a very rapid rate. Toenails grow quickly too, but are often soft and almost transparent, so they can grow long without you noticing.

Q **Do I need to cut my baby's nails, and if so, how can I make sure I don't hurt him?**

A It's important to keep your baby's fingernails short so that he doesn't accidentally scratch himself. For the first week or so you may want to put him in 'scratch mitts' until you pluck up the courage to cut his nails. Choose a time when he is relaxed, such as when he is feeding or even asleep. It's best to cut nails when they're soft after a bath, using special baby nail scissors that won't cut the skin (available from pharmacies). For older babies, make it into a game using the rhyme 'This little piggy' to ease any wriggling.

Take care when cutting nails: your baby is likely to wriggle about, making it difficult.

your baby's
clothes

You will probably receive plenty of baby clothes as presents or hand-me-downs from family and friends, so don't buy too much in advance. However, there are certain basic items that you cannot do without. Babies can get through two or three changes of clothes per day, so make sure you have enough of everything to allow for washing and drying.

getting dressed

Your baby might find getting dressed upsetting at first, particularly the sensation of being naked and cold. Try not to rush if she is crying, as this could make her more anxious as she picks up on your tension. Smile, talk to her soothingly, sing and give her lots of cuddles as you go along.

clothing essentials

Start with the following in newborn size, then add extras if you find you need more:

- Shawl or blanket to wrap your baby in or tuck around her in the pram or car seat.

All a baby needs in the first few weeks is a number of sleepsuits for comfort during the many hours she spends asleep.

- 6 sleepsuits to double as day- and nightwear initially, as your baby will be having lots of naps during the day and will need to be wearing something comfortable and soft. The suits have built-in feet, so you don't have to use socks.
- 6 vests/bodysuits with short or long sleeves, depending on the weather. They have poppers that go under your baby's bottom, so won't ride up. In cold weather, your baby can wear them under her clothes; in really hot weather, she may like to sleep in just her vest and nappy.
- Fabric bootees (also called padders or baggies) for outdoors.
- 2 cardigans or light hoodies/jackets.
- 3 pairs of socks.
- Sun hat or woolly hat, depending on the season.
- Pram suit and mittens for colder days.

Choose clothes that make it easy for you to access your baby's nappy for changing.

choosing the right clothes

When shopping for baby clothes, you should bear the following points in mind:

- Young babies grow incredibly quickly, so don't buy too many things in one size and allow lots of room for growing.
- Check that all clothes are machine washable and colourfast. You don't have time right now for hand-washing.
- Choose clothes that have wide, envelope necks or that open down the front in order to avoid having to pull clothes over your baby's face. Back buttons can also be fiddly, as your baby has to lie on her tummy while you do them up.
- Go for clothes in natural fibres such as cotton that allow your baby's skin to breathe, and soft things that she will be comfortable sleeping in.
- Baby socks tend not to stay on for very long, particularly if your baby likes to kick. You can avoid using them at all if you go for all-in-one suits or trousers with built-in feet.

caring for your baby's clothes

When washing your baby's clothes, use a non-biological powder that will be gentle to her skin. You don't need fabric conditioner, but if you want to use it, again choose a gentle variety.

As with all clothes, it's a good idea to separate white items from coloured ones if you want them to stay white. There's no need to wash your baby's things separately from the rest of the family's, provided you use a non-biological washing powder for everyone.

Newborn faeces are very liquid and tend to leak up the back of nappies on to vests and sleepsuits from time to time. If you want the stains to come out, you may need to remove them by hand before putting the items in the washing machine. The best way to do this is to use really hot water – preferably boiling from the kettle – directly on the stain and rub it with a bar of household soap.

Baby sick can often leave clothes looking a bit yellow, even after they've been washed. You can soak them in a whitening powder specially designed for babies.

'I used to be a bit snobbish about second-hand clothes, but since I've had my children I've changed my tune completely! They grow out of clothes so fast that it can cost a fortune, and some second-hand items are hardly worn, as their previous owner grew quickly too! I've found some brilliant buys in charity shops and nearly-new sales, and bought bags of stuff off the internet. I've also sold on some of the boys' outgrown things. Now my friends have children, we all pass on our clothes to one another, and it's lovely to see a new baby in clothes that I remember my own wearing.'

Charlotte, mother of
Keeley (6 years), Jamie (4 years) and
Joshua (1 year)

shared experience

dressing your baby

Prepare by setting aside an area where you will always change and dress your baby, with all her clothes and changing equipment close to hand. Make sure she's not lying on a cold or hard surface and that you don't have to bend too much, to avoid putting strain on your back.

getting dressed

A vest or bodysuit, with a sleepsuit on top, is the perfect first outfit for a baby. It is warm, soft and comfortable for either sleeping, kicking around on a mat or being tucked up in a pram or car seat.

Q **My baby is growing well and gaining lots of weight, but some of the clothes that fit her best are a couple of sizes smaller than those designed for her age. Does this mean she's small for her age?**

A   Not at all. The sizing of babies' and children's clothes varies hugely, and a top in size 0–3 months from one store can be identical in size to one from another store that's marked 6–9 months. In addition, sometimes clothes shrink slightly with washing and tumble drying, so you can find that a top that fitted your firstborn at 6 months is perfect for your second baby at 4 months! Your baby's weight is the best indicator of whether she's the right size for her age, so talk to your health professional and get her weighed if you are concerned.

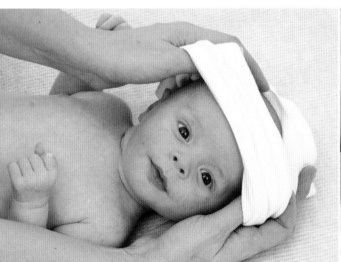

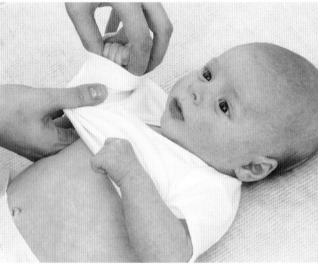

1 Lie your baby on her back. Hold the vest or bodysuit with the front facing you, and gather it up from the bottom. Pull the neck apart with your thumbs. Position the back edge at the top of your baby's head, and with one swift movement, slip it over her head.

2 Put the fingers of one hand down through one sleeve and stretch it wide. With the other hand, guide your baby's fist with your fingers and gently ease the sleeve over her arm. Now do the other sleeve in the same way. Lift up her feet with one hand and pull the back of the bodysuit under her bottom with the other. Fasten the poppers in between her legs.

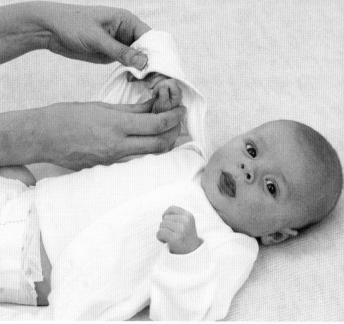

3 Now your baby is ready for her sleepsuit. Prepare it by opening all the poppers and laying it, front facing upwards, with the arms and legs spread out. Place your baby on top of the suit so that her neck rests in line with the neck opening and her shoulders are lined up with the suit's shoulders.

4 Gather up one sleeve like a concertina and stretch out the wrist end. Guide your baby's fist gently through the cuff. Now draw up the rest of the sleeve to her shoulder. Repeat for the other sleeve.

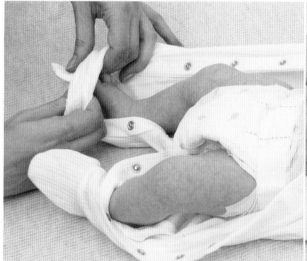

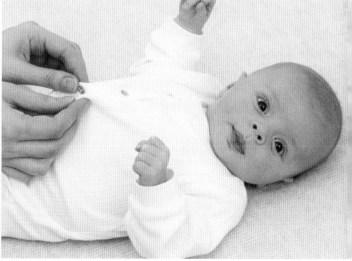

5 Gather up the fabric of one sleepsuit leg in your hands and open out the foot part. Slip it over your baby's toes and heels to cover her feet. Pull up the leg of the suit, making sure your baby's feet have plenty of room and aren't cramped. Repeat with the other leg.

6 Fasten the poppers inside the legs, around her bottom and up the front. If it's cold, your baby will need a cardigan as well. Begin by gathering the sleeves so that her fists slip easily through the cuffs, then draw the sleeves gently along her arms and around her back.

massaging your baby

In the first weeks and months with your baby, you may feel that you only do things to him: change him, bath him, dress him, feed him. It's rare at this stage that you get the opportunity to do something with him that is enjoyable and beneficial for both of you. Baby massage will not only help you to bond with your baby through the power of touch but will have many physical benefits for him as well.

how massage benefits your baby

As well as making your baby feel loved and secure, massage can soothe him in other ways, by:

Relieving digestive problems Massage helps to relax your baby's digestive muscles, which are tight and under-developed at birth, often causing trapped wind. It also encourages the movement of the colon to become stronger and more regular, so can help if your baby is suffering from constipation.

Improving feeding Massage can stimulate your baby's digestive system and he will be more enthusiastic about feeding, so be prepared to give him a feed as soon as he needs it. You may even have to stop to do this during massage.

Babies relish having a massage from birth and it can be a relaxing and enjoyable experience for both of you.

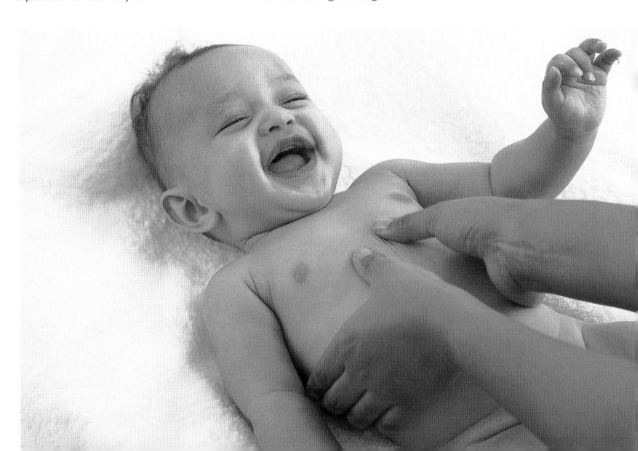

Regulating sleep Massage will soften your baby's muscles and give them a passive workout so that his body feels tired and ready to rest afterwards. It also boosts the flow of oxygen-enriched blood around the body, which encourages deeper breathing and in turn makes sleep more inviting.

Improving skin condition An almond or grapeseed massage oil can nourish your baby's skin and improve the texture. These oils keep the skin supple as it grows and encourage the elimination of toxins.

Boosting the immune system Your baby's lymphatic system under-functions from birth to around 3 months, but it can be stimulated by massage so that your baby is better equipped to fight off coughs, colds and minor infections.

how massage benefits you

Massaging your baby is real quality time. As you stroke and caress him, your mothering instincts and desire to nurture will come to the fore, and as you watch him move and respond to your touch, you will learn to identify his needs and feelings.

For many new parents, caring for their baby is not what they imagined or hoped it would be, and it's not unusual to feel discouraged or even disappointed. It can help to find something outside the daily drudge of nappy changing, laundry and feeding that you and your baby can enjoy together, to help you to feel useful, foster your relationship and enhance the bond between you.

Massage can be a quiet time that you and your baby share, just the two of you, which helps you both to feel relaxed and soothed, or it can be a sociable activity that you do at a class, helping you to meet other parents and babies and learn a new skill. Ask your health professional for details of classes and groups in your area.

what you will need

Carrier oil Some oil on your hands helps them to move smoothly over your baby's body. A carrier oil – so-called because it is often used to 'carry' essential oils, which should not be used for baby massage (but see page 236) – can be applied directly to the skin. Use a vegetable oil such as grapeseed, almond, olive, apricot, avocado or jojoba, which is absorbed into the skin. Mineral oils – which are present in commercial baby oils – can remain on the skin and block pores. Do a patch test first on your baby's ankle or wrist and wait for 24 hours to check that he isn't sensitive to the oil you are using.

Towel or mat This should be comfortable for your baby and one that you don't mind getting a little oil on.

Plenty of undisturbed time Switch off the phone, radio and television, and make sure you can focus completely on your baby. He may fall into a deep, relaxed sleep after a massage, so be ready to give a feed and tuck him up when you've finished. Don't massage straight after a feed – it's best to wait for 1½ hours to allow him to digest his milk.

Take care when choosing a carrier oil, as some are more suitable than others.

when not to massage

You can begin massage with your baby from birth. You should not massage if your baby:

- Is on medication – seek your doctor's advice first.
- Was born prematurely. Pre-term babies have much more sensitive skin and often prefer skin-to-skin cuddles only.
- Has a kidney problem.
- Has a heart problem.
- Suffers from epilepsy.
- Has a high temperature.
- Has high/low blood pressure.
- Has unexplained rashes or spots – eczema can sometimes be aggravated by massage.
- Has any cuts, swellings, abrasions, sprains, bruising or broken bones.
- Has recently been immunized.
- Has loose or clicky hip joints (see page 251), in which case there are some movements you should avoid.

starting
to massage

Before you begin your massage, gather together everything you need and make sure you will be undisturbed. The room should be warm enough for your baby to feel comfortable without his clothes on. Most movements in the following massages can be repeated four or five times, or as your baby likes. You do not have to follow these movements in any particular order, or necessarily do them all. Be guided by what you and your baby enjoy.

front of body massage

This routine for the face and front of the body is a gentle introduction to baby massage for both of you. Rub your hands together to warm them up and rub oil on to them. Remember to keep adding oil as you proceed through the massage, and to look at your baby and talk softly to him throughout the routine.

Find a position that's comfortable for both of you. Try sitting on the floor with your baby lying on a mat, or put him on a mat on a table so that you can sit on a chair or stand. Alternatively, lie or sit him on a towel on your lap, with your legs outstretched or bent up. This position creates a perfect distance between your face and his.

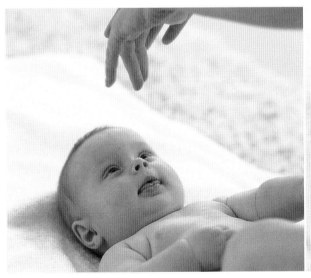

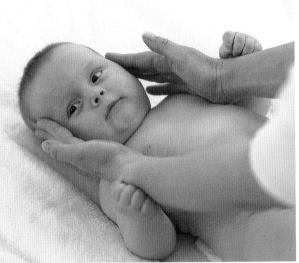

1 Lie your baby on his back. Wave your fingers over his face to attract his attention and to loosen and soften your finger joints. Try to have as much eye contact with your baby as possible.

2 Stroke your fingers outwards from the centre of his forehead and circle his temples a few times. Softly stroke both hands down to his jaw and down the sides of his neck. Now thumb-stroke with both hands from the edge of his nose to his jaw. This encourages lymphatic drainage.

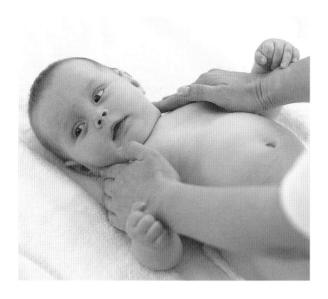

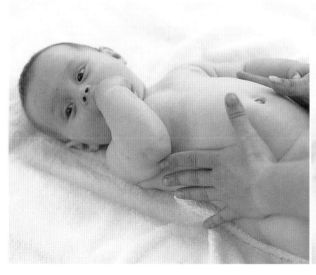

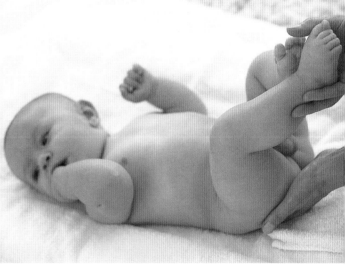

'I've got twin babies, and two older children as well. It sometimes feels that my babies never get my undisturbed attention, and they're always having to share me. From birth, I've given each of them massages, on their own. I may only get the chance to massage each of the twins once or twice a week, for a few minutes, but in that time I can focus completely on one baby, look her in the eyes and tell her how much I love her and how special she is. It's really special to me, and I know that my babies love it too.'

Terri, mother of Adam (7 years), Rachel (5 years) and Amy and Emily (4 months)

shared experience

3 Slowly and lightly stroke over his shoulders and into his armpits, ensuring you have enough oil on your hands for them to slide easily over his body. Remember that your hands will absorb the oil, depending on how dry they are.

4 Continue the same movement down your baby's sides and then over the front of his body, two or three times.

5 Hold up your baby's feet with one hand and slide the other under his bottom to the base of his spine. This area houses nerve endings to the digestive system and is an extremely soothing place to massage. Gently circle your fingers.

back massage

For this routine, lie your baby on his tummy. Place his arms so that he can push himself up, bearing in mind that he will decide how he wants to lie. If your baby isn't happy lying on his tummy, you could try lying him over your legs. Talk softly to reassure him, and have enough oil on your hands to sweep smoothly over his body.

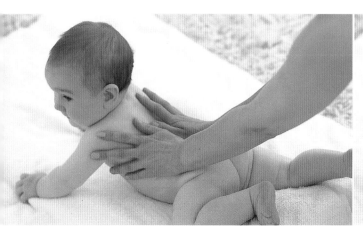

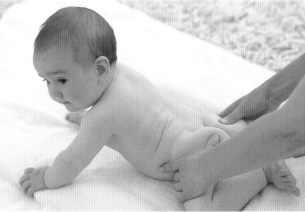

1 Sweep both hands all the way up your baby's body, from his feet to his shoulders, and down again several times. Massage out to his sides, gently following his ribs. Tap over his upper back to loosen any mucus.

2 Using your thumbs, very gently make little circles all over his buttocks, moving from the centre out. This helps to relax and tone the muscles around the hip joint. Gently stroke out to his sides with your whole hand, moving up towards his shoulders.

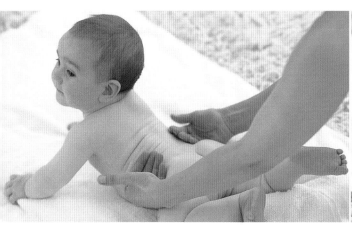

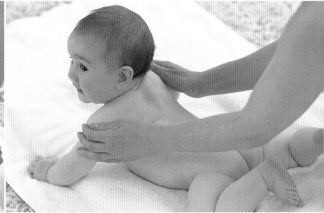

3 Starting at the base of your baby's spine, use the back of your hand to stroke your fingers from his spine outwards, in a flowing movement. Repeat this movement working up towards his shoulders. Now use your palms to sweep down his back and up again.

4 Gently pluck at the fleshy top of his shoulders to ease tension. This can be a sensitive area in need of a gentle touch. With your fingertips, gently massage outwards from his spine towards his shoulders. Sweep over his arms and come back to his back. Sweep down to his buttocks and up again, in one continuous stroke.

'At the hospital where I gave birth, they ran free massage classes twice a week for new mothers to come to with their babies. It was great – the teacher used a doll to show us the movements to do, and lots of them had songs and rhymes to go along with them. Kian really enjoyed the singing and stroking, and it was nice for me to meet other mothers with babies and to have an activity to do with him that didn't cost me a fortune.'

Angela, mother of
Kian (7 months)

shared
experience

leg massage

This massage is most easily performed with your baby lying on his back. The gentle movements are designed to relax and tone the thigh and calf muscles, and increase circulation.

1 Softly wrap one hand around the top of your baby's thigh and place your other hand around the back of the thigh. Slide both hands down to his ankle. Now, with the same hand position, smoothly glide one hand after the other from thigh to ankle. Do not straighten or pull the leg. Make sure the oil goes into the creases of his thigh.

2 Using your thumb or two fingers, gently make fast circular movements up and down the inside and outside of his leg twice. Try to merge your fingers into the fleshiness of the leg to stimulate the circulation. Repeat step 1.

3 Hold your baby's ankle and cup your other hand under his calf. Softly and lightly squeeze up from his ankle to the top of his thigh and down again several times. Repeat step 1, then repeat the whole routine on the other leg.

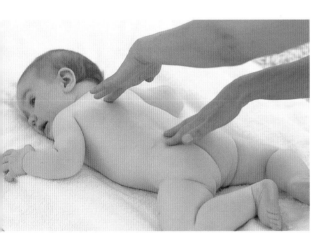

5 Finish the back massage by gently and repeatedly stroking down either side of his spine, from the top to his buttocks. Let the strokes start with your whole hand and diminish to a few fingers, then one finger only, light as a feather.

chapter 4
sleeping arrangements

Your baby's sleep requirements will change dramatically during the first 12 months, and establishing a routine that works may be one of the biggest challenges you face. Decide from the beginning where and when your baby will sleep, making sure you achieve a good balance between daytime naps and night sleeping. Disruptions to your sleep are inevitable – as are other problems, such as getting your baby to settle – so be prepared to adopt a number of different strategies as the year progresses.

when and where to sleep

Any parents of young children will be only too aware how important sleep is. After a series of interrupted nights, even the calmest of parents may be irritable, groggy and unable to concentrate. Babies and toddlers are also affected, to the extent that not enough sleep will eventually get in the way of their learning, physical development and ability to relax.

Avoid allowing your newborn baby to fall asleep in your arms, which could present you with problems later on.

when to sleep

Initially, the chances of parents getting a 'good night's sleep' are limited because newborns are unable to tell the difference between night and day. Their body clocks are governed by the need to feed at frequent intervals, regardless of whether it's dark or light, so although your baby will sleep for about 16 or 17 hours in every 24, his sleep is broken up into lots of relatively short stretches scattered randomly throughout the day and night (see pages 172–175).

A newborn's tummy is approximately the size of his fist, and his liquid diet of breast milk or formula will be absorbed quickly (breast milk is absorbed more rapidly than formula, as it is tailor-made for your baby). During the first few weeks of your baby's life, be prepared for him to sleep for 2–4 hours at a time before waking for a feed. Most babies start to make the day/night adjustment by about 10–12 weeks. You can gently ease them into this from an early stage, laying the foundations for a sleeping pattern that fits in with yours.

learning to settle

To build a basis for good sleep habits amid the unpredictable first weeks when your baby falls asleep whenever and wherever tiredness overtakes him, be aware of how you put him down to sleep. It's important to avoid creating 'negative sleep associations'. For example, if you rock your baby in your arms until he falls asleep, then tiptoe over to his cot to put him in every time you want to put him down to sleep, he'll quickly learn to rely on this. He may need the same help again when he wakes during the night. Also avoid making a habit of feeding or cuddling your baby until he sleeps.

Instead, try to look for signs that show he's getting tired, such as yawning or rubbing his eyes. When you think he's sleepy, put your baby down in his cot so that he is drowsy but still awake. He may grumble a bit, but if he's tired, he'll soon drop off to sleep (see also page 176). By doing this you are teaching him how to settle or soothe himself to sleep, which is a really essential skill to master. He will gradually learn to use these skills when he wakes in the night.

Many couples favour a Moses basket for their newborn – its size having obvious advantages if a baby is to sleep in his parents' room.

day and night

Another early-days strategy is to encourage your baby to recognize the difference between night and day. To help him figure this out, try:

- Creating a winding-down ritual that prepares him for bedtime. Keep the order consistent: for example, bath, followed by a feed, then a story or lullaby.
- Keeping night feeds as low key and peaceful as possible.
- Buying a night-light or fitting a dimmer switch so that you can feed in a darkened room at night.
- Changing nappies during the night only if it's really essential.
- Giving him lots of attention during the day and stimulating him by talking, singing and playing.

get your rest when you can

As friends, relatives and even complete strangers will be only too happy to warn you, exhaustion is part and parcel of the early weeks, so it's important to grab some rest whenever there's a chance. Resist the temptation to catch up on housework every time your baby sleeps during the day and instead take a nap. If you are breast-feeding, try expressing some milk and asking your partner, friend or relative to do the next feed so that you can catch up on sleep.

If you find that the lack of sleep is affecting your mood, talk to your doctor or health professional. Sleep deprivation is a recognized form of torture and it's hard to keep going if you're feeling stressed out through lack of sleep.

Q **Should we use a cot, Moses basket or carrycot for our baby?**

A Choosing a cot for your newborn has the advantage that he can use it until he's ready for a child-sized bed at around 2 years old (a cot-bed that transforms into a child's bed will last even longer – until he's around 5 or 6). But a carrycot or Moses basket will take up less room and can also be moved more easily for naps. However, your baby will grow out of these within a few months, and if you're using a stand for the basket, you must ensure it cannot be knocked over.

bed-sharing safety guidelines

If your baby is sharing your bed:

- Use a sheet and lightweight blankets, not a duvet.
- Never use pillows.
- Make sure his head is never covered by bedding.
- Check there are no gaps between headboard and mattress or bed and wall that could trap him.
- Avoid if there is a risk of your baby being squashed or falling out, if you have recently drunk alcohol or taken recreational drugs, are on medication that causes drowsiness or are excessively tired.

Babies find it hard to regulate their body temperature, so be sure to dress them appropriately for sleeping.

where to sleep

Many first-time mothers-to-be spend hours decorating and kitting out a nursery, only to find that their newborn spends most nights in the master bedroom. In fact, research into cot death or Sudden Infant Death Syndrome (SIDS) – the term used to describe the unexpected death of a seemingly well baby – shows a Moses basket, carrycot or cot in your room is the safest place for your baby to be when he's less than 6 months old. There is also the advantage that in the early months, when he is waking frequently at night, you'll be able to feed and settle him with the minimum of effort. It can be reassuring for both you and your baby to have him close by at night.

bed-sharing

Controversy has dogged the subject of bed-sharing in recent years. Experts warn that babies who share their parents' bed may be at a higher risk of SIDS if either parent smokes (even if they don't smoke in bed or in the house), has been drinking alcohol or taking drugs or medication likely to make them drowsy, or is very tired. Bed-sharing is also best avoided if your baby was premature (born before 37 weeks), weighed less than 2.5 kg (5½ lb) at birth or is under 3 months old.

The advantages of bed-sharing are that it minimizes the disruption of feeding at night and it has been praised as a way of getting breast-feeding established. Parents say it creates a close bond with their babies, although it can also make moving a baby into his own cot later on more difficult.

Most babies move into a room of their own by about 6 months.

buying a cot

It's an exciting moment, but with so many available, it can be daunting. Safety is crucial, so check bars on the cot are no more than 6.5 cm (2½ in) apart and there is a distance of 51 cm (20 in) between the top of the mattress and the top of the cot. On drop-side cots, ensure the mechanism works smoothly, is secure when upright and child-proof. A mattress should be 8–10 cm (3–4 in) thick and snugly fitting with a gap of no more than 4 cm (1½ in) around the edge.

your baby's own room

Create a welcoming bedroom for your baby. Some useful features are:
- Good storage so that everything you need is readily accessible.
- Room thermometer and effective control of room temperature – the ideal for a baby is around 16–18°C (61–64°F).
- Comfortable chair for you to feed in.
- Baby monitor that connects with your room.
- Dimmer switches and night-lights.
Non-essential extras:
- Baby sleeping bags so that your baby can't get cold if he's kicked off his blankets (choose the right size so that he can't slip down inside it).
- V-shaped pillow for back support when you are feeding.
- Blackout curtains, which help your baby to differentiate between day and night.
- CD player for music and story CDs, and a cot mobile.

SIDS safety guidelines

The following simple safety measures can reduce the risk of SIDS:
- Don't smoke during pregnancy; get your partner to quit as well.
- Let your baby sleep in a cot in your room for the first 6 months.
- Place him on his back to sleep.
- Keep his head uncovered: position him with his feet to the foot of the cot with a sheet and blankets tucked under his armpits so that he can't wriggle below the covers.
- Avoid using duvets and pillows for a baby under 12 months. A cotton sheet and one or two cellular blankets should suffice.
- Maintain the room temperature at 16–18°C (61–64°F) to prevent your baby overheating. This is the right temperature if he's wearing a vest and sleepsuit and has two cellular blankets and a sheet.
- A baby cannot regulate his own temperature, so don't put his cot either in a draughty place or near a radiator or a window where the sun shines in.
- Never allow anyone to smoke in the same room as your baby.
- Do not use cot bumpers, as they may contribute to overheating or suffocate your baby.
- If he seems unwell, seek medical advice immediately.

bedtime
routines

A consistent bedtime routine lays the foundation for happy sleep habits, the benefits of which will last for the rest of your baby's life. It's fine to start getting your baby used to the idea early on, although choosing when a newborn's bedtime begins is initially an arbitrary decision. Aiming for a bedtime routine will gradually help your baby adjust her body clock to coincide with your own.

parents' tips

- Devise a simple routine – it will be easier to remember and stick to!
- Keep distractions to a minimum at bedtime and let the answer machine pick up calls.
- Cotton nightclothes are the most comfortable for babies.
- Use a few drops of lavender oil on a handkerchief near the cot to soothe a restless baby.

Dress your baby in clothes that keep night-time nappy changes easy.

why have a routine?

Although not everyone likes a routine, babies do develop a sense of security and comfort from having one. Some of the benefits are:

- A consistent pattern of events will help your baby to respond to what is expected of her next.
- Parents regain a sense of control and order in their lives.
- It will help your baby learn how to settle herself to sleep, which will help her to sleep better.
- It sets aside a special quiet time for you to enjoy being with your baby.
- Other carers will find it easier to settle your baby, as they can follow the ritual she's familiar with.

Some parents dislike the restrictiveness and limits to spontaneity that a routine imposes and prefer to wait for one to emerge naturally. Choose what works for you and your family. If you work full-time, for example, and look forward to spending time with your baby in the evening, you may prefer her to have a late daytime nap and later bedtime. Routines can be hard work to stick to and require consistency and agreement between parents, so talk it through with your partner.

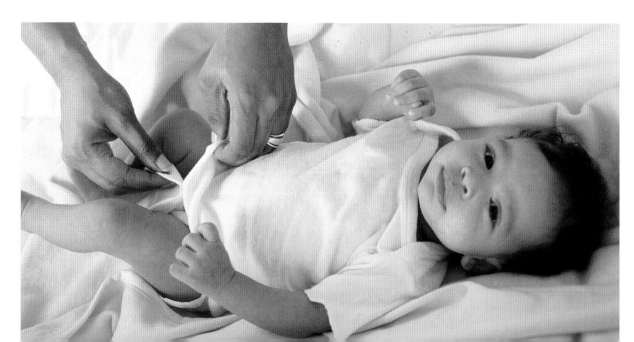

what do I do?

The idea is that over a period of weeks, your baby will learn how to respond to a situation by the sequence of events you follow. A typical bedtime routine – involving a feed, followed by a bath, changing into nightclothes, sharing a story and lullaby – will gradually prompt your baby to feel sleepy on cue.

The length of time your routine takes will depend on the age of your baby, but around 30–45 minutes is about right. Aim to start the process at the same time every day and follow the same pattern. You could include a massage (see pages 158–163), listening to music, talking through the day's events and saying goodnight to your baby's cuddly toys. Make it enjoyable for you both and keep activities calm and relaxed. As your baby grows, the routine will evolve, but in the early weeks, repetition is important to ensure success.

regimental routines

In the 1950s, it was thought best to feed a baby at 4-hourly intervals and never during the night. Mothers were warned they would spoil their baby if they 'gave in' to her crying. Over the past decade there has been a revival of a more regimented routine, one of the aims being to train young babies to sleep through the night as soon as possible. Experts' views vary and some do not recommend a very strict routine with newborns, preferring babies to be fed on demand.

Tuning in to your baby's needs and using your instincts to interpret when she is sleepy, hungry or ready for play will boost your confidence as a parent and help to build your baby's trust and self-esteem. Follow your baby's lead, and sleeping and feeding patterns will gradually emerge during the first 3 months.

bedtime routines with twins

The principles of introducing a routine with twins are the same as with a singleton, but the logistics of having two mean it's easier with two adults. Ask friends and family to lend a hand, or if you can afford it, hire a maternity nurse.

Aim for a bedtime ritual to signal sleep, but if you want to factor in some one-to-one time with each twin, allow longer for your routine. If you find that the twins differ in how much sleep they need, try getting them both to sleep at the same time in the hope that one falls in line with the other, or put the sleepier twin to bed first.

There are no hard-and-fast rules about where twins should sleep as long as you follow the SIDS safety guidelines (see page 169). Some parents choose to have their twins together in one large cot at first, although they will need to move into separate cots by about 3 months. Sleeping in the same cot can help twins soothe each other. How you feed your twins during the night will depend on what suits you, whether you're breast-feeding or bottle-feeding and if both you and your partner are waking up or if just one parent is dealing with night feeds. It is possible to breast-feed twins simultaneously.

Even with a splash about, a bath is always a relaxing start to her bedtime routine.

' When I knew I was expecting twins, I read everything I could on how to settle them at night and where they should sleep. Some advocated putting twins in the same cot, but I worried whether this was safe. In the end we bought two cots and put them side by side. We had a strict bedtime routine and having their twin close helped the babies settle. '

Sally, mother of
Rosa and Niall (2 years)

shared experience

changing
sleep patterns

Although the average newborn sleeps 16–18 hours in a 24-hour period, some sleep for 10–12 hours and others for around 20. There is also a lot of variation in how long newborns sleep for at any one time. While some go 3–4 hours at a stretch, others may wake every 1–2 hours. If he seems happy and alert when he wakes, then your baby has probably had enough sleep.

Q Can a newborn sleep for too long?

A If your baby sleeps for longer than 4–5 hours between feeds, health professionals recommend waking him up and offering him a feed. Contact your doctor or health professional if you are worried that he seems very sleepy and uninterested in feeding.

out of sync

During the last few weeks of pregnancy, when there's less space for him in the womb, you may have noticed that your baby becomes more active when you lie down to sleep. It's likely that he has more room to manoeuvre when you're stretched out; in addition, your movements are no longer rocking him to sleep. This topsy-turvy pattern persists for a while after he is born, but you can help his body clock adjust (see pages 166–167), and there are some babies who settle into sleeping through the night from as early as 4 weeks.

0–3 months

By the time he is 3 months old, your baby will probably be sleeping for about 15 hours in 24. As it dawns on him that day is playtime, when he's surrounded by noise, attention and people, daytime naps will drop from four to three and account for about 5 hours of sleep. The longer stretch of 10 hours' sleep will be more likely to coincide with

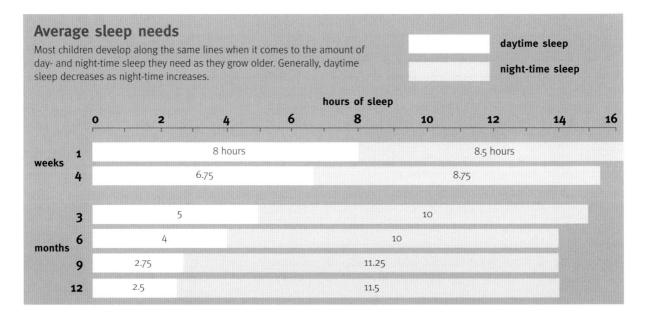

Average sleep needs

Most children develop along the same lines when it comes to the amount of day- and night-time sleep they need as they grow older. Generally, daytime sleep decreases as night-time increases.

daytime sleep

night-time sleep

hours of sleep

		0	2	4	6	8	10	12	14	16
weeks	1			8 hours			8.5 hours			
	4		6.75			8.75				
months	3		5			10				
	6		4			10				
	9	2.75			11.25					
	12	2.5			11.5					

night-time. Waking during the night is normal though, and may continue for some time, although it's estimated that at 3 months about 70 per cent of babies are sleeping from midnight to 5 am. When other parents claim their baby 'sleeps through the night', it may be that they are talking about a core sleep of around 5–6 hours rather than an uninterrupted 8-hour stretch.

3–6 months

This is a time of rapid development. By the end of his sixth month, your baby may only be having two daily naps of around 90 minutes to 2 hours and sleeping for a total of around 14 hours in 24. While there is still scope for variation, many 6-month-olds may sleep for 6 hours at a stretch at night and are showing signs that they have made the day/night adjustment and can settle themselves back to sleep.

6–9 months

The balance of daytime versus night-time sleep has shifted further by 9 months, and while total sleep is still around 14 hours, the amount of time your baby spends napping during the day will have dropped to less than 3 hours.

If your baby is healthy, gaining weight and moving on to solids, he is now, in theory, capable of sleeping through the night without a feed. Six months is a good time to introduce a bedtime routine (if you haven't already) and downscale or drop night feeds.

9–12 months

By his first birthday, your baby may have switched to just one nap during the day, which will help to consolidate his night-time sleeping. Babies vary in their need for daytime naps, and in families where there are older children, it can be harder to ensure an uninterrupted nap. On average, however, daytime naps around this age will last for about 90 minutes to 2 hours. The overall amount of sleep required is 14 hours, so approximately 11 or 12 hours of this will be at night. At 12 months most babies still wake at night but can fall back to sleep without help.

Many babies are sleeping through the night at 6 months.

'At 6 months old my baby was still waking every 3 hours for a feed. My friends' babies seemed to be sleeping for 6 hours a night. The constant interrupted nights meant I was really tired, so I made an appointment at a sleep clinic and saw a consultant who came up with a plan. I was advised to offer water instead of feeds and to go into my baby's room, speak a few reassuring words, then leave. I was to repeat this at intervals with no eye contact or fuss. It was very tiring for a few days, but after a week my baby got the message!'

Katy, mother of
Chloe (12 months)

shared
experience

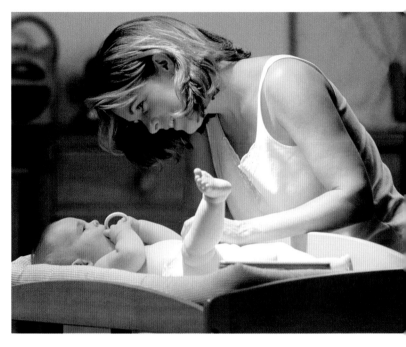

When your baby wakes at night, take care of him in subdued light to help him settle back to sleep more easily.

Q **Is it a good idea to wake my baby for a feed before I go to bed?**

A As long as your baby isn't premature or suffering from jaundice, some experts recommend that you should go with the flow and wait for him to wake when he is ready for a feed. The idea is that babies settle better and are quicker to sleep through the night if allowed to follow their internal clocks. If you wake him for a feed before you go to sleep, you are interrupting his natural cycle of sleep.

sleeping like a grown-up

It's not only the amount of time your baby sleeps that changes during his first year of life, the quality of his sleep alters too, becoming gradually more like an adult's. Adult sleep consists of rapid eye movement (REM) sleep, which is associated with dreaming, and non-REM sleep, or quiet sleep, which has four stages:

Stage 1 Feeling drowsy and beginning to fall asleep.

Stage 2 Light sleep during which the heart rate slows and eye movements stop.

Stage 3 Deep sleep when your body is relaxed and still.

Stage 4 Deep sleep when it can be difficult to wake someone.

As adults, we cycle up and down through the different states, moving from dozing, to light sleep, deeper sleep and lastly into REM sleep over a 90-minute period. During REM sleep, our bodies are usually relaxed and still, but our brains are active and we can be woken easily by noise or other disturbances. In an average 8 hours of sleep, we make about four or five circuits of REM and non-REM sleep, spending roughly 2 hours in REM sleep and 6 hours in quiet sleep.

babies do it differently

Babies have a very different pattern of sleeping to adults, which explains why they are a lot more wakeful. They spend almost 50 per cent of their sleep in REM sleep, in which phase they can be easily disturbed. This compares to an adult's 15–20 per cent. Very premature babies may spend as much as 80 per cent of their sleep in REM sleep.

When they are born and for the first 3 months, babies also tend to fall asleep and pass straight into REM sleep, unlike adults who move quickly into a deep sleep and then into light REM sleep some

90 minutes later. You can see this happening if you watch your baby once he's fallen asleep. For at least 20 minutes his eyes will flicker under his closed eyelids and he may startle at a sudden noise. Once he has dropped into his deep, non-REM sleep, however, he will lie still and relaxed, breathing steadily.

The other difference is that in the first few months, the time it takes him to move through each sleep cycle is 60 minutes or less, compared to 90 minutes for an adult. And as he makes the transition from one sleep stage to another, he is more likely to be disturbed by noise or woken by hunger or discomfort.

Spending more time in a light sleep state is a survival skill that your baby is born with – it means if he is hungry or in pain, he can wake easily and cry for help.

all change

As wakefulness is a central part of your baby's early sleep patterns, it's helpful to work out how you can cope best with the sleep deprivation and how you can teach your baby to soothe himself back to sleep when he wakes (see pages 166–167). Babies develop dramatically in the first 6 months, however, so rest assured there are significant changes to sleep patterns that will promote the transition from wakeful nights to peaceful nights:

- The amount of time your baby spends in REM sleep decreases, until by the time he's reached his third birthday it makes up only about 30 per cent of his sleep.
- At 3 months old, he will drop into non-REM sleep first rather than light REM sleep.
- His sleep cycles will become longer until by the time he is 3 months old they will last for 90 minutes.
- He learns to recognize the difference between day and night.

Q **My 8-month-old baby is still waking at least two or three times a night for a feed. Can he actually be hungry or is he just comfort feeding?**

A If your baby is healthy and gaining weight, then he doesn't need a night-time feed by this age. It may be that he's got into the habit of feeding in order to get back to sleep or he may be comfort feeding. Try offering cooled boiled water if he wakes during the night and increasing the last feed of the day.

baby sleep

REM sleep
This is the sleep state in which we dream, and scientists believe the ability to dream begins in babies before they are born. During REM sleep, your baby's body sends extra blood to his brain, which becomes very active, possibly digesting and storing the day's new experiences. REM sleep is believed to be essential for your baby's rapidly expanding brain and for boosting his learning and development.

Non-REM sleep
Growth hormones are secreted during your baby's deep, non-REM sleep, and this is an important time for the body to repair and rebuild its strength.

It is important that your baby learns to settle himself when going to sleep.

dealing with
disruptions

There are various developmental stages in the first year that may affect your baby's sleeping. There are also times when a baby's settled routine is thrown out of sync by everyday interruptions, such as illness or holidays (see pages 178–179). In many cases, the underlying solution is to help your baby learn how to settle back to sleep without your intervention.

Babies often cry out in their sleep, but will settle down again within a few minutes.

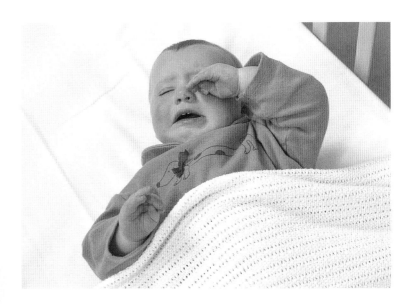

quick check

If your baby usually sleeps through the night and is suddenly wakeful, check:

- The temperature of the room (see box on page 169).
- Her tummy or the back of her neck, to assess if she's too hot or cold.
- If her temperature is raised (over 38°C/100.4°F) or she seems unwell.
- Whether her nappy is wet.
- If she is acting oddly.

If she hasn't been feeding well during the day, seems floppy or unresponsive or is crying inconsolably, seek medical attention right away.

the secret of sleep

If your baby is more than 6 months old, waking frequently and unable to return to sleep unless you go in to her, try the following tactics:

- Introduce a consistent bedtime routine.
- Put her in her cot while drowsy but awake so that she learns to drop off by herself.
- Avoid feeding or rocking her to sleep before putting her in her cot.
- Don't reward night-waking with lots of attention. Soothe her with the lights low and a quick reassuring pat.
- If she wakes and cries out, don't go in to her straight away – wait a few minutes to see if she can go back to sleep by herself.
- If your baby is healthy and putting on weight, she doesn't need a feed in the night after 6 months. Try offering her a bottle of cooled boiled water instead.
- Ensure your baby naps enough during the day and try to keep these times consistent (see pages 182–183).
- Avoid using props such as a dummy to help her fall asleep.

developmental changes

Whether your baby is sleeping through the night or you are still waiting for this to happen, there are various developmental milestones that may have an impact on sleeping patterns.

growth spurts

Your baby may seem to go through periods of frequent, almost non-stop feeding at various stages, so that instead of sleeping at night or during the day for 3–4 hours, she's suddenly feeding and waking every hour. This is usually the result of a growth spurt and these typically occur at 1–3 weeks, 6–8 weeks, 3 months, 6 months and 9 months. The abrupt changes in feeding and sleeping patterns may seem like a step backwards, but your baby's increased appetite is fuelling essential development and each growth spurt will only last a few days. If she's going to triple her birth weight by 12 months, your best strategy is to accept the temporary disruption to your routine and find other ways of catching up on sleep. Try to delegate chores or jobs that you feel need to be done. Another strategy is to try feeding your baby more in the early evening to fill her up.

teething

It's tempting to blame teething for disruption to a baby's sleep, but in fact research has shown that there is less connection than we imagine between teething and wakefulness at night. Although it can cause your baby discomfort, with lots of dribbling and loose stools, it shouldn't cause pain or a raised temperature. If she is crying out in pain, contact your doctor to check the cause of the problem.

Homeopathic teething powders, teething rings or soothing gels, which numb your baby's gums for a while, may help to relieve some of the aggravation. Aim to be consistent with the way you have previously put your baby down for bed and resettled her at night when she's woken. If you have weaned your baby off night-time feeds, try to resist going back to feeding her for comfort.

standing

Babies sometimes get the hang of standing up before they learn how to sit back down again. This can cause wakeful nights if your baby pulls herself into an upright position in the cot and then cries out because she can't get back down unaided. The best way to tackle this is to go in to settle her down again with the minimum of fuss. Keep the lights low, limit eye contact and speak quietly but firmly as you lie her back down in her cot.

During the day, encourage her to practise sitting down by holding her hands and pulling her up, then gently letting her down again. Once you know she's cracked it, you can let her try her new skill at night. It won't be long before she learns the knack of sitting down unaided and shouldn't cause a long-term disruption if you maintain a low-key response to her cries without getting up to help.

Encourage your baby to learn how to sit down again once she can stand in her cot.

Q **I've returned to work and my 9-month-old baby's sleeping and feeding routine seems to be upset. I'm worried she may not be feeding well at the nursery.**

A Ask your carer to write down the feeds and solids your baby has in the day to set your mind at rest. Try giving your baby an extra feed at bedtime if you think she may be hungry. At night-time when she wakes, reassure her without giving too much attention and resist the temptation to feed. Stick with your usual routine and she will settle down within a few weeks.

Moving house could be why your baby suddenly finds it difficult to settle at night.

separation anxiety

From around 8–9 months old, your baby is acutely aware of her surroundings and firmly attached to the people closest to her. When you go out of the room, she is capable of realizing that you are no longer there, but not sure that you will come back. You may notice that while previously you could leave her with a friend or relative without any problems, she now becomes upset and clingy if she's separated from you. This can cause problems during the day and at bedtime, even if she has been settling happily on her own previously.

To help her cope, be consistent with your bedtime routine, making sure you spend plenty of time cuddling and talking to her before putting her in her cot. It's then better to make a point of saying goodnight before leaving the room, rather than just creeping out when she's not looking, as this is likely to worsen feelings of anxiety. If she cries, pop back to reassure her, but make your return visit as brief and as calm as possible (see page 181). Remind yourself that this is a stage she's going through – she will come out the other side soon.

life gets in the way

As well as the developmental milestones that affect your baby's patterns of sleeping, there are the unavoidable ways in which everyday life can upset routine. For example, moving house, illness, holidays or an influx of visitors may all temporarily disrupt your baby's sleep. The good news is that if she has already established a regular pattern of settling and sleeping, it's relatively easy to get back on track.

moving house

Plan ahead so that you can limit the impact on your baby's normal sleeping routine. Make sure when you are packing up to move that the significant items your baby sees every day at bedtime are all clearly labelled and accessible so that you can create a familiar feeling in her new room straight away. Keep to her regular bedtime ritual as far as possible. And, as you are the main sources of security for your baby, consider how to make the event as stress-free as possible for you and your partner. If you are planning to start a sleep-training programme, it's best to hold off until after the upheaval of the move.

illness

When your baby is ill, it is very worrying and will inevitably have an impact on how you respond to her cries in the night. Treat this period as an unavoidable interruption to your routine, but try to keep disruption to a minimum. If your baby cries, resist the temptation to bring her downstairs or turn on the light in her bedroom. Keep soothing her in your normal way. If you're concerned that she may need help in the night – for example, if she has been vomiting – set up a camp bed on the floor in her room so that you can be nearby and settle her back to sleep easily. As soon as your baby is fit and well again, however, return to your normal approach to night-time waking.

holidays away

Routines often fly out of the window during a holiday, particularly if it involves a long flight or crossing time zones. Expect a period of adjustment when you return home, but aim to keep things consistent by following the usual bedtime routine while you're away, even if it is a pared-down version. Parents are often so worried about disturbing other guests in the hotel that they'll return to feeding or rocking their baby if she wakes in the night, even if they have stopped doing this at home. Avoid this if you can. It makes getting back to normal harder when you return.

Don't forget to bring along your baby's favourite toy or comforter, and pack her bedding too if you have enough suitcase space (a baby sleeping bag is ideal).

visitors

An influx of visitors over a few days can mean your baby finds it harder to wind down at bedtime after the extra attention of the day. She is also more likely to miss out on daytime naps, which tends to have a knock-on effect at bedtime, leaving her too tired and cranky to settle in the usual way. Ideally, aim to factor in a nap-time despite visitors, but if this is not possible, remind yourself that there are bound to be days when your routine and your baby's sleeping go a bit awry.

A baby's sleep pattern may change while on holiday, making it hard to return to a routine when back at home again.

sleep training

Some parents cope better with interrupted sleep than others, but there comes a point when most parents recognize that their baby's sleeping difficulties have to be addressed. For example, mothers may find the crunch comes when they return to work at the end of maternity leave. Sorting out sleep problems becomes top priority when napping during the day is no longer an option.

care with controlled crying

Learning to recognize whether your baby is tired, hungry, has a wet nappy or is just a bit disgruntled when he cries is an important part of getting to know him. Over the first few weeks you'll develop an instinct for what is needed. This process boosts your confidence as a parent and builds your baby's self-esteem and sense of security as he realizes his needs will be met. Babies learn most from how their parents respond to them – they have no idea that their night-waking is inconvenient, so ignoring their cries is potentially damaging. For these reasons, some health professionals have moved away from recommending sleep-training techniques that involve leaving them to cry, especially for babies less than 12 months old.

If you have tried the gentle sleep-training techniques described but your baby is still waking constantly, talk to your doctor or health professional for advice.

tackling wakeful nights

It is vital to be determined when you begin to tackle sleep problems. And it's essential that you and your partner agree how to do this and both stick to the strategy. It can seem daunting, and after many sleepless nights you may feel unable to take on the challenge, but getting your baby to sleep through the night is well worth the effort. Check the chart on page 172 to make sure you are being realistic about how long your baby can sleep at night.

Leaving your baby to cry may not be an effective way of tackling sleep problems.

can't settle at bedtime

If your baby protests at being put in his cot, there are some gentle techniques for teaching him to settle by himself:

Gradual withdrawal Establish a bedtime routine. If your baby is used to falling asleep while being held, rocked or fed, try gradually separating yourself so that he learns to drop off independently.

- Sit in a chair by the cot so that your baby knows you are near. If he needs more reassurance than this, place a hand on his arm.
- After a few days like this, take your hand away or move your chair a little further away from the cot. Carry on retreating every few days until you are sitting outside the room. Stay calm, resolute and resist pleas to stay or move nearer.
- Don't distract your baby. Keep eye contact to a minimum – try reading a book so that you're just a quiet presence in the room.
- This is a very gradual sleep-training programme, so it may take a few weeks to be effective.

Reassurance with words This is another gentle approach that can be used at bedtime and if your baby wakes at night.

- After following a bedtime routine, put your baby in his cot, firmly say, 'Night-night', or any other set phrase that you prefer, and then leave the room.
- If he cries out, return to the room, tuck him in again and repeat the 'Night-night' before leaving.
- Keep eye contact to a minimum and avoid picking him up. Stay firm and confident when you leave the room. You will need to be very patient, calm and consistent, but your baby will get the message after about a week.

waking and feeding

If your baby is 6 months or above and still waking for a feed at night, he may be doing it for comfort, out of habit or relying on this as a means of sending himself to sleep (see page 166). Teach him how to drop off by himself so that he can send himself back to sleep at night.

- Try giving him the last feed before changing him into his pyjamas to prevent him dropping off during a feed.
- Offer more milk and solids during the day.
- When he wakes, wait for a few minutes to see if he settles back to sleep by himself.
- Offer a bottle of cooled boiled water instead of a feed. If you are bottle-feeding, you can do this over a period of days by gradually watering down the milk. If you are breast-feeding, gradually reduce the amount of time your baby feeds or give water instead of a feed. It may be easier to get your partner to offer the water so that your baby isn't tempted by the close proximity of breast milk.
- It takes resolve to get out of the habit of feeding a baby back to sleep if you know this always works. Be prepared for disruption while you are in the process, but stay focused and within a few days your baby could be sleeping through.

Most sleep-training programmes are successful within a few weeks if you are consistent in your approach.

parents' tips for a peaceful night

- Give your baby a massage before bed to relax him.
- Avoid caffeine if you're breast-feeding at bedtime.
- Try playing the same music CD every night to signal that it's bedtime.

daytime naps

Babies need to nap, and the better your baby is at napping, the better she will sleep at night. This is because not getting enough sleep during the day will make her overtired and fractious, and result in her finding it harder to relax at bedtime. Regular naps also have an effect on your baby's mood and appetite, so she's likely to be more alert and active as well as enthusiastic about feeding.

Babies often rub their eyes to indicate that they're ready for a nap.

why nap?

Sleep is essential for both mind and body (see pages 174–175) and daytime naps are no exception. Even by the time she's 9 months old, your baby may still make up 20 per cent of her sleep during the day. Naps often involve a high proportion of REM sleep, so while your baby naps during the day her brain is busy assimilating all her new experiences. Sleep releases stress-reducing hormones, which probably accounts for the fact that a baby who misses her nap will be grumpy and out of sorts. Naps are also important because they give you a chance to catch up, either on much-needed rest or everyday chores.

where to nap?

Studies by SIDS researchers show that the safest place to put your baby down for her nap when she's less than 6 months old is in the same room as you, whether it's in a carrycot, Moses basket or travel cot. The same safety advice applies as for night-time: put your baby on her back with her feet to the foot of the cot (see box on page 169). If your baby is put down for a nap on a bed, you'll need safety rails and to remove any bulky bedding such as a duvet and pillows.

With an older baby, it's a question of working out by trial and error where is the best place for her nap. The solution will be one that best suits your baby and your family.

Babies have different levels of tolerance: while some are very obliging and may sleep happily in the living room, others are more easily distracted and sleep better in a quiet bedroom. Inevitably, naptime for second and subsequent babies may sometimes take place in a car seat or pushchair as you collect and deliver an older child from school or pre-school. Car seats and pushchairs are not recommended as a regular substitute for a cot or carrycot at nap-time, as the semi-upright position may put pressure on your baby's spine and young babies are at risk from suffocation (see page 230).

As well as deciding where your baby will have her naps, it's important to think about how you settle her (see page 181) and when she's likely to take her naps.

when to nap?

A very young baby has lots of short cat-naps in between her longer stretches of sleep during the day, but between the ages of 3 and 6 months, a pattern of sorts emerges (see pages 172–173) and your baby will become more receptive to being put down for a nap at a predictable time of day, which means you can influence when she sleeps rather than following her body clock.

Try keeping a diary over 2 weeks, noting when she naps during the day, and see if it follows a pattern. Some babies take three 45-minute naps, while others have two longer naps, one in the morning, one in the afternoon. There will also be babies who don't fall into any of the 'average' categories. At the age of 6 months, your baby needs roughly 14 hours of sleep in every 24 – about 10 hours will be during the night.

Q **My baby is 6 months old and her naps only last 30 minutes. She's often grizzly when she wakes. How can I help her nap for longer?**

A The amount of time it takes your baby to cycle through light- and deeper-sleep stages when she's napping tends to be shorter than at night, lasting only 45 minutes instead of 90 minutes. Listen out for when she reaches that vulnerable 30-minute stage in her nap, and if you hear her rousing, gently pat her back or shush her quietly to soothe her back to sleep. Try to ensure she can't be disturbed by any sudden loud noises and put her down to nap in a peaceful place.

Keeping a sleep diary can help you to determine whether a pattern is appearing.

Q My 8-month-old falls asleep when we go to pick up her older brother from school at 3 pm, which means she keeps going in the evening until about 9.30 pm. What can I do?

A Babies of this age may still need two naps a day, one in the morning and one in the afternoon, but you could try adjusting her routine so that she has her lunch a little earlier and her afternoon nap starts earlier. If she's woken from her nap sufficiently rested, she should be able to stay awake for the school run. Take toys and a snack to distract her from falling asleep again on the journey. You may need to adjust your routine gradually by moving your schedule 15 minutes each day over a period of days.

Take advantage of those occasions on which your baby shows signs of tiredness.

timing

To work towards a nap-time routine, check your nap diary to pinpoint when your baby is likely to be sleepy. If there are regular times in the day, use a shortened version of your bedtime ritual (perhaps just a drink and a cuddle) and put your baby down for a nap at these points. She may be so sleepy that she doesn't need the routine cues to encourage her to sleep, but will drop off almost as soon as you put her in her cot.

Once you notice your baby's sleepy signs, try to act on them promptly and offer a nap there and then, rather than changing her nappy or becoming involved in another task. A tired baby can work herself into an overwrought state quite quickly and will then find it hard to drift off for a nap.

Be sensitive to your baby's needs and remember that all babies have different sleep requirements. Some are more resistant to napping and you may need to spend longer on a winding-down routine or try a different environment. If she's not sleepy, then getting her to nap will be a struggle and it's worth leaving her to play for longer and trying again later.

Look out for the body language that shows your baby is ready for a snooze, such as:

- Rubbing her eyes.
- Eyes glazing over.
- Yawning.
- Becoming quiet and slower in her movements.
- Getting grouchy and irritable.
- Sucking her thumb or twiddling her hair.

The same principles apply at nap-time as when you are settling your baby at bedtime (see page 166). Put her in her cot or carrycot, drowsy but awake, so that she's not relying on being fed, rocked or cuddled to fall asleep. If your baby learns to fall asleep independently at nap-time, she'll be able to settle herself when she wakes at night too.

A baby that naps well during the day is likely to sleep far better at night.

nap difficulties

Problems may arise if your baby naps too late in the day, which will impact on how easily she will settle at bedtime. Most babies over the age of 9 months will be more wakeful at bedtime if their afternoon nap occurs after about 3.30 pm. At the other end of the scale, a baby who naps too early in the morning may start waking earlier.

Aim to adjust a late afternoon nap by gradually encouraging your baby to fall asleep for her nap about 15 minutes earlier over a period of days and moving the time back bit by bit. To alter the early naps, try delaying putting her down for the first nap of the day by 15 minutes or so and shifting this forward again after a few days until eventually there's a gap of 2–3 hours between when she wakes up in the morning and when she has a nap.

Parents with two or more children often find that the baby of the family never gets a routine of her own but simply has to fit in with that of her older siblings. If you are trying to establish a nap-time routine for a baby and have a toddler at home as well, you'll need to juggle the sleep needs of two different personalities, but it can be done. Try working towards a nap for both just after lunch, as this is a time when energy levels are at a natural low. Use the shortened bedtime routine to settle your baby and encourage your toddler to rest or relax listening to a story at the same time. You could create a special space in your baby's room with a comfortable beanbag for your toddler to relax in, or have your baby and toddler in separate rooms for nap-times.

Q **Why does my baby nap on the days she goes to nursery, but not at home?**

A Ask the nursery staff to tell you more about the routine they use to settle the babies. Find out as much information as you can about where your baby goes to sleep. Is it quiet? What time of day is it? Do the carers pat or stroke the babies if they stir? And so on. If it's possible to follow this routine at home, give it a go and keep trying for at least 2 weeks, being as consistent as you can. If your baby is capable of napping in the nursery at a regular time, then you know she can do it at home, so it's worth persevering.

chapter 5
feeding

Your baby will move from frequent milk feeds through first solids to regular meals during his first year. Whether you choose to breast- or bottle-feed initially, this is a good time to establish a routine that can be adapted as your baby grows. Make feeding fun as you introduce new flavours to your baby, and show delight in his first attempts to feed himself. Focus on suitable foods, avoiding potential allergies or choking hazards, and be prepared for a fussy or messy eater.

breast-feeding

Breast-feeding is the healthiest way to feed your baby. Breast milk provides her with everything she needs for the first 6 months of her life – many mothers breast-feed for longer than this – and there are enormous health benefits for both of you. Breast milk contains active cells that 'mop up' bacteria and antibodies that fight infections, giving your baby an extra boost to her immune system.

benefits of breast-feeding

It may help to protect your baby against:

- Asthma.
- Chest infections.
- Childhood diabetes.
- Ear infections.
- Eczema.
- Gastro-intestinal infections.
- Obesity.
- Urinary infections.

It helps protect you against:

- Breast cancer.
- Ovarian cancer.
- Weak bones later in life.

Other advantages:

- Breast milk is always fresh and at the right temperature.
- Menstruation may be delayed while you are exclusively breast-feeding.
- It can help you to get your pre-pregnancy figure back more quickly.
- Skin-to-skin contact is good for bonding mother and baby.

breast-feeding support

Initially, you may need help with breast-feeding, so make the most not only of your midwife but also of breast-feeding support workers. Ask your midwife for some contact numbers in case you need them. Other women who have breast-fed can also be great support, encouraging you to keep going, if and when the going gets tough!

It is important to take time finding the most comfortable position for breast-feeding your baby.

how the milk is made

From around 16 weeks into pregnancy, your breasts start to produce colostrum, which is yellow-orange, thick and sticky. Colostrum is all your baby needs in her first few days of life, before your milk is produced. It is high in carbohydrate, protein and antibodies, and low in fat. Some women are concerned that there won't be enough colostrum to satisfy their baby, but with a healthy full-term baby, you can be sure that this is all she needs. If you haven't experienced leaky breasts during pregnancy, don't worry, as this has no influence on your ability to breast-feed.

A newborn baby is not designed to take large amounts of fluids – her stomach is the size of a small marble. By feeding frequently, she stimulates the nipple and this sends messages to the brain to produce milk. Milk is therefore produced on a 'supply-and-demand' basis: the greater the demand, the bigger the supply. When the milk 'comes in' around the third day, your breasts may feel heavy and engorged, but this will pass within a couple of days. When your baby feeds, she will initially get the foremilk, which is watery and thirst-quenching, followed by the hind milk, which is thicker and packed with calories to make her feel satisfied. Even on a hot day she will not need any extra fluids – she'll just feed more frequently and will therefore naturally get more of the thirst-quenching foremilk.

If your baby tends to favour one breast, you can fool her into thinking she's feeding from that breast by placing her in the 'rugby ball' position on the other side.

breast-feeding problems

Uncomfortable It may be difficult, or simply take a period of time, for you and your baby to find a comfortable breast-feeding position. This is particularly the case if you have had a caesarean section and your stomach is sore. For some ideas on the most popular positions, such as the 'rugby ball', see pages 190–191.

Sore nipples These are nearly always caused by poor attachment at the breast. Make sure your baby is getting the areola in his mouth, not just the nipple. Babies can also get thrush in their mouth (see page 254), which can cause painful nipples. Ask your midwife to check if you are unsure.

Lumpy breasts Blocked ducts can cause breasts to feel tender and produce hard lumps. This makes feeding very painful, but persist if you can, as the breast needs to be drained. It can be useful to try feeding your baby in an alternative position to help drain the duct. Gently stroke the tender area as she feeds.

Mastitis This is inflammation of the breast tissue, which sometimes then becomes infected and tender. Mastitis can develop when the breasts aren't emptied properly at each feed, from a blocked duct, a bra that is too tight or where fingers have been too firm holding the breast. There is no danger of the baby receiving an infection from it, and the best cure is to continue draining the sore breast by allowing your baby to feed off it. If you develop flu-like symptoms, contact your midwife or doctor, as you may need antibiotics.

'I found it really odd that some people found it acceptable to see a baby drinking cow's milk, but not human milk. I refused on principle to go to the 'mother-and-baby room' to feed my baby. I wouldn't eat my lunch in a tiny dark room and I didn't expect her to either. Mothers should be proud to breast-feed their babies and not feel that they have to hide away!'

Priti, mother of
Sharan (3 months)

shared
experience

how to
breast-feed

Although breast-feeding your baby is the most natural thing in the world, it is also completely normal to feel self-conscious, especially in the early days when it might take a little time to get the hang of the feeding. However, as it gets easier, you will become more confident and will feel proud that you are giving your baby such a good start in life.

easy feeding

For ease of feeding, especially when you are out and about, you may feel more comfortable wearing a loose-fitting top so that you can position your baby at the breast quickly and unobtrusively, rather than having to remove layers of clothing.

It's good to experiment with different positions in which to feed your baby, and although it might not work one day, you may find that a couple of days later your baby latches on beautifully. It's also normal for your baby to favour one breast, but don't give up – keep encouraging her to feed at both using various positions.

Sitting up with your baby horizontal This can be used with a pillow on your lap.

Lying with your baby alongside Useful if your abdomen or bottom is sore, and also easy to do in bed.

Sitting or lying using the 'rugby ball' position This is a good position for feeding twins, and frequently successful for women who have large breasts.

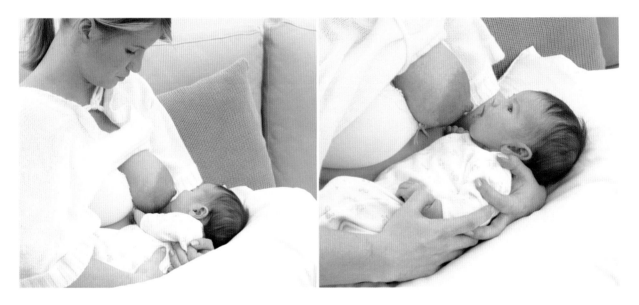

1 Sit down in a comfortable position, making sure that your back is supported. It can be helpful to rest your feet on a low stool. You may also find it useful to place a pillow on your lap.

2 Position your baby close to you to avoid him having to turn his head to reach your breast. Hold him horizontally so that his mouth and nose are facing your nipple. Gently support your breast, lining up the nipple with your baby's nose. Your baby will smell the milk and open his mouth wide.

are you attached?

Problems such as pain when breast-feeding, sore nipples or a baby that is unsettled between feeds are often caused by poor attachment. Ask for help if:

- Your baby makes a clicking sound as he sucks.
- He keeps sliding off the breast.
- He doesn't open his mouth wide when he feeds.
- He sucks his cheeks in as his jaw moves.

The position you choose will ultimately also depend upon the sort of birth you've had. Often women who have had a caesarean section initially prefer to feed lying down, as their stomach may be too tender for the baby to lie on.

steps to success

Offer the first feed soon after the birth when your baby's sucking reflex is strong. Even if your baby doesn't want to feed immediately, this is a chance to enjoy some skin-to-skin contact.

- Make sure that you are comfortable before you begin a feed. Have you emptied your bladder? Is your back well supported? Do you have everything you need to hand?
- Feed on demand. Don't expect a routine for the first few weeks.
- Keep your baby with you. Learn to recognize the signs that he is hungry.
- Avoid using teats too early, as it may confuse him (see pages 194–195).
- Use all the support available to you – midwives, breast-feeding support workers and other breast-feeding mothers.
- Remember to eat and drink. Breast-feeding uses lots of calories, so look after yourself.

3 Attach him on to your breast. If his mouth isn't open, brush his lips against your nipple. This will trigger the 'rooting reflex' and he will open his mouth. As you bring him to the breast, ensure his bottom lip makes contact with the areola, not the nipple. Your nipple should go towards the roof of his mouth.

4 Release your hand from your breast once he is feeding. Remember to relax your shoulders. If you are feeling pain, or that your baby is 'nipple sucking' rather than taking in the areola, detach him gently and try again.

expressing breast milk

Many women want to be able to express milk in order to leave their baby for a short period, return to work or involve their partner in the feeding. It is best to get the breast-feeding established first before you start to introduce expressing, and before you rush to buy a breast pump you could try expressing by hand. Expressed milk can be kept in the fridge at 4°C (39°F) or colder for 3–5 days.

Q **Are there certain foods I should avoid while I am breast-feeding my baby?**

A Although mothers who are breast-feeding often get given all sorts of advice, such as to avoid garlic or spicy foods, as long as you are eating the same sorts of foods that you have always enjoyed, it should not cause a problem for your baby. You may want to look at your diet, however, if your baby is suffering from colic. The food that was restricted during your pregnancy, such as soft cheese and pâté, is now fine to eat. If you have asthma or allergies in the family, it is sensible to avoid eating peanut products while breast-feeding, as they may increase the likelihood of your baby developing a nut allergy, but this applies only where there is a history of such conditions. Alcohol and caffeine can pass into breast milk, so consumption of these should be restricted.

Expressing your milk means your partner can take over sometimes.

hand expressing

Expressing by hand is the cheapest method of expressing milk, and for some women, particularly those who don't want to do it on a regular basis, it can work well.

- Wash your hands.
- Sit in a comfortable position with a wide-rimmed sterilized container into which the milk can be expressed.
- Support your breast with one hand and then massage it with the other, working downwards towards the areola, then all over the whole breast.
- Place your thumb 4–5 cm (1½–2 in) away from your nipple and your fingers below the breast, making a C-shape, then squeeze your fingers and thumb together, pushing your hand back against the chest wall, as though you are squeezing toothpaste out of a tube.
- Be patient – it can take a minute or two before milk appears.

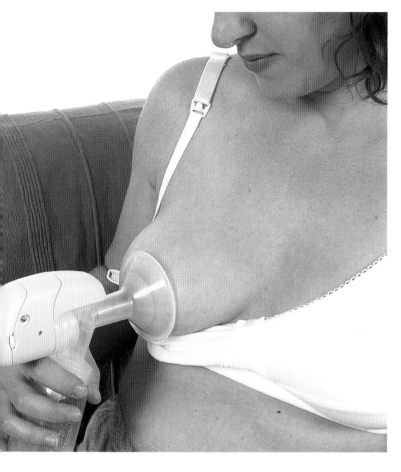

A breast pump is much quicker than expressing milk by hand.

successful expressing

Try in the morning when your milk supply might be at its greatest.

- Sit where you will not be interrupted by anyone.
- Try expressing from one breast as your baby feeds from the other.
- If your baby isn't in the same room, look at a photo of her or picture her in your mind.

using a hand pump

Various hand pumps are available and it's a good idea to ask around and see how friends get on with the different versions. Hand- or battery-operated pumps work by placing a funnel over the breast and then drawing the plunger in and out, which in turn draws out the milk.

electric pump

These mimic the action of your baby on the breast and are very efficient without causing pain. They are often used in maternity units when women are encouraged to express if they're having trouble breast-feeding or have a baby on the special care baby unit. They are more expensive than hand pumps, but can be hired from different organizations – ask your midwife for details.

Don't worry if when you start expressing you only get a few drops. This is very normal and it can take time and practice before you learn to express more milk. Women are often concerned about the colour of their milk, which can be anything from a very watery opaque to a yellow orange. If your baby was feeding at the breast, you wouldn't even be aware of the colour or amount of the milk produced, so trust in your body – it's managed to make your baby, so why would it not know how to provide her food too?

‘ My midwife told me to keep a Savoy cabbage in the fridge and when my milk came in and my breasts became engorged to put some of the leaves inside my bra. It was such a wonderful tip – the relief was instant! ’

Ruth, mother of
Sarah (4 weeks)

shared experience

the basics of
bottle-feeding

Whether from birth or following on from breast-feeding, feeding your baby with a bottle plays a huge part in modern parenting. While breast milk is undeniably best for your baby, it's not always possible to breast-feed. Bottle-feeding, although not necessarily the easy option, is sometimes the most appropriate. And with a little guidance, it can come naturally to both mother and child.

breast to bottle

If you decide to switch from breast to bottle, or want to start combining them, be prepared for your baby to need time to make the adjustment. Babies can be stubborn, but the mechanical differences in sucking from a nipple and feeding from a teat can also create what is known as 'nipple confusion'. Bear this in mind to help keep frustration – yours and the baby's – in check. The main differences are that when he breast-feeds, your baby opens his mouth wide and draws the nipple and surrounding tissue far back into his mouth. His gums compress

A baby's technique for feeding from a bottle is different to the one he uses to breast-feed.

All feeding equipment must be scrupulously clean before use.

tips for switching

- For breast-feeding mums wishing to move on to bottles at a later date, some experts believe offering expressed milk in a bottle at 5–6 weeks makes the transition easier. When to introduce a bottle is a personal choice, but seek advice from a health professional should you have any questions.
- The baby may associate his mother's smell with breast milk, so let someone else have a go.
- If you are combining and would like to keep breast and formula feeds separate, offer the formula in a cup from 4 months.

the milk sinuses underneath the areola and the tongue milks the breast. When given a bottle, gravity promotes a rush of milk. Your baby must use his lips to control the flow, not his tongue. Hold the bottle at an angle so that the teat is always full of milk. If your baby gulps air along with his milk, he may get trapped wind, which can be painful.

Once you get into the habit of using a bottle, be careful not to start offering one automatically in response to crying, as this can upset your baby's routine. Check that he is really hungry, not tired or in need of a nappy change or some attention.

why bottle feeding isn't bad

A sense of guilt is often attached to bottle feeding, but there are many reasons why, for mother and for baby, it can be the right choice.

Work Not everyone can be a stay-at-home mum, and inflexible working hours can make breast-feeding impossible.

Physical Various conditions or complications at birth may make it impossible for the mother to lactate, or the baby to feed.

Emotional Breast-feeding is not always simple. If a mother is finding it difficult, to the detriment of the bond between herself and the baby, or for any other personal reasons, she may choose to bottle-feed.

Whether the reasons are practical or emotional, bottle-feeding can offer flexibility and allow others to share in your baby's care.

Q How should I hold my baby to bottle-feed him?

A For the best swallowing position, align your baby's head with the rest of his body so that it is not twisted or arched, and have his head higher than his tummy. Because of the fast rate of flow in comparison with breast-feeding, he may prefer to be raised a little higher, perhaps in a seated position on your lap. Don't be afraid to experiment: try a variety of positions – sitting and standing – until you find one that feels right.

feeding
formula milk

With so many bottles, cans and take-away solutions, feeding with formula is well catered for. Although the list of ingredients may be daunting, the science has been thoroughly tried and tested to provide your baby with the next best thing to breast milk. All accredited formula manufacturers mimic breast milk as best they can, including fats, proteins, carbohydrates, vitamins and minerals.

Always check the temperature of the milk before feeding it to your baby.

choosing formula milk

It sounds simple enough, but with packaging that boasts 'new, improved' formula and endless benefits, it helps to know what you're looking at – and looking for.

First-stage milk is made from whey (most similar to breast milk) and is suitable for newborn babies.

Second-stage milk is based on casein (a protein found in milk) and is harder to digest. It is formulated for hungrier babies.

Follow-on milk is generally suitable for babies from 6 months old onwards. It contains extra iron.

Organic formula comprises ingredients that are mainly organically produced, although it does not mean that every ingredient is necessarily organic.

DHA-enriched milk has added DHA, an omega-3 essential fatty acid thought to improve brain development and function, and eye development.

Probiotic milk has added bacteria that are said to promote a healthy gut.

soya formula

Cow's milk is the common base for most infant formulas, but if your baby suffers from a cow's milk allergy or intolerance, there are alternatives. The most common alternative is soya milk, which is available from pharmacists and supermarkets. There have been a number of media-magnified concerns about the effect that soya formula has on the development of the reproductive system and the acceleration of puberty, due to its high levels of phytoestrogen (plant oestrogen); however, major studies have shown that the phytoestrogen does not mimic the human female hormone oestrogen and therefore does not affect testosterone levels in infant boys, as previously feared. Nevertheless, if you do have questions about any infant formula composition, you should always consult a health professional. Soya, along with low-lactose and lactose-free, formulas can also be prescribed by your doctor.

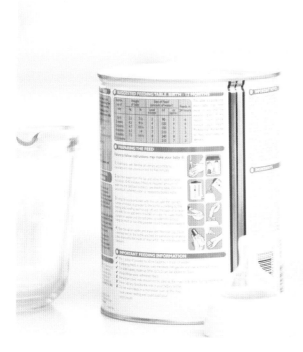

making up formula

It is necessary to make up formula milk strictly according to the manufacturer's guidelines in order to get the right amount of nutrition in the most easily digestible solution. Preparing milk in advance and storing it in the fridge used to be a bottle-feeder's blessing, but recent research suggests that such pre-preparation carries some health risks. Therefore, formula should be made up as and when you need it, following these guidelines:

- Make up formula using scalding-hot water that has cooled to no less than 70°C (158°F).
- Do not store formula in the fridge – pre-preparing increases the chance of contamination.
- When out and about, take some boiling water in a sealed flask and use this to make up fresh formula on the go.

how much formula?

The formula manufacturer will provide guidelines, but every baby has her own ideas. She should cease feeding once she is full, but bottle-fed babies sometimes overfeed.

Newborn Feed size: 30–60 ml (1–2 fl oz) at each feed, every 3 hours, for the first weeks. Babies with a low birth weight and premature babies will require a more specialized calculation, to be advised by your doctor or health professional.

1 month Feed size: 90–120 ml (3–4 fl oz); daily intake: 400–800 ml (14–28 fl oz).

2–6 months Feed size: 120–180 ml (4–6 fl oz); daily intake: 700 ml–1 litre or more (23–35 fl oz).

6 months Feed size: 180–220 ml (6–8 fl oz); daily intake: approximately 600 ml (20 fl oz).

Once your baby is on solid food, her daily intake of milk should gradually decrease to 500–600 ml (18–20 fl oz) of breast or formula milk, alongside a varied diet, until she is 12 months old.

Individual formula measurements are calculated to provide the most easily digestible solution for your baby, so be sure to read the instructions carefully.

Q Why can't I give my baby cow's milk?

A Cow's milk irritates young intestines, which can cause blood in the stools, contributing to iron deficiency. When your baby is 12 months old, is healthy and has no sign of anaemia, then you can give her cow's milk to drink. Under the age of 12 months, if it's not breast milk, it has to be infant formula. However, cow's milk can be used in cooking from 6 months, provided there is no evidence of intolerance.

bottles and other
feeding equipment

What could be easier than buying a bottle? Well, reading this for a start –
because there is mind-boggling choice when it comes to bottles and all their
accessories. Knowing what you are looking for saves time and money.

**Q I'm planning to bottle-feed
my baby. What will I need?**

A Although you don't need
much equipment to bottle-feed, it
helps to have at least six bottles
and teats. You must also have a
sterilizer and bottle- and teat-
brush for cleaning. If you are not
going to express your milk (see
pages 192–193), spend some time
choosing the most appropriate
formula (ask a health professional
for advice if you need it). Bibs and
muslin cloths are useful too.

There is a baffling choice of bottles
available on the market.

choosing a bottle

Plastic bottles Plastic bottles are commonly used because of their
versatility and flexibility. They are light and unbreakable under the
normal day-to-day pressures. They come in varied sizes, and the
smaller 120 ml (4 fl oz) size is all you will need for very young babies.
Don't use very old or cracked bottles.

Glass bottles Some parents prefer to use bottles made of heat-
resistant toughened glass, even though they are quite a bit heavier.
However, these can break or chip, so they are not generally
recommended by health professionals. These are available from
specialist outlets.

Travel bottles Bottles with disposable liners are great for travelling.
A sterilized liner is fixed to the bottle and the milk poured in. Teats
and seals must be sterilized in the usual way. The alternative is the
disposable one-use bottle, although it is expensive as a long-term
option and environmentally unfriendly.

Sterilizer bottles These are more expensive than the usual plastic
bottles, but do come with a great advantage – they steam themselves
clean! The teat and seal are placed in the large lid, along with a small
amount of water, and the bottle is snapped into place on top. The
entire upside-down bottle is placed in a microwave oven at the correct
power for the set time, and emerges ready for use.

Anti-colic bottles Gulping air when bottle-feeding is thought to

contribute to colic (see page 248). Anti-colic bottles are designed with funnels and vents that reduce the amount of air flowing through the milk and into the teat, or with vacuum-like bags to hold the milk. They are worth a try if your baby is suffering, but they don't work for everyone.

Breast-pump bottles Some bottles are compatible with certain breast pumps, removing the need to decant expressed milk. Check the descriptions given by the bottle and breast-pump manufacturers for more information.

teats

There is a wide range of teats available, with the emphasis on different needs and preferences. Ask friends what their baby likes or liked best.

- Latex teats are softer and more 'human', which may appeal to very young babies. However, they are not as durable as silicone, which are firmer.
- There are many different shapes available – round-topped, flat-topped, orthodontic and elongated. Choice really is subject to your child's preference.
- Various hole designs in the very tip of the teat denote the rate at which the milk can be sucked. With a very young baby, start by using a teat with a slow flow, to avoid choking. As your baby grows, the flow can increase.
- With all teats, the packaging will tell you when you should replace them with new.

Experiment with teat shapes to see which your baby prefers.

cleaning

Cleaning bottles with a bottles-only scrubbing brush is essential – but this is only the first step. To prevent harmful bacteria setting up home in the bottle, teat and seal, it is vital to follow cleaning with sterilizing, choosing one of the following methods. With any equipment or chemical cleaners, always follow the manufacturers' instructions.

Steam sterilizer Place the equipment into the sterilizer with the recommended amount of water and switch on the machine. Keep the lid on until the bottles are needed and clean the sterilizer once a day by wiping the inside dry.

Microwave steam sterilizers These units are specifically designed for use in a microwave oven. Check the microwave power needed to sterilize the equipment properly.

Sterilizing chemicals Sterilizing liquid or tablets are available from pharmacies and supermarkets. Most sterilizing products need to be mixed in a bowl with enough water to cover the items. Leave them to soak, usually for an hour, before removing and rinsing.

Boiling Place all equipment in a large saucepan and cover it with water. Tip and rotate the bottles to release all the air bubbles. Put the saucepan lid on and bring to a rolling boil for 5 minutes, to ensure any germs are killed, before allowing to cool. With clean hands, remove the bottles and store in a clean fridge. If they are not used within 24 hours, you will need to re-boil them.

In the first year, when your baby's immune system is fragile, sterilizing bottle-feeding equipment is essential.

safe and happy
bottle-feeding

Feeding is a perfect opportunity for some one-on-one time with your baby, which is why establishing a comfortable environment and a happy routine is so important. A baby can detect the slightest hint of stress, and a feeding experience that is fraught with frustration – or forced feeding – may create unwelcome associations for your baby, causing repeat mealtime upsets.

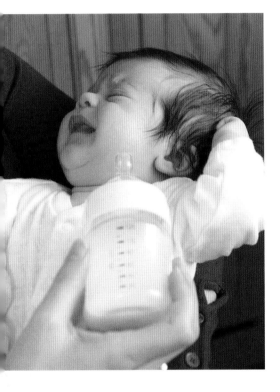

Never force a baby to feed – instead, look at the possible reasons why she won't and try adopting a different approach.

my baby doesn't want to feed

If your child is screaming, squirming or refusing to take the bottle, first rule out the possibility that she is unwell. Common illnesses that may affect feeding are viral infections (see pages 243, 246 and 248), ear and throat infections (see page 243), which make sucking painful, and oral thrush (see page 254). If in any doubt, or if your baby is losing weight, contact a health professional or your doctor, and in the meantime give her cooled boiled water to prevent dehydration.

If your baby is otherwise healthy and gaining weight, keeping a diary of when and how you offer feeds may help you to see a pattern in her behaviour and provide an answer to your feeding problems. Ask yourself the following questions:

- Are you misinterpreting discomfort/fatigue/boredom for hunger?
- Is she being distracted during feeds?
- Is she so hungry that she has upset herself to the point of being unable to feed?
- Has the formula been contaminated or taken on a smell, such as perfume from clothing or pungent food from the fridge?
- Is the teat flow too slow and therefore frustrating her?
- Is the teat flow too fast and therefore choking her?
- Is the formula the correct temperature?
- Have you started her on a new formula to which she may be intolerant – or simply unused to?
- If she's on solids, is she already full before you offer her milk?

my baby is spitting up her feed!

A certain amount of possetting and spitting up is completely normal, and some babies do it more than others. Apart from using a plastic-backed bib to prevent too much mess, there is often little else that can be done. Most babies overcome reflux at around 12 months.

If the spitting up is accompanied by weight loss, difficulty breathing, arching during and after feeds or coughing, there is a possibility that your baby could have gastroesophageal reflux disease (GERD). She will require evaluation by a health professional.

oral hygiene

Even if they are not fed sweet things and if their teeth are not yet visible, babies can suffer milk tooth decay. This is because baby teeth are at their most vulnerable when they first break the surface of the gum – and that might be some time before we actually see them. There are several ways you can avoid decay developing. When your baby falls asleep, the production of saliva, which washes the teeth and fights bacteria, drops dramatically, so don't encourage her to fall asleep while feeding. Sugary substances, such as sweetened water and some formulas, can affect the teeth beneath the gums. Following a feed, you can help by wiping the gums with a damp, clean cloth. If you are offering diluted juice, which is high in natural sugars and acids, do so in beakers, which allow the fluid to pass the teeth quickly.

from bottle to cup

After 12 months, babies should have no need for bottles, but the earlier you introduce a cup, the easier the transition will be. The danger of leaving it late is that your baby will have come to associate the bottle teat with comfort, much like a pacifier. There are two methods to stop using a bottle:

Withdrawal Cut down bottle feeds gradually, offering instead a sippy cup until your baby is weaned off the bottle altogether.

Cold turkey This is a battle of wills. Have a few snacks and cups of feed at the ready, but don't be surprised if it takes a few days and a lot of screaming. If you have steely nerves, it's the quicker option.

bottle-feeding don'ts

At all costs, do not do the following:
- Force feed your baby. This may lead to choking and will establish bad associations with feeding. Remain calm wherever possible. Encourage her to feed by gently teasing the edges of her mouth with the teat.
- Feed lying down. Giving a bottle in the lying-down position can cause choking and inhalation of milk into the lungs. Fluid can travel up and into the ear, causing ear infections, or sit in pools in the mouth, increasing chances of tooth decay.
- Add solids. Mixing solid matter into the milk increases the likelihood of choking and overfeeding.

Using a cup decreases the chances of tooth decay.

weaning –
just for starters

Within a few months, milk will not be enough to support your baby's speedy development. When to wean will depend, in part, on your baby – but no matter how eagerly he watches your fork, solids under 4 months are inadvisable, unless recommended by your GP. And the recommended age is 6 months.

Weaning can be an exciting time for carer and baby – if somewhat messy.

first foods

Baby rice is ground rice with added vitamins and minerals. It is mixed with breast milk or formula to create a runny solution with a soft texture and bland flavour that is perfect for a baby's first food. However, not all youngsters like baby rice, and simple fruit and vegetable purées, such as apple or pear, are good alternatives to start with.

Generic cereals can contain high levels of sugar and salt, which your baby will struggle to process, so use only baby-formulated cereals or baby rice.

If your baby is not yet 6 months old, solid feeds should be 'tasters' of what's to come – he may only eat half to one teaspoon, once a day. Don't be tempted to drop the volume of milk feeds to make him hungrier. In addition, don't give babies under 6 months products

Beginning weaning A sample timetable

Meal	Week 1	Week 2	Week 3	Week 4
breakfast	milk	fruit purée and baby rice	variety of fruit purées with baby rice	variety of fruit purées with baby rice
mid-morning	part milk and 1–2 tsp baby rice, progressing to milk with fruit or vegetable purée	vegetable purée and baby rice	vegetable purée and baby rice	vegetable purée and baby rice
lunch	milk	milk	milk	medley of vegetable purées
tea	milk	variety of vegetable purées	variety of vegetable purées	variety of fruit or vegetable purées
bedtime	milk	milk	milk	milk

containing gluten, because of an increased risk of developing coeliac disease, which damages the small intestine.

An increasingly popular trend is baby-led weaning, which misses out the purée stage and gives babies solid food from the first day of weaning (see page 213).

foods to try

If you are going to feed purées, start with steamed or boiled carrot, butternut squash, sweet potato, yam, apple or pear. Dilute these with breast milk or formula, or cooled boiled water. Later you can introduce avocado, apricot, courgette, broccoli and cauliflower. It is thought that introducing fruit purées first may encourage a sweet tooth, so try to alternate fruit with vegetables. Avoid adding flavourings, such as salt or sugar (see box on page 204); for cooking methods, see page 214.

learning to wean

Weaning is an exciting time for both mother and baby, so make sure you are relaxed and happy, and armed with bibs! Sit your baby upright – in a high chair, car seat, bouncer or on your lap – and let the adventure begin.

Timing Choose a time when your baby is perky: mid-morning or lunchtime is best. Cut short the usual milk feed and offer just a teaspoon or two of solids before finishing off the remainder of the milk feed.

Technique Place the spoon only a little way into your baby's mouth and raise the spoon handle as you withdraw it so that the food is caught behind his upper gum. Don't be surprised if he uses his tongue to push it straight out – just try again. If he becomes agitated, leave it and try again the next day. It may take him a few days to adapt to the new experience.

Had enough? Your baby's stomach is very small and he will not take more than a couple of teaspoons, probably less. If he shuts his mouth or turns his head, he is full.

Progressing After 2 weeks of weaning, add in a teatime feed. From there you can start to build up the quantity of food, stepping up to three feeds a day over the next few weeks. From 6 months the quantity of food that your baby will want may increase very quickly and this is completely normal.

planning ahead

It is easy to make extra purées for the freezer. Buy some ice-cube trays with lids, fill with purée and pop out a food cube when required.

Follow this routine to ensure your purées are in perfect condition when you come to feed them to your baby:
- Sterilize the ice-cube trays (or containers).
- Put the freshly cooked food in and allow to cool, loosely covered.
- Seal and label with the flavour and date, then freeze.
- Use within 6 weeks.

ready for solids?

Your baby may be ready if he is:
- Aged 6 months. Some babies may be ready earlier than this, though not before 4 months. Talk to your health visitor for further advice.
- Holding up his head unsupported.
- Sitting well, with support.
- Unsatisfied after a full milk feed.
- Trying to put things in his mouth.
- Waking in the night with hunger.
- Watching you eat.
- Making chewing motions.

you will need

- Bibs
- Rubber-tipped baby spoons
- Small feeding bowls

Q **Why can't I feed my baby solids before he is 4 months old?**

A Your baby's digestive system is simply too immature for weaning before the age of 17 weeks. Weaning too early is also thought to increase a baby's chances of developing food allergies, and young babies cannot let you know when they are full, making it too easy to overfeed them. In addition, a baby's swallowing abilities are not fully developed until he is 4 months old, so feeding solids may cause your baby to choke. Early weaning may also increase the risk of later obesity.

your baby's
diet

Six months old is a turning point in your baby's life. Previously dependent on milk, she must now rely on a more varied diet to obtain all the nutrients she requires for healthy growth and development. It is important to recognize what you should – and shouldn't – include in her diet. If your baby takes to solids well, it won't be long before she's ready to try something more interesting.

foods to avoid under 12 months

- Salt
- Sugar
- Honey
- Nuts
- Blue and unpasteurized cheeses
- Smoked and salted meats and fish
- Pâté
- Offal (liver once a week is fine)
- Strong spices
- Carbonated drinks
- Caffeine
- Soft-boiled or raw eggs

components of a healthy diet

Iron By 6 months, your baby's natural store of iron will be depleted, so fresh supplies must be provided by her new, varied diet. The most easily absorbed form of iron is found in meat. Other sources of iron include apricots, beans and lentils, green leafy vegetables and fortified cereals. Vitamin C aids absorption of iron, so offer a piece of fruit or some diluted fresh juice with meals. However, some vegetables, such as broccoli and cauliflower, have a high vitamin C content so can be offered without the need for fruit or juice. This will help to get your baby used to drinking plain water. Avoid feeding too much dietary fibre, such as lots of wholegrains, beans and lentils, as this can inhibit iron absorption and it makes the diet very bulky.

Calcium This is very important for bones and teeth; good sources of calcium include dairy products, such as cheese and yoghurt. For babies with lactose intolerance, green vegetables, wholemeal bread, lentils, ground almonds, sesame paste and tofu also contain calcium – get advice from your health professional before feeding these.

Protein Your baby's rapid growth means she needs plenty of protein. Include a variety of sources in her diet to ensure she obtains a good

You should make sure that your baby's everyday diet includes plenty of fresh fruit and vegetables.

left Fruit is naturally sweet and delicious, and full of vitamins and minerals.

below Apricots are renowned for being a good natural source of iron.

balance of amino acids, the 'building blocks' of protein: well-cooked eggs, meat, poultry, fish, tofu and dairy products are all good sources, as are beans, lentils and peas.

supplements

Healthy babies under 6 months should be receiving everything they need from milk. After 6 months, it is advised that a baby who is having breast milk as her main drink should be given vitamin A and vitamin D supplements, as should a formula-fed baby who is having less than 600 ml (20 fl oz) of formula per day. Premature babies, those with a low birth weight or babies of mothers who have diabetes may require iron supplements. You should discuss this with your doctor or health professional. Vegetarian babies may also need supplements (see below).

a vegetarian baby

If you are bringing your baby up as a vegetarian, you need to be careful to ensure she gets the nutrients she needs. After 6 months, it is important to make sure she is getting enough iron, calcium, essential fatty acids, minerals and protein. These are all readily available from cereals, beans, lentils, nuts and seeds, dairy and soya products, such as tofu (allergies allowing, see page 206), cooked eggs and fruit and vegetables. There are very few sources of vegetarian long-chain omega-3s, so you might choose to include flax seeds or flax seed oil in your baby's diet, but it's best to consult a health professional first.

Beans and lentils play an important role in the vegetarian baby's diet.

Porridge is a popular choice for babies over 6 months.

Q What can I give my 6-month-old daughter to drink other than milk?

A Under 6 months, the only drink you should offer is tap-water, boiled and cooled. Avoid bottled water, as it can contain high levels of minerals and sodium. After 6 months she can have real fruit juices, diluted to reduce the concentration of natural sugar and acid, which can erode tooth enamel. One part juice to ten parts water is ideal. Avoid squashes, cordials and drinks with added sugar, as they are bad for your baby's teeth and offer little or no nutritional value.

allergens to avoid

If you have a family history of eczema, asthma or allergies, you may choose to avoid these foodstuffs until your baby is 8 months old.
- Cow's milk products.
- Fish and shellfish.
- Soya beans.
- Tomatoes.
- Citrus fruit and juices.
- Eggs.
- Peanuts, sesame seeds and kiwi fruit (avoid until 3 years old).
- Gluten products (bread, flour, pasta, some breakfast cereals and rusks).
- Follow-on milk.
- Additives.

To be sure your baby is getting enough protein and iron, include two servings of pulses (lentils, beans, chickpeas) or tofu per day. Nuts and nut products are also a useful source of protein, unless there is an adverse reaction or a family history of allergies. Quorn® products can be used, but they should not be relied on, as they are low in calories. Textured vegetable protein (TVP) may be difficult for young babies to digest and you should check the salt content carefully.

allergies and intolerances

Some foods are linked to allergies and intolerances and are best avoided if you have a family history.

What is a food allergy? This is when the body's immune system overreacts to an ordinarily harmless food, mistaking it as harmful and producing antibodies. This may not cause any symptoms, but at some point in the future when this food is eaten again, the antibodies are ready to act. This causes mast cells to release chemicals such as histamine, which in turn leads to physical symptoms.

What is a food intolerance? This is a gut response, occurring when something in a food irritates the digestive system or when the necessary digestive enzymes are lacking in the gut.

Recognizing a reaction Allergic reactions vary from diarrhoea to vomiting, hives and rashes. Although rare in babies, in extreme cases a reaction can cause anaphylactic shock (see page 255), a potentially fatal reaction in which the mouth, tongue and airways swell and blood pressure falls. Intolerance reactions usually create gastric problems, such as bad wind and diarrhoea.

Preventing reactions The longer a baby is breast-fed and the older she is when she starts being fed solid food – six months – the more likely it is that her digestive system can process proteins normally. However, the routine steps to avoid problems should always remain the same:

1. Introduce new foods one at a time, leaving 3–4 days between bringing in another new food, and watch for adverse reactions.
2. If you do observe wheezing, coughing, discomfort or rashes, stop offering the food and see if the symptoms go away.
3. If the symptoms are severe seek medical help immediately.
4. If you are unsure whether it's an illness or allergy speak to your doctor for advice.

making progress

Texture Don't be tempted to stick with a runny consistency just because it works. Once your baby is used to the feeling of 'solid' food in her mouth, you can start to introduce some soft lumpy bits. Gradually altering the texture of her food to soft and lumpy at approximately 7 months and to a coarser mash by around 9 months. This is essential for speech development. Also, if she is not given lumps in her food at this stage she may refuse them later on.

Self-feeding Likewise, this should be encouraged, and although you may feel as if you are clearing a disaster zone at the end of every meal, it will be worth it. Consider it target practice – it won't be long before your baby is hitting the spot. Try giving her a small bowl of food and her own spoon, and have a set yourself. Every time she misses her mouth, you can fill the gap with a spoonful of your food. Babies love to copy, so try eating alongside her, and with slow movements, play follow my leader.

adding some spice

Encouraging your baby to be adventurous with flavours now can help to avoid fussy eating habits later. Don't use anything fiery, though.

- Cinnamon is a sweetener and is great with stewed fruit, especially banana. However, it can cause an allergic reaction, so check this carefully (see left).
- Coriander gives a tang and is delicious with puréed avocado.
- Ginger provides spice and helps to combat wind. Try it with cooked carrots and stewed fruit.
- Rosemary has a great flavour and encourages relaxation. Mix it with mashed potato and lamb.

Self-feeding is a messy business – but with the right attitude it can be good, clean fun!

making a
meal of it

If you started weaning early, then he should be ready to tackle two meals a day by 6 months and three by 7 months. If you are starting at 6 months, pass through the purée stage quickly, as your baby will be better equipped to eat solids. You can expect him to be ready for three meals a day by the age of 7–8 months.

severe choking

Always watch your baby while he is eating. If he has a severe case of choking and is unable to breathe, cough or cry, act quickly as follows:

Lay him face down along your forearm, with his head low and deliver up to five back blows between the shoulder blades with the heel of your hand. Check his mouth quickly after each one and remove any obstruction.

If back blows do not clear the obstruction, turn him onto his back and deliver up to five chest thrusts, with two fingers in the middle of his chest, pushing inwards and upwards. Check his mouth after each one.

If the obstruction does not clear after three cycles of back blows and chest thrusts, call the emergency services. Continue cycles of back blows and chest thrusts until help arrives, and resuscitate if necessary. Seek medical advice if your baby has been given chest thrusts.

adapting family food

When your baby is enjoying similar tastes and textures to you, commonly around 9–12 months, there is no reason why he shouldn't be ready to eat some of the family meal – unless, that is, you are having a take-away, which will be laden with bad fats, salt and sugar.

You may have to adapt your meals to avoid overloading your baby's system with additives and seasonings, so remember to check the label of any food product you use. Many pre-packaged sauces, soups, cereals and ready meals are high in salt and sugar – avoid these. Put the seasoning on the table, not into the food. Provided that your family meal contains carbohydrates, proteins, good fats and vitamins, it should be satisfying your baby's needs. If you need to adapt your meal to meet your baby's healthy requirements, then all the better.

Offering finger foods gives your baby a chance to take control.

Always check the temperature of hot food, especially if heated in the microwave.

finger foods

Between 7 and 8 months, your baby will probably enjoy getting to grips with his food. He may find spoons fiddly, but should have good control of his fingers. Allowing him to feed himself will help him to build a healthy relationship with food. Don't offer anything that has too many loose crumbs, as these could be inhaled. Try:

- Toast, pitta, naan or chapati soldiers.
- Cubes of cheese, apple or pear.
- Cooked pasta shapes.
- Cooked carrot sticks or green beans.
- Bananas.
- Rice cakes.

Meal suggestions:

- Roast dinners
- Risottos and stews
- Lentil hotpot
- Shepherd's pie
- Macaroni cheese
- Spaghetti Bolognese

how to cook...

Tomato sauce Heat together olive oil and canned tomatoes with a dash of balsamic vinegar to sweeten.

Cheesy sauce Heat milk and grated Cheddar cheese with a little cornflour to thicken.

Gravy Heat stock (chicken, vegetable or both, see below) with tomato purée, adding some cornflour to thicken.

stock

Stock cubes can contain a lot of salt, but you can make your own. It's easy, and a terrific base for sauces, stews, risottos and purées. Home-made stock can be kept for 3 days in the fridge or 3 months in the freezer (use the ice-cube tray method, see page 203).

- Place a chicken carcass into a deep pan, cover with water and boil.
- After an hour, add chopped onion, celery, carrots and herbs.
- After another hour, remove the chicken carcass and strain the liquid.
- Leave the liquid to cool and then skim off any fat.

Q My baby is always hungry. What can I give him to keep him happy between meals?

A While adults try to avoid picking between meals, babies need to eat little and often, and healthy snacks should be part of your baby's diet, especially as he gets increasingly mobile and burns off more energy. Try these:

- Vegetables with home-made cream cheese dip or hummus.
- Fruit pieces and yoghurt.
- Dried apple rings and apricots.
- Bread with vegetable purée or fruit spread.
- Cream cheese sandwiches.

6–9 months

Remember that smooth purées should have become much lumpier by 9 months. Each time you introduce a new food, be aware that your baby might have an adverse reaction, so introduce it slowly, mixing it only with foods you know he is fine with.

New foods	• Cow's milk, mild cheeses, cream cheese, yoghurt, eggs (cooked)
	• Bread, porridge, rusks (if there is no adverse reaction or history of gluten allergies)
	• Peas, lentils, beans, tofu
	• Lamb, beef, pork
	• Plaice, sole, trout (filleted, de-boned)
Offer daily	• 2–3 helpings of carbohydrate
	• 2 helpings of fruit and vegetables
	• 1 helping of protein

Serving suggestions

First thing	Breast-feed *or* milk (200 ml/7 fl oz)
Breakfast	Cereal with cow's milk and mashed banana or fruit purée
Mid-morning	Some fruit or rice cakes
Lunch	Red lentil dhal with carrot and courgette, plus yoghurt *or* Macaroni and cauliflower cheese, plus apple and pear purée *or* Turkey with vegetables and rice, plus apple purée
Mid-afternoon	Breast-feed *or* milk (200 ml/7 fl oz) and toast slices
Tea	Cheesy vegetable medley purée (parsnip, carrot, broccoli) *or* Chicken and peach purée *or* Creamy sole and potato, plus fruit salad
Bedtime	Breast-feed *or* milk (200 ml/7 fl oz)

9–12 months

As your baby is far more energetic now, he will need more solids to fill the hunger and nutrition gap. It's time to introduce even more new foods, with richer flavours and coarser textures.

New foods
- Ground nuts, ground seeds (if there is no adverse reaction or history of allergies)
- Canned tomatoes, canned tuna, oily fish
- Eggs (well cooked)
- Ham (low salt)

Continue to use previous weaning ingredients and recipes, but be more adventurous with combinations and textures. This is a great time to adapt nutritious family meals (see below).

Offer daily
- 2–3 helpings of carbohydrate
- 2 helpings of fruit and vegetables
- 1 helping of protein

Breakfast	Cereal with cow's milk and mashed banana or fruit purée
Mid-morning	Breast-feed *or* milk (200 ml/7 fl oz) and some fruit or rice cakes
Lunch	Mediterranean chicken: chunky puréed cooked chicken with red pepper, courgette and carrots, plus fruit *or* Macaroni cheese, plus apple and pear purée *or* Ratatouille: vegetable chunks simmered in tomato purée, stock and herbs until tender and then sprinkled with grated cheese, plus rice pudding
Mid-afternoon	Breast-feed *or* milk (200 ml/7 fl oz) and a snack, if wanted
Tea	Vegetable medley purée (parsnip, carrot, broccoli) with rice, plus fruit salad *or* Chicken and peach purée, plus yoghurt *or* Creamy cod and potato, plus fruit salad
Bedtime	Breast-feed *or* milk (200 ml/7 fl oz)

fussy eaters

Most children go through a stage when they're a bit picky about what they eat. Babies soon learn that food thrown on to the floor provokes a reaction, but refusing to eat is not always a struggle for independence or a ploy for attention – teething or illness can affect appetite. In all cases, handle your baby's moods carefully, because the approach you take will affect future mealtimes.

Q My little girl generally likes her food, but we have a problem when it comes to vegetables. Have you any suggestions?

A Some children, even babies, don't like the taste of vegetables. Try disguising it by adding some puréed fruit or cooking the vegetables in home-made chicken stock. Dilute their taste in a sauce for pasta or fish. Make sure you don't overcook vegetables, as they lose their vibrant colour and taste mushy. Offer vegetable finger foods at the beginning of mealtime. Your baby is more likely to eat them when she is hungry.

eat together

In many busy families, the baby's mealtime can become a kitchen corner job, while you try to get on with myriad other tasks. However, babies take their cues from their environment, so if you take time to eat around the table together, as a family, it will reinforce the notion that mealtimes are to be relished. New foods will be more acceptable if your baby sees her parents eating them too. Eating together all the time is a big challenge, as family schedules are generally hectic and depend on external commitments. But 'getting on' with something else in the kitchen – leaving your baby to feel pushed aside – may cause her to seek attention. And not eating is probably one of the most popular tactics. So even if you can't be eating alongside her, sit with her and have a drink. Spend some time talking about your baby's food, praising her when she chews and smiling throughout. Make shapes, faces and stacks with finger foods. If it can't be a family meal, it can still be a sociable occasion.

It is not unusual for a baby to reject a food with an unfamiliar texture or taste.

Some foods have both nutritional and entertainment value.

baby-led weaning

There is a school of thought that babies should not be given purée, but instead offered food in its purest and unpuréed form so that they can decide for themselves whether they are ready to tuck in. If you want to try this, wait until your baby is 6 months old and can chew and reach out for the food. The theory is that by allowing her to go at her own pace – and at her own taste – your baby will develop a healthy relationship with food. If you try this, remember to follow the guidelines regarding inappropriate foods for babies under 12 months (see page 204). Offer finger foods that are easy for your baby to grasp, such as broccoli, pieces of fish and bits of potato.

coping with a picky eater

Stay calm. Getting uptight or shouting will exacerbate the situation.

- Don't keep offering unwanted food in the same sitting.
- Don't prepare a string of meals in desperation.
- Check for teething, as sore gums make it painful for your baby to grind or chew. Offer something softer, like purée, banana or yoghurt. Go back to something chewier on another day.
- Remove distractions, such as toys, books and the television.
- Keep a food diary: it may reveal some fad patterns.
- If you are concerned about your baby's eating habits or she starts to lose weight, get advice from your doctor or health professional.
- Babies are sometimes put off by huge portions, especially if they have already shown signs of being picky. Offer smaller portions and then seconds, if required.

more tips for avoiding fuss

- Serve unwanted foods a different way next time round. Don't pile it up – make food faces on the plate, vary the texture and make mash patterns with a fork.
- Never make an issue over pickiness in front of your baby. She will soon realize that high-chair antics make her the centre of attention. Instead, give lots of attention and praise whenever she eats well.
- Try, try and try again. So she may not like cheese now, but food fads are fickle and change week to week. Keep offering a wide variety of fresh, nutritious foods at regular intervals.
- Before it becomes a plate-tipping disaster, let her win. Even little babies can be stubborn and you must learn to keep the situation under control. Say: 'Okay, not today. But maybe tomorrow?'
- Promote mealtimes as fun, sociable events – an extension of playtime.
- Give her a spoon as soon as she can hold one.
- Let her pretend to feed you if she finds it fun.
- Don't rush meals – it's not a chore.
- Let her play with her food.

cooking and
storing food

Home cooking sounds so rewarding and wholesome, but to ensure it really is, you need to maintain high hygiene levels, use healthy cooking methods and be prepared for plan B. Because when the fridge is bare or you're in the mood for a take-away, your baby isn't going to be able to follow suit. Stocking the freezer with portions of baby food can be really helpful when time is tight.

safety first

Use-by date indicates the date after which the food should not be eaten. **Best-before date** is more of a guide to food quality, but with babies and meat or dairy products it is best to err on the side of caution.

Puréeing is a great way of getting your baby to eat nutrient-rich foods.

cooking methods

Steaming is the best way to cook vegetables and fruit, as it requires no extra fats and keeps the nutrients locked in – especially vitamins B and C. It also preserves disease-fighting flavonoids. If you don't have a steamer, you can improvise by placing the food in a bowl with a small amount of water and covering it with clingfilm, which you then pierce. Heat in a microwave until the food is tender and cooked through – take care when removing the clingfilm, as the steam produced is hot. Alternatively, put a little water in a saucepan on the hob and allow it to boil. Then place the food in a colander or sieve on top of the open pan and put the lid on top of this. Steam until tender or cooked through.

Boiling vegetables and fruit leaches many of the nutrients into the water. Use the cooking water in the purées and sauces to ensure that you are re-introducing as much of that leached goodness as possible back into the food.

Baking is great for juicy foods like meats and ingredient combinations with sauces such as shepherd's pie. Bake fruits on their own in their skins in a little water, then allow them to cool, for an extra-sweet treat for dessert.

Microwaving doesn't always heat evenly, so be sure that the food is piping hot throughout. Stir thoroughly to dispel 'hot-spots' and taste-test before serving.

Warm food is great for bacteria, which just love cosy environments. If you want to give warm food to your baby, heat it until it is piping hot first and then cool it to the required temperature.

Puréeing is a great way to blend and combine soft or softened foods. When puréeing meats, ensure that the meat is pre-cooked and broken into small chunks.

Whichever cooking method you use, always make sure meat is cooked right through – when pierced, the juices must run clear and there should be no 'pink' areas. Don't allow food to burn, as the crispy black bits contain chemicals that could be carcinogenic. Wash vegetables and fruit thoroughly, especially if you are serving them raw.

It is a good idea to steam vegetables in large quantities and freeze puréed batches.

organic matters

Non-organic produce can contain additives and by products of farming. For example, fruit and vegetables may have been treated with pesticides, and intensively farmed meat can contain residues of antibiotics (fed to the animals to keep infection at bay) or hormones (which make animals grow faster or fatter). Organic meat and non-farmed fish should not contain such 'additives'. However, organic foods can be pricey, which might mean you cannot afford so much of them. On balance, it is better that you buy regular products and provide your children with the full set of nutrients rather than they miss out.

frozen and storecupboard foods

Cooking meals from fresh is not always practical. For such times, it is easy to have something in the cupboard, fridge or freezer that can be turned into a quick, no-fuss meal. Freezing is an excellent way to preserve food, as the nutrient losses in foods that are reheated from frozen are negligible.

Frozen vegetables such as cauliflower, broccoli and spinach can be used to rustle up a quick meal: steam cook and serve alone or in a cheesy or tomato sauce for pasta and risotto (see also page 203). Vegetables begin to lose nutrients as soon as they're harvested, so freezing is a great way to limit this.

storecupboard standbys

These suggestions are for babies of 6 months and above. Always check the salt content of any prepared foods.

Breads Pitta, naan, chapati, unsalted crackers, water biscuits, rice biscuits and bread sticks. These can be spread with a little unsalted butter, or dipped into fruit or vegetable purée, cream cheese or hummus, all of which can even be home-made.

Cans Tuna or salmon in spring water, sweetcorn. These make a wonderful sandwich filling or pasta sauce (for babies of 9 months plus). Canned tomatoes are useful for making quick sauces.

Pasta Stir in some cream cheese for a super-speedy meal.

Dried fruit Apple rings, dried mango and apricots, among others.

Grains Rice makes a quick risotto or rice pudding, while couscous and quinoa are quick-cooking, nutritious alternatives to rice and pasta.

Baked beans Choose low-sugar, low-salt varieties (for babies of 9 months plus).

Ready-prepared baby foods Baby-food manufacturers try to jam-pack their jars with nutrients, so they're great for quick and easy meals. Before purchasing, check the 'use-by' and 'best-before' dates, and that seals have not been broken.

fridge tips

- Keep uncooked meat at the bottom of the fridge in sealed containers where it cannot touch or drip on other foods.
- Keep refrigerated food out of the fridge for as short a time as possible.
- As soon as they have cooled, put leftovers in the fridge in suitable containers. Eat them within 48 hours or follow any advice on the label.
- Defrost frozen food in the fridge overnight. If defrosting at room temperature, ensure the food is heated until piping hot throughout before cooling and feeding.
- Never reheat cooked foods more than once.

chapter 6

your baby's health

Your baby's health will be of paramount importance to you in the first year, all the more so because she is unable to protect herself during these first few months. In addition to familiarizing yourself with the most common ailments likely to occur, make sure you know how to protect your baby from pets and pollutants in the home, check up on car and travel safety and, once she is on the move, make sure all areas of your house are secure and safe from potential harm.

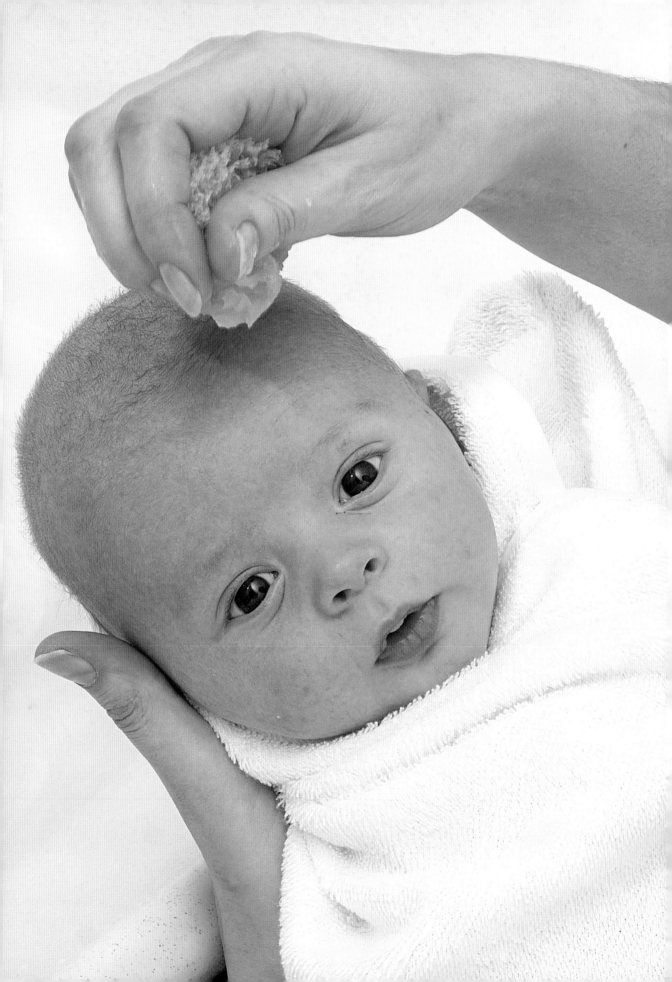

your baby's world

When you become a parent, the world can seem a frighteningly dangerous place for a young baby, but don't let it paralyse you. Realize you are not alone – partners, relatives, friends and health professionals are all sources of advice and support. Accept that you will get it wrong sometimes, but the important thing is to ensure that you keep your baby as safe and as happy as possible.

Buying organic fruit and vegetables is a good way to avoid unwanted residues in your baby's food.

hidden poisons

We are surrounded by chemicals and pollutants, and young babies and children are particularly vulnerable. Common pesticides and household chemicals may disrupt hormone levels, and fast-growing youngsters are more likely to accumulate persistent chemicals in their bodies. Many chemicals in everyday use are relatively new and their effect may not have been studied over long periods of time – evidence for or against potential health hazards is not always proven. For example, phthalates – used in some shampoos, moisturizers, perfumes, PVC and previously an ingredient in some children's plastic toys – are now thought to cause birth defects and have been linked to asthma as well as reproductive problems in animals. In Europe they are banned in teething toys for children under the age of 3 as well as other plastic toys.

If this is something that worries you, environmental groups can provide you with more information.

food – good or bad?

About a quarter to a third of all fruit and vegetables contains some pesticide residues. Proportional to their body weight, children are estimated to eat twice as much fruit and vegetables as adults, so they are more susceptible. You can help to reduce your baby's exposure to potentially toxic substances by feeding him certified organic food. Alternatively, wash or peel fruit and vegetables and ensure that meat is good quality and from a reliable source. Studies have shown there may be a link between some food 'E numbers' and behavioural problems and some physical illnesses, such as asthma and eczema. Be wary of tartrazine (E102), ponceau 4R (E110), allura red AC (E129), carmoisine (E122), quinoline yellow (E104), sunset yellow (E110) and sodium benzoate (E211). Check for these in cakes, biscuits, drinks and processed foods.

Some people are also concerned about the effects that hydrogenated or trans fats that are found in many processed foods can have on the body.

how healthy is clean?

Most of us use chemicals to clean our houses and eliminate germs such as salmonella, which can cause unpleasant or serious illnesses. However, not all germs are bad. For example, bacteria are everywhere: they cover our skin and live in our bowels, and when they are in the right balance they cause us no harm and even give us some protection from other illnesses. However, with their immature immune systems, young babies are more vulnerable to germs, and milk (their only food) is a breeding ground for harmful bacteria, so hygiene is vital. Here are some guidelines:

- Ordinary soap and water, or an eco-friendly detergent, are sufficient to clean most household surfaces (apart from toilets) exposed to normal use.
- Any surfaces that have been in contact with raw meat and eggs must be cleaned thoroughly to ensure that potentially harmful bacteria are eradicated.
- Food (particularly meat) must be cooked well and if being kept should be cooled and frozen or chilled quickly in covered containers (see page 215). Make sure your fridge and freezer are working at the correct temperature.

avoiding infections

All babies get infections, more commonly during the colder months of the year. While this is distressing, most of these health problems are mild and nothing to worry about. In fact, there is increasing evidence that early infections protect against certain diseases, such as leukaemia, by promoting a strong immunity. If you have other children, or your baby goes to nursery or playgroup or has regular contact with other children, you may be shocked by how many 'bugs' he picks up. Don't worry; this is normal – germs can be easily spread around groups of youngsters.

Diet is important in combating infections. For example, breast-feeding transfers antibodies from you to your baby. Breast milk also contains substances that discourage some problems such as gastroenteritis (see page 248). Make sure your baby continues to have a good diet once he is weaned (see pages 202–215). After the age of 6 months babies may benefit from supplements of vitamins A, C and D. However, seek advice from your health professional, as over-supplementation can be harmful.

It is also beneficial to keep people that are obviously ill away from your baby. Be thorough in your everyday hygiene – remember to wash your hands when you come home from work or if you have been around people who are suffering from illness. Washing your hands after preparing food (particularly meat) and going to the toilet is vital – and make sure you dry them thoroughly. Also wash your baby's hands before he eats. While serious infections are rare, they are more worrying. Follow the advice above and ensure your baby is immunized (see pages 220–221).

Consider replacing regular household cleaners with eco-friendly ones.

Q **My husband and I like to smoke occasionally, but we never smoke in the house. Will this affect our baby?**

A The effect of tobacco smoke on a baby's health is very well known: it increases the risk of cot death (see pages 168–169) as well as asthma, ear infections and meningitis. Even where parents smoke only outside the house, carbon monoxide levels in their children are higher than in those of children of non-smokers. The best thing to do is to stop smoking.

your baby and immunization

Vaccination is an important way of protecting your baby from serious and potentially life-threatening diseases. As a result of immunization, even within the last 10 years, diseases that were previously common are now rare. In the UK, the Council of the Faculty of Homeopathy recommends that children are immunized conventionally to ensure they get the best protection possible.

keep on schedule

The immunization schedule is specially designed to protect your baby against those diseases she is most vulnerable to at the time. The gaps between vaccinations are set with this in mind. If she is unwell or you are away, make sure she is immunized as close as possible to the 'ideal' date. Where immunity wears off over time, your baby will be offered a booster as the best way to give long-lasting protection.

Your baby will be automatically booked in for routine immunizations and you will be notified through the post.

targeted diseases

Diphtheria A bacterial infection that causes fever, sore throat, nausea, vomiting, headache, difficulty breathing and heart problems. Up to 10 per cent of sufferers die – the young are particularly vulnerable.

Tetanus Bacteria in soil and manure release a toxin that causes muscle spasm and breathing problems. It can kill.

Whooping cough or pertussis A bacterial infection that causes severe bouts of coughing, leading to breathing difficulties. It can be particularly serious in young babies and has a higher death rate in babies under 1 year old.

Polio A highly contagious viral infection that affects the nervous system and can cause paralysis and death. Polio vaccination has been so successful that, for example, there have been no natural cases of polio in the UK in over 20 years.

HIB Haemophilus Influenza B is a bacterium that can cause meningitis, pneumonia, epiglottitis and ear infections. It was the most common cause of bacterial meningitis before the introduction of the vaccination.

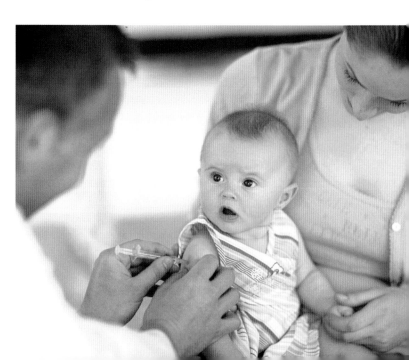

Meningococcal C A bacterium (not the only one) that can cause meningitis and septicaemia. It used to cause about 150 deaths a year – since the vaccine was introduced, cases have fallen by 95 per cent.

Pneumococcal The streptococcus pneumoniae bacterium can cause chest infections, ear infections, meningitis and septicaemia, which has a 1–2 per cent death rate.

MMR Measles, mumps and rubella are viral infections that are often mild but have serious potential complications, including meningitis and encephalitis. Deaths from measles are still common in the world, although they have fallen significantly thanks to vaccination. (See MMR controversy, below.)

Tuberculosis An infectious disease caused by a bacterium that primarily affects the lungs. Vaccination against tuberculosis is not routinely given to all babies in the UK – it is usually offered in areas where the risk is considered to be high or if a parent or grandparent was born in a country where the risk is higher. In older babies, testing to ensure no contact with TB may be carried out with a skin-prick test (BCG).

Meningococcal B Vaccines against Meningococcal B have proved difficult to develop. However, they are currently undergoing final clinical trials. Group B accounts for 80 per cent of meningococcal disease in the UK, and if successful, the vaccine should reduce the incidence of meningococcal meningitis and septicaemia.

what about side effects?

There are very few reasons not to vaccinate a baby – even premature babies are usually vaccinated as normal procedure – but if you have any worries, talk to your health professional. They should also explain any potential risks.

After vaccination your baby may develop a sore, slightly swollen, red area around the site. If this area becomes very large, have it checked by a health professional. Your baby may also develop a mild fever (up to 38°C/100.4°F) and may feel unwell for 24–48 hours.

After MMR your baby may be unwell for 1–3 weeks following the vaccination and may develop a mild rash.

the MMR controversy

Although MMR has been used for 30 years in 100 countries, and the suggestion of links between the vaccine and autism/inflammatory bowel disease has not been supported by further research, for some parents a degree of anxiety remains. The risk to your child from measles, mumps and rubella is relatively high. If vaccination levels drop, the diseases will become more prevalent and so the risk of your child catching them will increase. There is no evidence that single vaccines are any safer, and they increase the time for which your baby is at risk. Giving your baby the MMR vaccination is by far the best way to protect her against these three serious infections that cause many serious illnesses and deaths worldwide each year.

Q Does my baby have to have her jabs before I can take her to the swimming pool?

A Check with your local pool. Although babies can swim at any age, some swimming pools suggest that they have some or all of their vaccinations beforehand. If that's their rule you will have to stick with it – the reason dates from a time when the authorities were worried about the spread of polio in swimming pools.

Not all swimming pools accept babies unless they have had their vaccinations, so it is wise to check before going.

is my baby normal?

There is nothing like babies to bring out the competitive spirit. Don't take it seriously – babies are all individuals, and they all develop at different rates. While friends can be a great help, they can also cause you a lot of concern. If you are worried, talk to a health professional – they will be able to reassure you or, if there is a reason to be concerned, instigate appropriate action.

You will be invited to attend regular routine checks on your baby's health throughout his first year.

checking your baby's health

Most healthcare systems offer babies and children routine developmental health checks, including hearing, vision, growth, hand–eye coordination and motor skills (see pages 16–19). The first of these is usually done at birth to check for any physical abnormalities, but also to assess basic neurological reflexes. Your baby's heart will be checked for murmurs (see page 243) and his hips for clicks (see page 247). These are all rechecked at around 6 weeks.

Subsequent routine checks will continue to assess your baby's sight, hearing and interacting skills, and also, as appropriate, other

development such as speech. They will also monitor any physical conditions such as undescended testicles and hydrocoeles (see page 250). Your baby will be assessed in comparison to other babies of the same age – if he is not yet doing something, your health professional will check him in a few weeks to ensure that he has progressed.

understanding centile charts

Centile charts are derived from the average growth of thousands of babies. There are different ones for boys and girls, but not much allowance is made for racial variations. The charts plot a graph of a baby's weight, head circumference and, once he is standing reliably, height against his age. The 50th centile is the average – half of all babies will be above this and half below this.

Your baby should settle on to a centile. Although this may vary from week to week, he should generally grow along this line. If he crosses over two or more centiles, you need to discuss this with a health professional, although it may be normal. Two per cent of normal babies will be on or below the second centile and 2 per cent will be on or above the 98th. However, a disproportionate difference between weight, height or head circumference may suggest something is wrong.

head start

Just as tallness runs in some families, small or large heads run in others. Take this into account when assessing your baby's head size. At his 6-week check, any distortion of his head caused by the birth should have settled down. His head should then grow along his centile. If it deviates significantly, crossing centile lines, consult a health professional. Most deviations will settle down in time, but there are a few problems to be aware of:

Hydrocephalus The spaces within the brain are filled with fluid that circulates. If any excess fluid accumulates, it causes a condition known as hydrocephalus, which can cause the skull to increase in size; it may also cause vomiting and sleepiness as well as seizures. It is treated with surgery.

Craniosynostosis A condition where one or more of the suture lines (joints) of the skull fuse before brain growth is complete. Closure of a single suture line is most common and causes an abnormally shaped head. Where multiple sutures fuse, the baby will have a small head. It may require surgery.

Positional plagiocephaly, or flat head This is usually caused through a baby's preference for lying with his head on one particular side, which causes a flattening of the skull. The condition is usually mild or moderate and corrects or reduces when the baby grows older and as the baby becomes more mobile. Early intervention to encourage the baby to lie with the other side of his head down can help the problem. Some medical experts advocate the use of wearing helmets, but they need to be worn over a long period of time and their long term benefit is not as yet fully established.

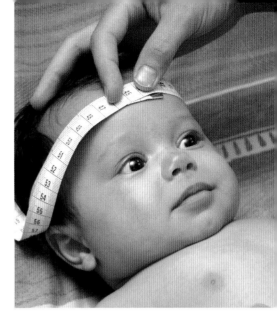

Your baby's growth is closely monitored in the first few months after birth.

failure to thrive

This is when a baby's weight crosses two centiles. It generally requires investigation. Possible causes are:

Drop off / catch up post-pregnancy A baby may grow large in pregnancy but is not meant to be that big genetically – so initially he will grow comparatively slowly after birth to allow for this. Conversely, a baby may be smaller than he is meant to be genetically (this might occur if the mother had pre-eclampsia) and is likely to grow rapidly to reach his natural centile after birth. This will need confirmation.

Reflux Gastroesophageal reflux (see page 249).

Urinary tract infections, which can have no symptoms in children.

Feeding difficulties due to breast-feeding problems, cleft lips and breathing problems.

Digestive problems such as milk intolerance or wheat intolerance.

Chronic medical conditions, such as cystic fibrosis (see page 234) and metabolic problems.

safeguarding your
home and garden

Most accidents involving children happen in the home, so it's important to make your home and garden as safe as possible. Think ahead and be prepared – use your common sense and supervise your baby at all times. Make the most of child-proofing equipment, and remember: you need to be extra-vigilant when visiting friends and family whose homes are unlikely to be baby-proofed.

Stair gates are an effective barrier for small children once crawling and walking.

general home safety

Inspect every room at floor level so that you can see the world from your baby's perspective. Things to look out for include loose carpets or rugs, electrical cabling, small, sharp or dangerous objects that your baby could put in her mouth and uncovered electrical sockets. The following tips should help to make your home a much safer place:

- Install stair gates at the top and bottom of the stairs.
- Make sure the gap between banister railings is no more than 10 cm (4 in) to prevent your baby getting her head between them.
- Fit smoke and carbon monoxide alarms throughout your house.
- Cover any sharp corners on furniture with padding or special self-adhesive corner protectors.
- Fit window catches that will only allow windows to open a safe amount so that your baby can't fall out.
- Cover electrical sockets with socket covers so that your baby can't poke something inside them.
- Cover electrical leads with a lead tidy, to prevent your baby pulling or chewing them.
- Secure unstable furniture that your baby could pull down.
- Move or put away breakable objects and houseplants.
- Cut the loops of cords on blinds or curtains and/or tie up the cords so that they are well out of your baby's reach.
- Check for loose carpet or rugs that could cause you to trip when carrying your baby.
- Fit door-slam protectors. These clip over the edges of doors to prevent them shutting on your baby's fingers.
- If you have an open fire, use a fireguard.
- Keep cigarettes, matches and lighters out of sight.
- Keep hot or alcoholic drinks out of your baby's reach – hot drinks can still scald a baby 15 minutes after they have been made.
- Check your floor regularly for small objects on which your baby could choke, including pet food and older siblings' toys.
- Ask guests to place coats and handbags out of reach so that your baby cannot remove potentially dangerous items.

kitchen safety

The kitchen is perhaps the most difficult room to make safe for your baby – and it's also the most hazardous, with saucepans full of boiling liquid, hot oven doors, sharp utensils and dangerous cleaning products. If possible, install a gate and keep your baby out altogether. Accidents are more likely to happen when you are busy and distracted, so try to keep your baby out of the kitchen when you are cooking. However, if your kitchen is open plan and you can't limit your baby's access, adopt the following safety measures and keep a close eye on her at all times.

- Buy the least toxic cleaning products and store them in a lockable cupboard or high up out of your baby's reach. Many small children learn how to open child-proof lids – don't give them the opportunity.
- Store knives and sharp utensils in a locked drawer.
- Use the back rings on the cooker when you can, and make sure all saucepan handles are turned inwards. You could also fit a specially designed hob guard.
- Fit safety locks on your washing machine, dishwasher, tumble dryer and wastebin.
- Keep a fire extinguisher near the cooker.
- Store glasses and china out of reach.
- Keep the flex from appliances out of reach and use a cordless iron, if possible – otherwise, ensure you always unplug the iron when it's not in use.
- Have a 'safe' cupboard away from the cooker, and use it to store items such as small saucepans, plastic containers, kitchen foil and wooden spoons. If your baby is allowed to open and explore this cupboard, she is more likely to leave the others alone.

bathroom safety

Scalding hot water, cleaning products, medicines, slippery surfaces and sharp objects like razors and scissors can all make the bathroom a dangerous place. However, the greatest risk is drowning. Babies can drown in just a few centimetres of water, so it's very important to take extra care at bathtime. Take these precautions:

- Never leave your baby unattended in the bath, even for a few seconds. If you need to leave the room, take her with you.
- Set your water temperature to below 46°C (115°F) to avoid scalding. Always run cold water into the bath first and test the temperature with your elbow or a bath thermometer – it should be approximately body temperature (29.4°C/85°F) before putting your baby in.
- Turn the thermostat on heated towel rails to below 46°C (115°F) to avoid burns.
- Buy a padded protective cover for the bath taps and spout.
- Use a non-slip suction mat on the base of the bath.
- Consider buying a bath seat (for babies over 6 months) or bath support (for babies under 6 months) so that you have both hands free to bath your baby.

Consider fixing safety locks on low-level cupboards in kitchen and bathrooms.

smoke alarms

Fire poses one of the greatest risks to children, so it's vital to install smoke alarms around your home. Smoke alarms can reduce the risk of dying in a house fire by 50 per cent, so fit one near your kitchen, on the stairs and outside your baby's bedroom. Check them every month to make sure they are working, and replace the batteries every year.

puppy love

Pets can help a child to develop social skills and non-verbal communication, increase her self-esteem and self-confidence and enhance her understanding of sharing, compassion and empathy. A pet can provide activity, love, loyalty and affection. It can also teach valuable lessons about life, such as nurture, illness, reproduction and death. Health benefits from owning a pet include lowering stress and boosting the immune system.

While these benefits are undeniable, you must ensure your baby is safe at all times during interaction with any pet. Clear pet faeces away and take great care with exotic pets, such as turtles, as these carry a wider variety of germs. Here are some don'ts:

- Never leave a young child alone with a pet, even one with no previous history of aggression.
- Don't let your pet lick your baby's face and hands.
- Don't allow your baby to hit or pull at a pet.
- Don't allow children to play with venomous animals.

- Keep the toilet lid closed with a special latch.
- Keep all medicines and sharp objects out of reach in a cabinet or on a high shelf.
- Store cleaning products, including the toilet brush, and cosmetics, toothpaste, nail polish, shampoo and lotions safely out of your baby's reach.

safety in the nursery

Health professionals recommend that your baby should sleep in your bedroom until she is 6 months old to reduce the risk of Sudden Infant Death Syndrome (see pages 168–169). Until then, use the nursery to change, dress and play with her or for daytime naps. Even if you only spend short spells of time in there, there are still several important safety considerations to bear in mind:

- Never leave your baby unattended on a raised surface, such as a changing table, in case she rolls off. It is better to get into the habit of placing your baby's changing mat on the floor.
- Place your baby's cot away from windows and radiators to avoid excessive heat or draughts.
- Place a thermometer in the nursery so that you can make sure your baby isn't too hot or too cold. The correct temperature is around 16°C (61°F).
- Always place your baby to sleep with her feet against the foot of the cot so that she can't wriggle under her blankets.
- Buy a baby monitor to use at night and during nap-times.
- Always put your baby in her cot if you need to leave her alone for a few minutes.
- Duvets and pillows are not recommended until your baby is at least 12 months old. Until then, use sheets, cellular blankets or a baby sleeping bag.

Check whether or not your baby is allergic to cat or dog fur before investing in a pet.

Always wash your baby's hands after a romp in the garden.

garden safety

It is important not to overlook your garden in terms of safeguarding your baby. As she gets older, your baby is likely to spend more and more time outdoors. Gardens can be dangerous, but many of the most common accidents are easy to prevent.

- Never leave your baby outdoors without supervision. Even if she is sleeping in her pram, she could be at risk from household pets such as cats and dogs.
- Consider fencing off an area of your garden for your baby to play in safely without risk of accidents.
- Garden ponds are a major hazard to babies and young children. If you have a pond or water feature, make sure it is covered or fenced in so that your baby can't walk or crawl into the water.
- Check your garden for animal droppings, which may harbour worms or diseases such as toxoplasmosis. Even if you don't have pets, neighbours' cats or foxes may still come into your garden.
- Make sure that sandpits are covered, as cats like to use them as a litter box.
- Many flowers and plants can be toxic or poisonous to children. Ask for advice at your local garden centre about what is safe to plant. Common culprits include foxglove (*Digitalis*), hellebore, hyacinth and lupin. Teach your baby not to touch or eat plants to reduce any risk.

first-aid kit

No matter how careful you are, accidents do happen, so it's vital to have a well-stocked first-aid kit to hand in case of an emergency. It is possible to buy complete first-aid kits over the counter, but it's usually cheaper to tailor-make your own (see page 239).

travelling with your baby

Going on holiday with your baby can be a daunting experience. This is mainly because a baby needs so much equipment that it can be difficult to know exactly what to pack. Parents also worry about how their baby will cope with long plane or car journeys. However, with a little forward planning and careful organization, you can still have a relaxing and enjoyable break.

before you travel abroad

Your baby will need his own passport. Send for a passport in good time, as it can take a few weeks to process passport applications.

- Make sure all your baby's vaccinations are up to date. Check whether any special immunizations are required.
- You also need travel insurance to cover the whole family for medical treatment. Make sure your insurance covers you for the loss of your luggage too, as losing a suitcase full of your baby's essentials can be very costly to replace.
- Make several lists of various helpline numbers and keep them in different places so that you will always have a copy to hand if your luggage goes astray.

flying

It is safe for your baby to fly when he's just a few days old, although you may wish to check with your doctor if he is under 4 weeks, particularly if he has recently had a cough, cold or ear infection. If you have the option to choose when to fly, book flights that fit in with your baby's routine. Explain that you are travelling with a baby when you book, as you may be able to reserve a sky cot and seats with extra leg room.

You will need to check in your pushchair before you board the plane. If your baby can sit unaided, you may find it easier to use a lightweight foldable version, as some airlines will let you store it in the overhead locker. If not, a sling or papoose can be very useful.

Feeding your baby on take-off and landing should help to prevent the ear-ache and ear popping caused by the changing pressure inside

Make sure you always give your baby adequate protection from sunlight.

Keep a close eye on children whenever they are playing near open water.

the ear. If you aren't breast-feeding, you will need to bring formula and cooled boiled water, as babies can get very dehydrated during flights. If your baby is already on solids, bring jars and packets of baby foods and a variety of finger foods. It's a good idea to pack extra food and drink, just in case there are any delays to your journey. Check what you are allowed to take on the plane with you before you leave home. To keep your baby occupied during a long flight, take a selection of favourite and new toys and books. Be prepared to take an older baby for regular walks up and down the aisle, as he is likely to get bored and irritable if he has to sit still for too long.

sun safety

Even on cloudy days, babies should not go outside without adequate sun protection. Their delicate skin can burn in less than 15 minutes, and they can overheat very quickly, so you should be particularly careful when travelling in hot countries.

A baby under the age of 1 year should remain in the shade at all times to keep him cool and protect his skin. This is particularly important between the hours of 11 am and 3 pm, when the sun's rays are at their strongest. Fit a canopy or parasol on to your baby's pushchair. For total protection, opt for a UV cover, which completely covers the pushchair, like a rain cover.

Always put a sunhat on your baby to reduce the risk of heatstroke. Look for one with a wide brim to give him the most protection, or choose a 'legionnaire' style, with a brim at the front and a flap at the back. You could also consider protective sunglasses, which can be worn from the age of 6 months.

If you can't keep your baby out of the sun, make sure he is dressed in loose, comfortable clothing. He should wear a t-shirt at all times when playing – and it should be changed for a dry one if it gets wet. You will need specially designed swim-nappies if you take your baby swimming, and you should protect any bare skin with a children's sun cream with a sun protection factor (SPF) of at least 20. Apply at least 20 minutes before sun exposure, and reapply at least every 2 hours.

checklist of what to pack

Don't forget to pack the following essential items:
- Travel cot (unless your accommodation provides one – check that it is suitable and safe).
- Pushchair.
- Baby sling/papoose.
- Nappies.
- Fold-up changing mat.
- Baby wipes.
- Muslin squares.
- Food and formula.
- Bottles.
- Breast pump (if you are breast-feeding).
- Cup, bowl and spoons.
- Sterilizing equipment.
- Blanket/baby sleeping bag.
- Bubble bath and lotion.
- Dummies.
- Bibs.
- Clothes (allow for two outfits per day).
- Favourite toys.
- Sunhat and sun cream.
- First-aid kit.

car
safety

Choosing the right car seat for your baby's age and weight is very important. Fortunately, many stores now offer a fitting service, which will help you to find the perfect seat for your car and install it safely. Aim to buy a car seat several weeks in advance of the birth and practise taking it in and out of your car, as this can be tricky until you get the hang of it.

Q **A friend of mine has offered to give me her baby's old car seat, but someone else has said that this is not a good idea. What's the problem?**

A It should be fine to have a car seat from someone you know and trust, but you should never buy a second-hand car seat from a stranger. Such a seat could have already been damaged in a car accident, but you may not be able to tell this by looking at it. For peace of mind, it's best to buy a new car seat and save money on other items instead.

infant carriers

Newborn babies should always have a rear-facing car seat, as this provides more protection for their head, neck and back if you are involved in an accident. Many infant carriers come as part of a 3-in-1 'travel system', which means they can be clipped straight on to the frame of your pram without you having to take your baby out. They can also be used outside the car as a carrier, chair or rocker. This is particularly useful during the first few weeks when babies tend to sleep a lot, as it means you can lift the seat in and out of the car using the carrying handle, without disturbing your sleeping baby.

Infant seats are placed on the back seat, where they are held in place by the seatbelt. They recline at a 45-degree angle and have detachable soft head supports, which you can use until your baby is able to hold her head up by herself. As this type of seat provides a snug fit for your baby, it is inadvisable to leave her sleeping in it for long periods, as this can put pressure on her developing spine. Young babies are also at risk from suffocation if left sleeping in a car seat, as they find it difficult to keep their heads up for any length of time.

Always follow the manufacturer's instructions for installing a baby seat.

It's not advisable to let your baby fall asleep in his infant carrier when you're not in the car.

Rear-facing seats should be used for as long as possible – at least until your baby is 9–12 months old and 9 kg (20 lb). If your baby's head sticks up above the top of the seat, or she exceeds the maximum weight before this, you will need to buy a second-stage or combination car seat and use it in the rear-facing position until your baby is ready for a forward-facing seat. However, if your baby weighs less than 9 kg (20 lb) at 1 year old, continue to use the rear-facing seat until she grows out of it.

combination car seats

Combination car seats can be used in a rear-facing or forward-facing position and are suitable from birth to approximately 4 years old, depending on your baby's weight. Use them in the reclined, rear-facing position for babies under 1 year who weigh less than 9 kg (20 lb), and in the upright, forward-facing position thereafter. This design tends to be a better investment, as it lasts for much longer. However, it can seem rather large for a newborn and, as it stays in the car, you will have to lift your baby in and out of it at the beginning and end of every journey. This type of seat should have a five-part harness, which has five straps: two at the shoulders, two at the hips and one at the crotch – safety experts agree that this offers the best protection. The seat is held in place by your car's seatbelt. As with all car seats, make sure it is fitted correctly. If you are in any doubt, ask for it to be checked.

car seats and airbags

Never place a rear-facing car seat in the front passenger seat of your car if you have a front-seat airbag. In the event of an accident, the pressure from the inflating airbag could seriously injure your child. If your car is not fitted with an airbag, then you can travel with your baby in the front of the car, provided the seat is pushed back as far as it will go, leaving plenty of space between your child's seat and the dashboard. Bear in mind that the safest place for your baby to travel is in the back of the car.

caring for a
sick baby

The best way to cope with a sick baby is to temporarily suspend normal life and focus on your baby. Carry him around if necessary, and if he wants an unscheduled nap, then allow him to have it. Don't be afraid to give age-appropriate medicines for a few days – they should make him more comfortable, but take him to the doctor if you are at all worried.

If your baby suddenly becomes very clingy, he may be feeling poorly.

body temperature and fevers

Fevers are part of the body's defence mechanism to kill off bacteria or a virus (for taking temperatures, see page 238). However, when the fever becomes too high, a baby may feel very unwell, stop drinking and lose too much fluid through sweating. In susceptible children, a rapid rise can even cause a febrile convulsion (see page 243).

when to call a doctor

When your baby seems ill, you are bound to be worried. With minor illnesses, you may be able to soothe him with the help of medicines such as paracetamol and/or ibuprofen (see page 239), but if you have any concerns over his health, **always err on the side of caution** and arrange to see your health professional. If a baby is very unwell, he must be examined as soon as possible; if he is mildly unwell for 2 days, it's also worth taking him to the doctor. Doctors understand that the health of your baby is very important to you.

Responding to temperature rises If temperature does not reduce in 1–2 hours, seek advice.

Range	Temperature	Action required
Normal	36–37.5°C (96.8–99.5°F)	No action.
Mild	37.6–38°C (99.7–100.4°F)	Remove layers and/or blankets, keep hands and feet warm. Monitor.
Moderate	38–39°C (100.4–102.2°F)	As above and give paracetamol and/or ibuprofen if distressed. Seek advice if under 3 months.
High	39–40°C (102.2–104°F)	As above and seek advice.
Very high	More than 40°C (104°F)	As above and seek advice.

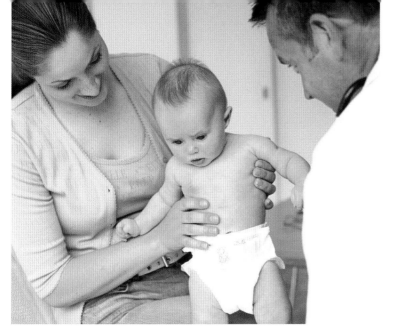

You should always consult a doctor if you suspect your baby might be seriously ill.

when to call an ambulance

Do not hesitate to call an ambulance if your baby:

- Has reduced responsiveness.
- Is breathing either very slowly or very fast.
- Is choking.
- Is suffering from major bleeding.
- Has burns bigger than a baby's palm size.
- Has blue lips.
- Has a rash that doesn't fade under a glass (see meningitis, page 243).
- Has a fit or convulsion (see febrile convulsion, page 243).
- Is pale, mottled, ashen or blue in colour.
- Is making a weak, high-pitched or continuous cry.
- Has a bulging fontanelle (or neck stiffness and dislike of light in an older child).

hospital

It is very traumatic for you and your child when he is admitted to hospital. The staff will inform you as much as possible and involve you in your child's care, but you may feel isolated and out of control. Take heart, and remember that while children do get sick quickly, they also recover quickly.

Hospitals are tiring and you will probably get very little sleep because of the combination of worry and noise. If you can, take turns to be there with your partner or a friend so that you get a break. Your health is important – once he is a little better, your baby will need some entertaining, especially if he is older, and this can be hard if you are exhausted. Don't be afraid to ask the play specialist, nurses or anyone to help you!

When you finally get your baby home following a period of hospital treatment, it is quite common to feel traumatized. Give yourself some time to recover and take life easy for a week or two. Talking it over with a good friend may help.

Q How can I tell if my baby is dehydrated?

A Dehydration occurs quite easily in babies. Signs to watch out for are if your baby becomes lethargic, has fewer wet nappies, his eyes or mouth are dry or his fontanelle is sunken. If you are concerned, take him to the doctor.

signs that your child is unwell

In babies, ill health is commonly indicated when they are:

- Off their food.
- Clingy, refusing to be put down or leave your sight.
- Grizzly or whining.
- Lethargic.
- Pale in colour.

Other signs include:

- Raised temperature.
- Rash.
- Diarrhoea or vomiting (can occur in numerous illnesses).
- Fast breathing or heart rate.
- Fever.

chronic conditions

Having a child with a long-term illness changes your life, even if your child is relatively well. If it is a life-threatening illness, it will be much more difficult. Try to enjoy your child and make things as easy for her as possible. But be aware that there may come a time when you experience a sense of loss for your 'healthy' child and for what might have been.

'When William was born by emergency caesarian, routine checks noticed that oxygen levels in his blood were low. A heart scan showed he had a serious heart problem. When he was 2 days old he had his first operation to help send blood to his lungs. The doctors did not want to operate again until the oxygen levels dropped to a certain level because they wanted William to grow as much as possible. At 17 months he had his second operation – the major restructuring of his heart – which went well. He will need more surgery when he is older, but for now he is a happy, healthy little boy.'

Isobel, mother of William (3 years)

shared experience

cystic fibrosis

This genetic disease eventually causes internal organs to become clogged up with sticky mucus, leading to inflammation and infections. The main organs that are affected are the lungs and pancreas, which causes breathing and digestive problems. The disease is usually diagnosed through neonatal screening programmes (heel-prick test, see page 19), so your baby will usually be well when she is first diagnosed. The early diagnosis means appropriate treatment can begin as soon as possible.

A baby with cystic fibrosis may be born with a bowel obstruction, leading to an earlier diagnosis. At present there is no cure. Treatment is usually managed by specialists and will include physiotherapy, diet and medication. The baby will probably have lung problems as she gets older. She may have difficulties digesting food and may develop diabetes. Fertility can be affected. Long-term health can suffer and eventually lung transplantation may be needed.

cerebral palsy

This is a permanent disorder of movement or coordination that is noticed in infancy or early childhood and does not worsen over time. The disorder can range from mild to severe, and it is caused by damage to an area of the brain during pregnancy or infancy. It may have a variety of symptoms. The condition is usually suspected due to clinical symptoms, and a brain scan may be carried out to confirm the diagnosis. Symptoms that are severe usually lead to an earlier diagnosis of the condition.

Many people with cerebral palsy have no learning difficulties and live normal lives. Although there is no cure, the treatment – which includes physiotherapy, occupational therapy and speech therapy – can often improve a child's capabilities. In addition, as she grows, she will probably learn to compensate for mild or even moderate problems. Drugs may be required to help relieve muscle spasm, while surgery might be used to correct tight tendons. Orthotic devices and communication aids are also used.

Babies with Down's syndrome develop more slowly than other children, but can be helped to reach their milestones through play and everyday activities.

sickle cell anaemia

This is an inherited disorder that is more common in certain racial groups (see page 19). In sufferers, the shape of the red blood cells changes in a characteristic way, and they are more fragile and last a shorter time, which leads to anaemia. Infants are usually diagnosed because they have anaemia and jaundice due to the increased turnover of red blood cells. Their spleen will also be enlarged, as it has to break down these cells. A blood test confirms the diagnosis.

There is no cure for sickle cell anaemia. Good health and diet are important, as is vaccination against pneumococcal disease (see page 221). Normally there are no symptoms. However, a baby will be more prone to serious infections, and infections that are minor in most youngsters (such as slapped cheek disease, page 253) may cause serious illnesses. Sufferers must avoid a reduction in oxygen levels (such as at high altitude), as this leads to the blood cells becoming more rigid and sickle-shaped. Their shape means that they stick together, slowing the blood flow and leading to the blockage of small blood vessels. Called a sickling crisis, this requires urgent treatment – hydration, often intravenous, is essential to stop clogging of the blood vessels, and strong painkillers and transfusions may be needed. Long-term kidney, bone and lung damage can occur, as can bone infections.

Down's syndrome

This genetic condition is caused by an extra chromosome 21 (all or part of it); nothing you did before or during your pregnancy caused this. The baby will usually have a collection of characteristic signs that may alert a health professional, but the definitive diagnosis is made by analysing chromosomes. She will need her heart checked, as heart problems are more common with this condition.

There is no cure. Most babies with Down's syndrome reach their milestones more slowly, but eventually most will learn to walk, talk, read and write. Feeding problems are common, but usually settle within the first few weeks. A physiotherapist will advise you on games and exercises to do with your baby. The level of learning disability can vary.

Q **My baby was born 10 weeks early and on special care for 2 months. She still has breathing problems and I don't feel I can leave her. How will I cope when she gets older?**

A We all want to protect our children – this instinct comes to the fore even more when your child has been unwell. As any child grows, they naturally gain more independence – and while it's wonderful to watch them gain new skills, it can be hard to let them go. Your natural protective instinct is overwhelming and it will be hard not to 'wrap her in cotton wool' as she grows. While it is important to ensure her safety, it is also important to make sure she gains as much independence as possible to allow her to reach her full potential. The support of other mums who are in or who have been through similar situations can be invaluable. Talk to your health visitor about support groups.

235

complementary health

There are many complementary therapies; some can be useful or pleasant, but not all are proven and some might be harmful. If you decide to use one, choose a therapist who is registered with the recognized organization. Your baby should always receive conventional care, such as immunizations (see pages 220–221). And if he has a medical problem, the best first stop is a doctor.

Lavender is particularly good for soothing your baby when it comes to night-time, and encourages sleep.

relaxation

Both you and your baby can enjoy relaxation techniques. Knowing how to relax is a valuable skill and it will help your child as he grows. Massage (see pages 158–163) has been shown to help weight gain and development in premature babies. Cognitive behavioural techniques and hypnotherapy are widely used. Generally, babies will settle with quietness, touch, music and rhythmical movement. Warmth also helps, but make sure your baby is not too warm (see page 169).

aromatherapy

Aromatherapy is most commonly used in conjunction with massage, to treat a wide range of conditions. Essential oils can also be added to baths in order to enhance mood and inhaled via vaporizers to clear a stuffy nose.

Essential oils should not be used on babies under a week old and, apart from lavender oil, should only be used under the advice of a practitioner trained in their use with babies. The most common adverse effect is a rash on contact; this can be severe and include blistering. Some oils cause a reaction in sunlight; others may result in allergic reactions (see page 255). Oils should not be swallowed.

osteopathy and chiropractic

These two therapies work on the structure of the body, its muscles and bones, to improve and maintain function. Children with physical disabilities such as cerebral palsy often find osteopathy helpful. However, perhaps the most common form used in babies is cranial osteopathy, which involves extremely gentle manipulation of the bones of the skull to release tension throughout the body. It is used following a traumatic birth and to treat babies with colic, poor feeding, sleep problems, glue ear, ear infections, eczema, constipation and many other conditions. Usually following treatment a baby is relaxed and sleeps well – although there are always exceptions!

There is evidence that osteopathy and chiropractic benefit conditions of the muscles and skeleton, but no definitive evidence for other conditions for which they are sometimes used as a treatment. The most serious side effects of treatment – stroke or spinal cord injury – are rare and follow manipulation of the spine or neck. More common are minor side effects, such as pain around the area of manipulation, headache or fatigue.

herbalism

Herbalism is the use of plants as poultices or in medicines. It aims not only to treat symptoms but also to address body imbalances, thereby encouraging the body to heal itself. In babies, it is used to treat recurrent infections, colic, poor growth and skin conditions, as well as allergies.

One of the main problems with herbalism is that the dosage is not as standardized as conventional medicines, and the products are not as carefully tested. Some remedies are inadequately regulated and may contain toxins, heavy metals or man-made drugs. In one review of complementary medicine, herbalism caused the highest incidence of paediatric adverse effects, although the relationship between the remedy and the effect was at times uncertain. Reactions are widespread and include skin rashes, liver and heart problems, coma, breathing difficulties and even death, although again serious side effects are usually uncommon.

acupuncture

Acupuncture usually follows one of two main schools, traditional Chinese or modern Western. It uses fine, sterile, single-use needles, which are inserted into the skin in particular places and then subtly manipulated. The aim is not only to improve but to maintain health; in babies, it is commonly used to treat musculoskeletal problems as well as teething pain. In young children, between four to six needles are usually used. Initial insertion of the needle may cause a slight prick and its manipulation may cause a little discomfort, but this usually settles quickly.

The needles can cause mild problems such as bruising or skin reactions, or more rare and severe problems such as a lung collapse. Infections may occur around the site of the needle or in the blood stream. Rarely, needles can break.

homeopathy

Homeopathy is the use of certain substances in an extremely diluted and shaken form, normally taken as a white tablet. It is not usually harmful and can be used alongside conventional medicine. In babies, homeopathy is commonly used to treat teething pain and symptoms of hayfever. Recent reviews of numerous studies that matched homeopathic treatments against placebo treatments failed to show any benefit of homeopathy over taking a placebo; there was no single condition that showed a better response to homeopathy compared to the placebo.

Many complementary therapies use flower or plant extracts as a base.

Q **Can diet help to treat certain illnesses?**

A Babies with eczema, asthma, autism and glue ear may benefit from a review of their food intake, but particularly with young babies it is extremely important not to restrict diet without proper advice. Those suffering from food allergies need extra care in their diet. For example, if your baby is allergic to dairy products, you may need to cut these out, but it is vital to ensure she has sufficient calcium intake to maintain healthy bone growth (see also pages 204–207.)

first aid
in the home

It is worth putting in some effort to ensure that you are ready for minor problems when they occur and you will never regret doing some basic first-aid training. Hopefully, you will never need to use these skills, but it is better to be prepared. Aim to keep a basic first-aid kit – always replenished after use – in the house, and some commonplace medicines.

Q Which type of thermometer is the best to use for taking my baby's temperature?

A A digital thermometer is easy to use. It is usually placed in the armpit and will bleep when it is ready to give a reading (usually after about 30 seconds). Ear canal thermometers are not recommended for a baby under 1 month old. The narrowness of the ear canal can mean they are less accurate in babies under 1 year, but they give a reading in a few seconds, so are very convenient. Temperature strip thermometers generally take 1–2 minutes to give a reading and can be inaccurate.

first-aid skills

From bleeding and burns to choking, drowning and poisoning, there are many things that could potentially happen to your baby. The best way to make sure you are prepared in the event of such an awful situation is to attend an emergency first-aid course that is run by a bona fide first-aid organization.

There are courses that are designed specifically for new parents – ask for information about these from your health professional. Although some useful information is given here about various conditions, a book can in no way teach all the practical skills that are needed to assess injuries, resuscitate or treat life-threatening conditions. To acquire these skills, consider attending a recognized first-aid course. Such courses are updated frequently and are the best way to learn how to respond to emergency situations with confidence.

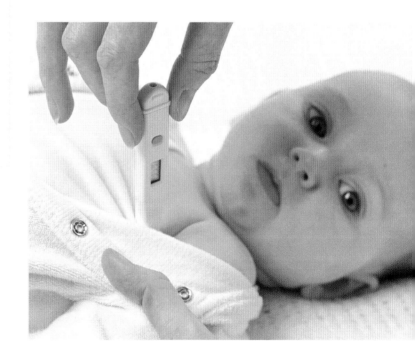

It can be difficult to persuade a baby to keep still for a thermometer reading.

If you have to treat a very young child, it may be easier to administer an oral medicine using a syringe.

what to do in an emergency

If your child is very unwell or badly hurt, you are likely to panic, but these basic tips should help you through any situation.

Assess
• Exactly what has happened.
• Who is injured.
• How the injuries occurred.
• What needs to be done.
• Who is there to help. If you are not alone, send someone for help; if you are alone, start shouting, as someone may hear you while you are getting on with the treatment.

Ensure safety
• Resist temptation to rush in before ensuring your own safety.
• Make sure any source of danger is removed from any injured person.
• Only move an injured child if you need to remove them from danger.

Life-threatening injuries first
• While a screaming child with a broken arm may demand attention, a silent child may be struggling to breathe, which is life threatening. A child who can talk (or scream) can breathe.
• The other immediate life-threatening condition is major bleeding.
• While treating breathing problems and bleeding, it is essential to call for urgent medical help as soon as possible.

Call for help
If possible, get someone to do this earlier, but if you are alone, call for help as soon as you can.

first-aid kit and basic medicines

Get the basics together before your baby arrives:
• Thermometer.
• Antiseptic wipes, spray or cream.
• Plasters or plaster spray.
• Bandages.
• Non-stick sterile dressings.
• Ice/cool pack.
• Antihistamine spray (medicine as your baby gets older).
• Paracetamol suspension.
• Burn shield (in pad or gel form, for dressing burns).
• Eye bandage.
• Eye bath.
• Tweezers.

Medicines:
• Infant paracetamol.
• Ibuprofen (if the baby is over 7 kg (15½ lb), not suitable for some children with asthma).
• Rehydration sachets.
• Teething gel.

cold compresses

These are highly effective in reducing swelling and bruising. They can be used for up to 30 minutes, although small children may not tolerate them for this length of time and the temperature of their skin should be checked regularly. They can be bought ready-made to put in the fridge or freezer from pharmacists, or you can make your own at home. There are various different ways of making a cold compress:

- The easiest way is to soak a small cloth in cold water and apply to the injury. The cloth will need replacing regularly, as it will warm up quickly.
- Wrap a bag of frozen peas (or similar) in a towel and apply to the injury. Ensure there is a good layer of cloth between the frozen middle and the skin. Check regularly that the skin is not becoming too cold (older children can tell you).
- Use ice cubes in a plastic bag wrapped in a towel as above. Always make sure children are supervised when plastic bags of any sort are being used.

first aid for minor injuries

If your baby suffers a cut, bruise, burn or other injury, try to keep her calm; the advice below may be useful. **If you are ever in doubt about minor conditions, seek medical advice, and with life-threatening ones, call an ambulance immediately.**

cuts

- Using clean dry hands, clean the cut under warm running water if possible, otherwise use antiseptic wipes.
- Dry the cut and cover with a clean non-stick dressing.
- If the cut is bleeding, use pressure (see below).
- Seek medical help if the cut is large, deep, on the face, bleeding heavily or your child is unwell.

bleeding

- Apply direct pressure to the wound with a pad (such as a folded cloth) or your fingers until a sterile dressing is available.
- If blood comes through the dressing, put another one over the top – do not remove the original one.
- Raise and support the area if possible (take care if you suspect a fracture or severe injury).
- Maintain pressure until the bleeding stops.
- Seek medical advice.

bruises

- Use a cool pack or cool compress (see box left), if your child will tolerate it, to reduce swelling.
- Seek medical advice if the bruise is severe and on the head.

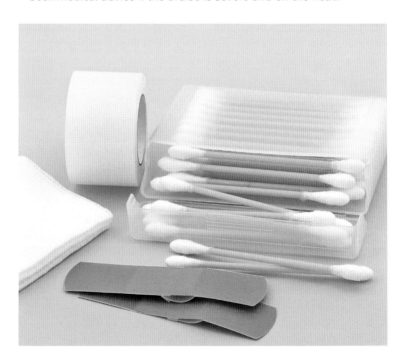

It is a good idea to keep a basic first-aid kit, including a range of plasters and bandages, in the home for emergencies.

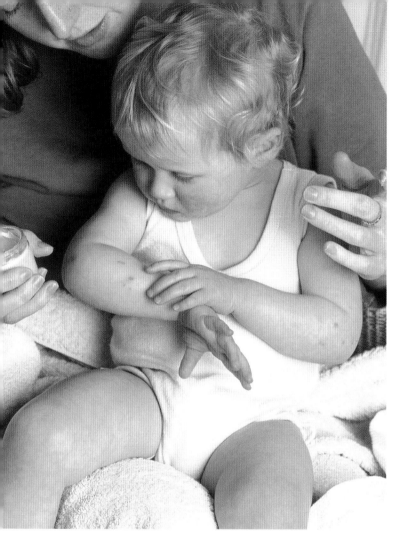

Antihistamine is available in both spray and cream forms, and can soothe the sting or itch of an insect bite.

insect bites

- Remove the insect (or sting) if still present.
- Use antihistamine spray, cream or medicine (depending on age).
- Use a cool pack or compress (see box opposite) to reduce swelling and painkillers if the baby is sore.
- See a doctor if the bite is on the face, or the swelling is large or inflamed or your baby is unwell.
- If the area of redness continues to increase, seek medical advice.

minor thermal burns

- Hold the burn under cool running water for at least 10 minutes.
- If possible, remove surrounding clothing or jewellery.
- Wrap the burn in clean clingfilm (not if facial) – take care not to make it too tight – or a non-stick dressing or a clean, dry smooth cloth.
- Give a painkiller if needed.
- Leave blisters intact.
- Do not use creams unless medically directed.
- Seek medical advice if the baby is under 1 year old, the burn is bigger than palm size or if the face, hands or feet are involved.
- If burns are severe or your child is unwell, seek urgent medical help.

'When Annie was 11 months we went on a picnic. She toddled towards me, but stumbled and fell on to a picnic table, hitting her chin. She started screaming and there was blood everywhere. I checked her over – her face seemed OK, but there was blood pouring from her mouth. We took her to a minor-injuries unit, where they found that she had bitten through her tongue. They gave Annie an ice-lolly to help the swelling go down. For the next week, every time she ate her tongue bled slightly, but it healed well.'

Sarah, mother of
Annie (7 years)

shared experience

241

common
ailments

In the first year of your baby's life, there will be many times that you are worried about him. Fortunately, it is the minor ailments that are most common, but it is natural to worry that your baby will suffer from one of the rarer but more serious conditions. If you *are* worried, see your health professional – always trust your instincts. If a baby is very unwell, he must be examined as soon as possible.

is he ill?

Generally, the younger the baby, the harder it is to tell how ill he is, as there are fewer indications and for many illnesses the early symptoms can be quite similar – the baby may be a bit more clingy and grizzly than usual, go off his feeds, have a mild temperature and runny nose and he can't tell you what's wrong! So, if he is not feeding well, has a temperature (particularly if higher than 38°C/100.4°F) or is vomiting, arrange to see the doctor without delay. If your baby has been seen by the doctor and is receiving treatment – or was given the all-clear – but you think his condition has since worsened, do not hesitate to seek further medical advice.

While unpleasant at the time, a lot of the minor infections that your child will encounter and fight off as he grows are an essential part of his developing immune system. However, it is very hard to cope with seeing your baby unwell – even a minor cold can be distressing. Not only can it be physically tiring caring for a clingy baby but it is also emotionally wearing. In addition, your sleep is often disturbed more than it normally is, and because you are in such close contact with your child (and often tired and stressed), you tend to pick up their illnesses more easily. At these times, try and do only what is essential – some things have to be done and some can wait. Help from family and friends and advice from pharmacists, health visitors and doctors can make a real difference.

One of the things that a lot of new parents find difficult to judge is when to take their baby to the doctor. Few people like to 'bother' their doctor unnecessarily. However, it can be hard to assess how ill your baby is. If you are unsure whether your baby or child needs medical attention, you can always ask a doctor to call you to discuss what is wrong with your baby and decide if they need to be seen. As a lot of symptoms in babies can be non-specific (for example, a baby can go off their feeds with a simple cold or a serious infection), most doctors are happy to see small children if the parents are concerned.

The charts that follow are intended as guidance. If you are worried, **always consult your doctor.**

If your baby's temperature is consistently high over a period of three days, you should take him to see a doctor.

Neurological

Complaint	Description	Action
febrile convulsion or fit	Convulsion occurring with fever – usually one that is rapidly rising. The baby will lose consciousness, jerk all over and then go limp before gradually coming round. Although frightening, such fits rarely cause any harm as long as the illness causing the fever is dealt with. If a baby has had one febrile fit, he is more likely to have another. There is a slightly increased risk of non-febrile fits in children who have previously had a febrile fit.	Protect your baby from the surrounding environment, turn his head to one side and **call an ambulance**, particularly if he is under 3 months, the fit lasts longer than 5 minutes, affects only part of his body, recurs in the same illness, he does not have a temperature, is very unwell or does not regain consciousness. He may be admitted to hospital for observation. Keep his temperature down. **Seek medical advice** if not calling an ambulance.
meningitis and septicaemia Immunization (see pages 220–221) will help your baby to avoid these illnesses. If your baby has had meningitis or septicaemia, you will have had an extremely traumatic experience, even if the outcome was good. Consider joining a support group.	Meningitis is infection and inflammation of the lining surrounding the brain caused by a virus, bacteria or rarely other organisms, such as tuberculosis. Septicaemia is infection of the blood. **These are life-threatening illnesses**, requiring urgent medical attention. They have numerous complications, from hearing loss to brain damage. The rash (see action) is not always present or may not be present early on. A baby may show a combination of the following: off feeds, irritable, dislike being handled, generally unwell, fever, pale or mottled skin, rash, decreased alertness or responsiveness, high-pitched cry, bulging fontanelle, dislike lights, stiff jerky movements, be floppy, be listless.	Always **call an ambulance** if you suspect either condition. If your baby has a rash, place a clear glass over the spots and press down firmly – the dark red-purple rash typical of meningococcal septicaemia will not fade. If the doctor does not diagnose meningitis, ask for clarification so that you don't continue to worry. If your baby remains unwell and you are still concerned, have him reassessed – trust your instincts.

Heart

Complaint	Description	Action
heart murmur 	An extra sound heard when listening to the heart, due to the flow of blood over the heart valve or blood vessels. In babies there is often nothing wrong with the heart; this is called an 'innocent murmur', caused by their rapid heart rate (particularly when they have a temperature or are stressed). Murmurs caused by structural heart problems need specialist attention.	Many children have a heart murmur at some time (up to 80 per cent). A doctor will usually pick it up during an examination. If the murmur is persistent, the doctor may refer your baby for an echocardiogram (an ultrasound of the heart). If this is abnormal, the specialist will discuss whether treatment is required.

Eyes

Complaint	Description	Action
blocked tear duct	Watery eye or eyes, usually from birth as the tear duct has not joined from the eye into the nose. This condition occurs in about one in five babies (particularly in premature babies). A baby is prone to sticky eyes and conjunctivitis (see below) while the tear duct is blocked.	The tear duct becomes patent (open) within a few weeks or months following birth. Daily gentle massage of the corner of the affected eye (near tear duct) helps exude any pus that has collected. **Seek medical help** if you need to be shown how to do this. If the problem is still present at 1 year, your baby will need referral to an eye specialist – a simple operation will open the tear duct.
sticky eyes	A symptom usually caused by blood or discharge entering the eye during birth or by a tear duct being blocked, either temporarily during a cold or persistently (see above). May also be due to conjunctivitis (see below) or an eye infection. A sticky discharge is found on the eyelashes, typically first thing in the morning, and it may stick the eyelids together.	Clean the baby's eyes with cooled boiled water using fresh cotton wool and wiping from the inner to outer corner (see page 140). **Seek medical help** if the eyes become red or it isn't settling after a week of cleaning. If it occurs in the first few weeks after birth, your doctor will need to ensure that it isn't a birth infection. These must be treated to avoid damage to the eye.
conjunctivitis 	Eye condition, often occurring with a cold and causing inflamed, pink or red and sore eyes. The baby may rub his eyes and be grizzly. There may be a pus discharge, possibly copious, sticking the eyes together, particularly in the morning. Conjunctivitis is more common if the baby has a blocked tear duct (see above). It can also be caused by infections caught during birth, which can cause eye damage.	Clean the eyes regularly with clean cotton wool and cooled boiled water. Conjunctivitis is usually viral and often occurs with a cold. Occasionally, it is caused by a bacterial infection, which requires antibiotic eye drops or ointment; you may need two people to get these into the baby's eye(s). **Seek medical help** if it occurs within 1–2 weeks of birth to ensure it is not a birth infection (see above). If the eyes are swollen, very red or getting worse, or don't settle within a few days, go to the doctor.
squints	The eyes do not look in the same direction. Under 4 months, this is normal, as long as it is intermittent – it occurs as the baby learns to look at things. A family history of squints may warrant a referral to an eye specialist. Most persistent squints are due to refractive errors (the two eyes focusing differently) and may be treated with an eye patch, spectacles or a combination. Rarer causes include cataracts, which may require surgery.	**Seek medical help** if your baby always squints, appears not to see you or still squints after 4 months. Don't delay, as squints can cause problems with sight development. If your baby's eye does not seem to move at all or the squint develops suddenly, consult your doctor urgently.

Ear, nose and throat

Complaint	Description	Action
colds	Viral infections causing a runny nose, mild temperature (<38°C/100.4°F) and maybe a mild cough. Bacterial infections can occur on top of the cold, making matters worse.	Give painkillers if distressed (see page 239). **Seek medical help** if he gets worse or his temperature increases, or if he stops producing wet nappies.
croup	Viral infection of the larynx (voice box) and trachea (windpipe), most common in winter and spring. It causes a barking cough (sounds like a seal), a raised temperature, loss of appetite and a hoarse voice. It is usually worse at night and bad for one to two nights. If the baby develops breathing difficulties, he needs hospital care, which may include steroids and oxygen.	Try to keep your baby calm. Encourage him to rest between bouts of coughing, and see if he will drink. **Seek medical help** if your baby's alertness is reduced or he has an increased breathing rate or difficulty breathing, or other symptoms such as harsh breathing between bouts of coughing. Also take him to the doctor if he is not drinking.
tonsillitis 	Inflammation of the throat, with infection of the tonsils (two glands at the back of the throat), which become swollen, pink or red and may show a white discharge. The breath may be smelly. Symptoms include a temperature and lack of appetite; the baby may have a cough. Older babies (12 months) may complain of a sore throat. Rarely, the swollen tonsils cause breathing difficulties or abscesses may occur. Glands in the stomach may enlarge (mesenteric adenitis) and cause pain, which can be mistaken for appendicitis. This can occur with any respiratory infection.	Most cases are viral and will settle with painkillers (see page 239). **Seek medical help** if your baby is under 3 months, is very unwell or has a high temperature (>38°C/100.4°F). Also see a doctor if he is not drinking or is no better after 3–4 days. Some doctors prefer to treat tonsillitis in babies under 1 year with antibiotics.
ear infection	Infection – viral or bacterial – of the middle ear, causing painful inflammation and sometimes pus. It may occur with or after a cold. Typically, the baby runs a temperature and may scream or pull at his ear due to the pain, which is often worse at night, as lying down increases the pressure in the ear. The eardrum may actually perforate (burst), causing a discharge of pus (see page 246). Recurrent infections may cause glue ear (see page 246) or temporary hearing problems.	Painkillers are usually needed for both temperature and pain relief (see page 239). **Seek medical help** if your baby seems unwell or has a high temperature (>38°C/100.4°F). Antibiotics may be required. If his eardrum perforates, it will need to be checked a few weeks later to ensure it has healed, which in most cases it does.

Ear, nose and throat (continued)

Complaint	Description	Action
glue ear	Sticky fluid accumulates in the middle ear, causing fluctuating deafness; no other symptoms appear. It may occur after ear infections or colds. Persistent loss of hearing can lead to problems with speech.	Seek medical help if you are concerned about your baby's hearing or speech development. Glue ear often resolves itself, but if he repeatedly fails hearing tests at intervals, then he may need grommets – an operation inserts small tubes into the eardrum, allowing air behind the eardrum. The grommets eventually fall out spontaneously.
ear pain	Pain in the ear, usually the middle ear (behind the eardrum), typically causing pulling at the ears and crying, and an unsettled child, sometimes with a fever if caused by infection. Sometimes throat infections can cause ear pain, as they can cause the tube that allows fluid to drain from the middle ear into the throat to block, causing pressure in the ear to build up. Pressure changes (e.g. on planes) can cause ear pain that lasts after pressure changes settle.	If pain continues, try painkillers. If unwell or ear pain does not settle, seek medical help.
burst eardrum	If pressure behind the eardrum becomes too great, the eardrum can burst. This is often due to infection, but occasionally occurs due to other causes (e.g. on planes). Acute pain is suddenly relieved when the eardrum bursts. If due to an infection, there may be a fever or a discharge.	Seek medical help to confirm that the eardrum has burst. Often your doctor will want to recheck the eardrum a few weeks later to ensure the eardrum has rehealed. In most cases, the eardrum heals itself.
ear discharge	Discharge, usually pus from the ear canal. Sometimes after acute illness with fever and pain. The pain and fever sometimes settles as the discharge starts. Ear discharge usually means the eardrum has burst (see above); it may settle on its own.	Seek medical help if your child is unwell or the discharge is not settling; antibiotics may be needed. The doctor may want to recheck the ear a few weeks later (see above).
rhinitis	Inflammation inside the nose, which, if persistent, tends to be due to an allergic reaction. It causes a stuffy, runny nose and mouth breathing. Children with rhinitis may be hypersensitive and may suffer from diseases such as asthma (see page 248), enlarged adenoids or eczema (see page 254).	A reduction in house dust mites may help. Seek medical help if the inflammation persists. Your baby may need steroid nose sprays or antihistamines. The condition may need further investigation, such as skin-prick testing for allergens.

Mouth

Complaint	Description	Action
teething 	Some of a baby's teeth may come through with no problems, others may cause you and him many sleepless nights. He will drool and chew on anything, and may be distressed at times. He may have slight bleeds from the gums.	Give your baby plenty of things to chew on. Try different textures: soft, hard, cold. Use teething gels and, if he is distressed, painkillers (see page 239). **Seek medical help** if your baby is unwell or has a fever.
ulcers	Small, shallow, painful lesions in the mouth, often associated with a viral infection. The baby may be reluctant to eat or drink, which can lead to dehydration.	Try painkillers (see page 239) and teething gel. Provide cool, soft, non-acid food and drink. **Seek medical help** if your baby is not drinking or having wet nappies, or is lethargic.
oral thrush	A recurrent fungal infection in the mouth caused by thrush (candida). Small cream, slightly raised plaques appear on the lining of the mouth. If scraped off, the area underneath may bleed. Antibiotics can make thrush more likely. Feeding may be affected, although usually the thrush does not cause soreness.	Check for nappy rash (see above), as they can occur simultaneously. **Seek medical help**, as your baby will probably need an antifungal medicine. If you are breast-feeding, you may be asked to use a cream on your breasts between feeds. With bottle-fed babies, new teats should be used and old ones disposed of.

Musculoskeletal

Complaint	Description	Action
clicky hips 	A click may be heard or felt in the baby's hip. This is usually discovered as part of the hip examination during a routine baby check (see page 17).	Clicky hips are often normal, but may indicate a slightly loose hip joint. Although it is important to get it checked, it may need no treatment. With persistent clicks, your baby may be referred for an ultrasound for further investigation (see below).
congenital dislocation of the hip (CDH) and developmental dysplasia of the hip Treatments for these conditions can make life difficult – find a support group.	In CDH, the joint is dislocated or dislocatable, while in dysplasia the socket part of the joint is usually too shallow. Abnormalities may be discovered at routine baby checks (see page 17). The baby may have unequal skin creases, different leg lengths or bear weight unequally. You may notice unequal hip movement when changing his nappy. As he grows, his mobility may be affected.	When the problem is found, your baby will be referred for an ultrasound. The sooner these conditions are discovered, the better – earlier treatment is easier and usually more successful. It usually consists of splinting. If this doesn't work, surgery may be needed. Occasionally, treatment is not totally successful and the joint is at risk of arthritis as the child ages.

Chest

Complaint	Description	Action
bronchiolitis	Viral infection of the small airways (bronchioles), causing inflammation and mucus. A cold-like illness develops into an irritable cough and increased breathing rate with difficulty feeding over 2–3 days. In severe cases, the baby may need hospitalization to receive oxygen and help with feeding, either via a small tube put through his nose into his stomach or intravenously.	Watch your baby's fluid intake – ensure he is having wet nappies and is alert. **Seek medical help** if he is lethargic, less responsive, unable to drink or has fewer wet nappies. If he has difficulty breathing or his breathing is fast, his condition needs to be assessed by a doctor.
chest infections	Acute inflammation of the airways due to infection, either bacterial or viral. The baby will feel unwell and have a high temperature (often ›38°C/100.4°F). He will have an increased breathing rate, lack an appetite and often, but not always, a cough. In some cases he may need hospital admission for intravenous antibiotics and fluids or help with breathing.	**Seek medical help.** Chest infections often need treatment with antibiotics. **Call an ambulance** if your baby has difficulty breathing, with increased breathing rate or reduced responsiveness.
wheeze	A whistling sound on breathing is usually caused by viral infections, although other causes, such as foreign bodies (a swallowed toy, for example) need to be considered. Often the baby may wheeze with every viral infection, although he appears otherwise well. Wheezing does not necessarily mean he is or will become asthmatic, although some wheezing children do develop the condition.	If your baby is well and not distressed, the wheeze may require no treatment, although the first time it occurs it should be assessed and may be treated with inhalers or other medicine. **Seek medical help** if a foreign body may be the cause. Your baby will be X-rayed and most likely assessed in hospital. If he has a high temperature (›38°C/100.4°F), he may have a chest infection and may need to be prescribed antibiotics. **Call an ambulance** if he is distressed or has difficulty breathing, becomes less responsive or changes colour.
asthma	Long-term sensitizing condition of the airways in which they become swollen and narrowed. Asthmatic attacks, with wheezing and shortness of breath, can require hospital admission. Typically, a baby may have a repeated chest infection, be a viral wheezer or the only symptom may be a persistent cough at night (a common sign of childhood asthma). Asthma is rarely diagnosed in children under 1 year.	Do not smoke. Reduce house dust mites. Encourage activity and a good diet. **Seek medical help** if your baby has difficulty breathing. If asthma is confirmed, the treatment aims to make sure a child's life is not restricted and he can take part in normal activity.

Tummy

Complaint	Description	Action
gastroenteritis	Tummy bugs are often viral but can be bacterial. They cause vomiting and diarrhoea, and maybe a mild temperature (<38°C/100.4°F) and mild tummy cramps. Dehydration can occur and may require hospital admission for intravenous fluids – smaller babies are more at risk. An uncommon infection causes kidney problems – bruises or bleeding can occur as well as reduced (and red) urine output – often up to a week later in a pale, listless child. **Contact your doctor urgently.**	Be rigorous with hygiene to prevent spread. If your baby is vomiting, continue breast-feeding but do not give formula. Offer small sips of water or rehydration solution frequently. If he wants solid food, give something bland and non-dairy. **Seek medical help** if he is lethargic, unwell, less responsive, having fewer wet nappies, has a high temperature (>38°C/100.4°F) or keeping nothing down, or if it goes on for more than 2 days. Treatable bacterial causes can be diagnosed with a stool sample. A urine sample may be taken, as urine infections can cause similar symptoms.
reflux	Acid from the stomach flows back up into the food pipe (oesophagus). The baby may be in pain (typically worse on lying flat) and may vomit (particularly with a full stomach). Reflux may cause him to have disturbed sleep, feed fitfully or fail to thrive. Very occasionally a baby may also be prone to chest infections or breathing difficulties.	**Seek medical help**, as treatments to reduce inflammation can be added to bottles or given after breast milk. These reduce the production of acid and its effects, and increase the speed at which the stomach empties. Feed thickeners may be used. Keeping your baby upright after feeds and propping up the legs of his cot at the head end may help. Most babies improve over time, particularly when they start solids and become mobile. If it persists, seek assistance.
colic If your baby has colic, get some support for yourself, as this will be a tough time. Seek professional help if you feel you cannot cope. 	Persistent crying with an unknown cause in an otherwise healthy baby. About 20 per cent of babies get colic, the symptoms being crying for more than 3 hours a day for more than 3 weeks. Typically, it starts in the evening. The baby may pull his legs up, feed fitfully and be difficult to settle, but is otherwise well and growing normally. Colic has no complications and babies grow out of it, usually by 4 months old. Other conditions cause symptoms similar to colic. Check with your doctor to ensure these are not missed.	Soothe him as much as possible — different things work for different babies (see pages 132–135). If you are breast-feeding, continue; if you are bottle-feeding, talk to a health professional about trying whey hydrosylate milk, as this is more easily digested. Try lactase enzyme drops (to help digest the sucrose in milk) and colic relief remedies – some babies find them helpful. Rhythmical movement, massage and limiting stimulation by not patting, lifting or jiggling your baby may all help the problem. **Seek medical help** if he continues to cry, seems unwell or isn't growing.

Tummy (continued)

Complaint	Description	Action
undescended testicles	The testicles develop within the abdomen and usually descend into the scrotum before birth, but in 3–4 per cent of full-term babies one or both testicles stay within the abdomen or along the path of descent. Undescended testicles can be associated with slightly lower sperm counts; they are lower still if the testicles are not brought down into the scrotum. The risk of testicular cancer is also slightly higher. It reduces, but is still slightly higher than normal, if the testicles are brought down into the scrotum.	If your baby's testicles are not in his scrotum, he will be observed either by your doctor or by a specialist. By 9 months old, 65 per cent of cases will have descended with no treatment. If they have not descended at this stage, surgery or hormone treatment will be needed.
hydrocoeles	Fluid in the sac surrounding the testicle is common in newborns, especially premature babies. He will usually have a lax swelling around one or both testicles. It is harmless and rarely painful.	The hydrocoele will be assessed by a doctor, to ensure there is no underlying abnormality, and needs observation, but will usually settle after 6–12 months with no treatment. **Seek medical help** if it becomes larger, tense or red. If it persists beyond 1 year, it may need surgical treatment.
constipation 	Faeces are hard and usually painful to pass. Babies fed only breast milk rarely become constipated, as it is easily digested and contains a hormone that increases gut motility. Formula milk is less easily digested and may cause constipation as your baby's digestive system adapts to it. A change of formula or a change of diet when weaning, for example, can cause constipation. Small splits in the skin will make passing stools even more painful. If he seems very distressed or passes a redcurrant jelly-like substance, **seek urgent help** – he may be suffering from something other than constipation.	Prevention is best. Act early. If it becomes painful for your baby to pass a stool, he may try not to and become more constipated. Fluid intake (once weaned) and activity are essential. Cooled boiled water is good for older babies. If he is on solids, try green leafy vegetables, and apricot or prune purée. Take care with fibre: without fluid, it can be constipating. Gentle massage of the tummy may help, as can leaving his nappy off and bending his knees up. If your baby is bottle fed, a formula with pro- and prebiotics can help. **Seek medical help** if your baby is under 4 months or the condition doesn't improve. He may need laxatives. Use these with care – it is better to continue until the problem is completely resolved than risk it recurring.

Tummy (continued)

Complaint	Description	Action
diarrhoea	Abnormally frequent, watery or runny stools. Diarrhoea can be a symptom of a tummy infection (see gastroenteritis, page 249) or other illnesses, such as urinary tract infection (see below). Diet can also cause it – high fibre or lots of squash, fruit juice or artificial sweeteners are common culprits. Dehydration is uncommon but may warrant hospital admission. Prolonged diarrhoea may indicate coeliac disease (wheat intolerance).	Ensure your baby is getting enough fluid and be careful about hygiene. Toddler's diarrhoea (beyond the age of 1 year) is thought to have dietary causes. **Seek medical help** if there is blood in the stools or the condition persists beyond a week. Also see a doctor if your baby seems unwell. A stool sample may need to be analysed.
urinary tract infections	Bacterial infection of the bladder or kidneys. The baby may have a temperature and vomit or be off feeds; he may have diarrhoea. His urine may smell and an older child may complain of tummy pain or pain on urinating. Occasionally, urinary infections in children do not present as an acute illness but can cause diarrhoea or failure to thrive. Urine can flow back up to the kidneys and damage them. About a third of child sufferers have the potential for this to happen, but will grow out it.	**Seek medical help** as soon as possible, as your baby needs antibiotics. Medical attention is urgent if he feels unwell with a high temperature (>38°C/100.4°F) and is unable to keep anything down. His kidneys may require investigation, during which time he may need to remain on a low dose of antibiotic.
inguinal hernia	A weakness in the muscle wall, allowing a bowel loop to protrude into the groin. The baby may have a small bulge in the groin or scrotum; it may be there all the time or may come and go. Inguinal hernia occurs in about 5 per cent of children and is more common in boys. Part of the bowel may become stuck in the hernia, affecting its blood supply, which may lead to damage.	Most hernias are soft and non-tender. They need assessing and will require a non-urgent operation. **Seek medical help** if the hernia becomes hard, tense, painful or your baby seems to be in pain. A portion of bowel may have become trapped and his condition needs urgent assessment.
umbilical hernia	A protrusion of the abdominal lining through the abdominal wall, around the umbilicus, because the muscle ring has not closed completely after birth. Part of the bowel may be contained within the hernia. The area around the belly button will bulge. The hernia is usually soft, but will protrude when the baby sits or cries.	A hernia of less than 1 cm (½ in) will probably close by itself by the age of 3–4 years. **Seek medical help** if it does not resolve or if it becomes hard or painful. It may need to be surgically repaired.

Skin

Complaint	Description	Action
urticaria	An allergic rash like nettle rash, producing raised red-white wheals that may be itchy.	Remove the source of the allergy, if known. **Seek medical help**, as your baby may benefit from antihistamine. **Call an ambulance** if his condition gets worse or he has difficulty breathing.
nappy rash	Several different types of rash may occur in the nappy area. The most common is irritant dermatitis, where urine and bacteria in faeces create ammonia, which in moist conditions produces an irritating alkaline solution (see pages 136–139).	Use a nappy cream and clean the area with cotton wool and water, rather than wipes. **Seek medical help** if the rash worsens. If small red spots are present, it may be thrush (candida), which needs to be treated with an antifungal cream.
jaundice	Yellow or slightly 'sun-tanned' skin due to deposits of bilirubin. When a baby is born, the foetal blood is broken down to be replaced by normal adult blood. Bilirubin is a by-product of this process. In some babies the liver cannot get rid of the bilirubin fast enough and some is deposited temporarily in the skin. Jaundice is common in newborns, particularly breast-fed ones, as substances in breast milk can reduce the rate of bilirubin excretion. There are some rarer causes of prolonged jaundice that may need treatment.	If the jaundice is mild and your baby is alert and feeding well, his urine is pale and his stools not pale, then no treatment is needed – it will usually settle by 2 weeks of age. **Seek medical help** if the jaundice starts within the first 24 hours after birth, is severe and your baby is sleepy, unwell or not feeding, his stools are pale or his urine is dark. If the jaundice persists beyond 2 weeks of age (3 weeks if premature), he will need further investigations. Some babies require light (photo) therapy to reduce the level of jaundice.
impetigo	Bacterial skin disease causing an infectious red rash that may include small, fluid-filled blisters and will develop a yellow crust. It is often on the face, but can be (or spread) anywhere.	The rash is very contagious – use careful hygiene to avoid spread. **Seek medical help**: your baby will need antibiotic cream or medicine. See the doctor again if it doesn't settle in a few days, as he may need to be given a different antibiotic.

Skin (continued)

Complaint	Description	Action
chickenpox There is a chicken pox vaccine available, but in the UK this is currently not given routinely. However, it can be given if close contacts are particularly vulnerable (such as undergoing chemotherapy). If you are in contact with chickenpox and are pregnant and have never had chickenpox, see your doctor urgently. There may be a risk of complications, and possible effects on the baby.	Contagious viral illness that often begins with mild cold-like symptoms, then blister-like spots appear, becoming widespread. Babies often only get a few spots. After recovering, the child has lifetime immunity. The spots can become infected. Ear and chest infections can occur and, rarely, meningitis.	Depending on his age (see page 239), give your baby paracetamol or ibuprofen if distressed. Antihistamines can ease itching, as can calamine lotion. Sodium bicarbonate in a bath can reduce itching. Once the rash has scabbed over (about a week) he is no longer infectious. **Seek medical help** if the spots become infected – antibiotics are needed. You must consult a doctor if your baby's temperature is high (>38°C/100.4°F), he is unwell or not drinking, or if area around the spots is very red.
slapped cheek disease (parvovirus) If you are in contact with slapped cheek and are pregnant and have not had this virus before, contact your doctor, as it may affect the baby – two blood tests will show whether you have caught it.	Viral illness that usually makes the baby mildly unwell, with a runny nose and mild fever (<38°C/100.4°F). It is characterized by bright red cheeks and may cause a widespread pink, lacy rash over the body that may come and go (especially in the bath or after exercise). It may be itchy and can cause joint pains (in older children and adults).	Use paracetamol or ibuprofen, depending on his age (see page 239), if he is distressed. **Seek medical help** if he becomes unwell with increasing fever or joint pains, or if your child has a pre-existing medical condition, such as sickle cell anaemia.
hand, foot and mouth disease	This illness is caused by a group of viruses. The baby may be mildly unwell and will have small blister-like spots on his palms, soles or in his mouth (ulcers), and often nappy rash (see page 252). He may be off his food, drool and have a mild temperature. He may become dehydrated due to not drinking because of pain from the mouth ulcers.	Give your baby paracetamol and ibuprofen for pain if his age allows (see page 239). Try teething gel on the mouth ulcers. Encourage drinking (avoid fruit juice, which will sting) and soft or cold food. **Seek medical help** if he is not drinking, his nappies are not wet, he is unwell or lethargic or has a high temperature.
non-specific viral rash	Any rash that is suggestive of a viral infection but not caused by a particular virus. The baby will have a pink, slightly raised rash, mainly on the trunk. He may be suffering from a cold or be mildly unwell.	**Seek medical help**, as you need to have it checked. There is no treatment. Visit the doctor again if your baby becomes more unwell or the rash gets worse, as the diagnosis will need to be confirmed.

Skin (continued)

Complaint	Description	Action
eczema 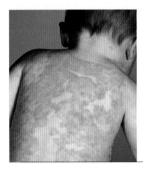	Reddened dry skin or spots. The baby may scratch it and it may become sore or infected. Many children grow out of their eczema. If they continue to suffer, it is important to treat it carefully, as it can cause hardening of the skin.	Use moisturizers specifically for eczema (see page 151) on the baby's skin. Avoid soaps and other chemicals. Hard water and house dust mites may aggravate the problem. Diet may also be contributory. **Seek medical help** if initial treatments don't work. The baby may need antihistamines to reduce itching. Steroid creams will ease inflamed skin and help to stop scarring; use under medical supervision. Infected eczema will need antibiotics.
heat rash	Bright red, raised pimply rash that is worse in areas where the skin rubs together, such as in the groin.	Keep your baby cool and take his clothes off where possible. Use cotton clothing. Don't use creams or calamine lotion: these can make things worse. **Seek medical help** if the rash worsens or your baby seems unwell. It may be that there is a different diagnosis.
seborrhoeic dermatitis or cradle cap	Scaly, often yellow patches on the baby's scalp. It can also cause nappy rash (see page 252).	This usually clears up on its own, but you can treat it by massaging with olive oil or with a cradle cap shampoo. **Seek medical help** if it spreads on to the forehead. It may need to be treated with antifungal or steroid cream.
haemangioma (strawberry naevus) 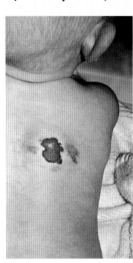	Small flat, red or blue area on the skin at birth or developing a few weeks later. It will slowly increase in size and prominence. Haemangiomas often grow until the age of 1 year. Occasionally, bleeding or ulceration occurs and sometimes excess skin needs to be removed once the haemangioma has resolved. Facial haemangiomas can interfere with the eyes, nose or mouth, or breathing. Multiple haemangiomas need investigation to ensure no more are present.	If small and not on the face, just mention it to your doctor. Most resolve spontaneously by the age of 5 years – although it can take up to 10 years. **Seek medical help** if it is large, on the face, is causing problems or your baby has multiple haemangiomas. Laser treatment may be the suggested course of action.

Allergies

Complaint	Description	Action
general allergies	Allergies can cause all manner of symptoms, from rashes to a runny nose. Children can grow out of some allergies, but they can also recur and worsen.	Try to work out what is causing the symptoms and remove it. **Seek medical help**, as antihistamines can help, and also steroids in certain situations. **Call an ambulance** if the reaction is severe.
anaphylaxis	Severe reaction to food, insect bites or stings, or a variety of other allergens. The breathing and blood circulation are badly affected. The baby may wheeze or suffer from breathing difficulties, become less alert or collapse. Anaphylaxis may recur.	**Call an ambulance.** If your baby has been prescribed either antihistamine or an adrenalin injection (epipen), give these. If this is the first occurrence of the problem or the cause is unknown, your doctor will investigate and discuss future management.
hayfever	Allergic reaction to any one or more of a variety of pollens (or mould spores) caused by an over-reaction of the immune system. Symptoms include a runny nose, sneezing and watery, irritated eyes.	Avoid pollen (or other irritants) as much as possible – early morning and evenings are the worst times. When outdoors, put sunglasses on your baby if possible. When you come in, bath him, including his hair. If his eyes become very swollen, **seek medical help** for an antihistamine prescription. **Call an ambulance** if he is suffering from breathing difficulties.
food	Food allergy can be severe, causing anaphylaxis (see above), or milder, causing rashes and vomiting with diarrhoea. Some food allergies (such as milk) tend to reduce with time. However, only reintroduce such food under medical supervision, as the reaction may get worse.	Do not feed your baby any more of the suspect food. **Call an ambulance** if the reaction is severe, otherwise **seek medical help** as soon as possible to discuss any suspected reaction.
bites	Usually cause pain and discomfort, and produce a small area of surrounding redness. Subsequent stings or bites by the same insect may produce a more severe reaction.	Remove the insect and sting, if present. Apply antihistamine cream/spray depending on the baby's age and a cool flannel or cool pack to reduce swelling (see pages 239–241). Painkillers may help (see page 239). **Seek medical help** if the area of redness increases. Stings and bites can cause anaphylactic reactions (see above). **Call an ambulance** if there are breathing difficulties or your baby is unwell. Seek urgent medical attention if your baby has been stung near the mouth or nose.

chapter 7

learning

Your baby has come into this world ready to learn. Over the next 12 months, she will develop from a helpless newborn into an infant approaching toddlerhood. Her capacity for learning during this time is astounding. Everything she does is a first-time experience, a new discovery – she observes all that she sees, absorbing vital information and storing it for later. Although she has little control over her movements to start with, your baby tries to make sense of the world around her from the word go and is remarkably successful in learning on every level, be it physical, intellectual or emotional.

nature versus
nurture

There has long been a debate as to how each baby develops into the complex character that he will be by the time he reaches adulthood. Referred to as the 'nature versus nurture' debate, the issue centres on whether a baby is born complete with a set of inherited characteristics, or is a 'blank slate' on which the experiences of life itself influence the kind of person he will become.

what does this mean?

The 'nature' argument is based on heredity and focuses on the idea that our innate characteristics and personality traits are determined before we are born. We inherit them from our parents and they develop as we grow. For the most part, they make us who we are and there is little we can do to change them.

There is certainly plenty of scientific evidence to suggest that a number of physical qualities are inherited from our parents and are, without doubt, part of our genetic makeup: eye and hair colour, for example, or the size of our adult feet. The nature argument suggests that if such physical qualities are inherited, so too must be certain psychological characteristics. This might explain why we can share aspects of our personality with our parents. The same hand gestures and facial expressions are particularly common, for instance.

A combined approach to the nature versus nurture debate might suggest that a baby's innate creative potential is fostered through stimulation of his visual senses.

The 'nature' view is supported to some extent by scientific trials in which twins separated at birth and raised by different parents have continued to develop similar personality traits and abilities as they grow older. The same has been found to be true of adopted children, who display characteristics similar to those of their natural parents, despite having never lived with them.

Central to the 'nurture' argument, which is based on environment, is the idea that, although we inherit some character traits from our parents, the majority are influenced by the surroundings in which we are raised, and our upbringing. Some people might even argue that a newborn baby has no inherited personal characteristics at all and that his unique persona develops through experience alone.

a combined approach

Most child-development professionals accept that children are influenced by a combination of both nature and nurture. There is no doubt that genetics play a crucial role in a baby's makeup and that a certain potential is there from the very start. However, in many instances, the way in which a child is brought up decides whether that potential comes to fruition. One could argue, for example, that a boy inherits, genetically, a skill for drawing from his mother, but that he may only discover and develop that skill if he is raised in an environment in which he is encouraged to practise drawing, and where he is not only praised for his successes but also coaxed through his failures. If his efforts are routinely ignored or denigrated, his confidence may well be shaken, in which case he is less likely to want to continue (see page 261).

By considering arguments from both sides of the debate, it is possible to see how a host of genetic traits – a musical ear, a sense of humour or being left-handed – may be inherited, and how the environment in which a baby is raised can influence the development (or not) of those traits.

birth order and gender

Scientific research has shown that where a child comes in the family – youngest, oldest or middle – can have an effect on his learning skills and temperament, primarily owing to the amount of quality time and attention he receives from his parents. Older siblings are likely to have more one on one interaction with parents and so tend to be brighter. Younger siblings tend to have less parental attention and so are less dependent on them. More often than not, middle children prove milder tempered and more diplomatic than their siblings.

Similarly, a baby's gender will influence his personal development. Baby boys are naturally more adventurous than girls and are more likely to take risks. This can be compounded by the fact that parents expect boys to be more rough-and-tumble and, without being particularly aware of it, tend to encourage this behaviour in a boy but not in a girl.

A baby's environment can play a pivotal role in his ability and desire to learn.

Q Even though he is only 2 weeks old, my baby already seems to have quite a strong character. Is this possible?

A A baby begins to show his personality from the day he is born – perhaps making a fuss at changing time or often being grumpy on waking – and certain traits grow stronger as he gets older. An older child may be determined to feed himself, or love bathtime or be afraid to go to sleep with the light off.

how you can help

There is much you can do to aid your own baby's progress – not least by ensuring that she is encouraged to thrive in a positive environment. Central to the development of a newborn baby is her desire to explore and discover. She will be on the move constantly, whether mentally or physically, deliberately seeking new challenges and learning opportunities.

Q **Is there a link between physical interaction and a baby's learning ability?**

A Scientists believe that there is. At birth your baby's brain has 100 billion cells, but at first the connections between them are underdeveloped, and she is capable of only the most basic biological functions. By stroking her cheeks, hugging, kissing and tickling her, you can stimulate the brain cells to connect. Your physical attention and her early learning experiences are crucial in producing a child who is able to plan, reason and solve problems.

the right environment

Relaxed and comfortable surroundings are paramount. Be wary of noisy places or those where there are too many distractions. Use different parts of the home for different activities – variety is just as important for your baby as it is for you. If your baby has siblings, avoid creating an atmosphere in which one child is favoured over another. Above all, promote a warm, loving environment, have plenty of physical contact with your baby and tell her you love her.

It can be a comfort for your child to know that you are by her side as she plays.

Leaving your baby alone with a toy will encourage her to explore for herself.

one-to-one

One-to-one attention is essential for learning more quickly and for boosting confidence. Take pleasure from her achievements – make a big deal of her first smile or early babbling. Join in her activities without dominating them: show her how to play with a toy that she is finding difficult, or introduce new ways of playing when she is bored. She will benefit from having time to play alone. Talk to her to stimulate her language skills (see pages 270–273).

gauging your baby's ability

The toys you choose for your growing baby, and the games you play, can influence her development (see pages 274–275). Offer something beyond her ability and she will quickly become frustrated; opt for something too easy and she will get bored. Try to find activities that challenge her, without stretching her too far. For example, putting a toy just outside her reach will stimulate hand control, movement skills, vision and attention, while rolling a ball towards her will improve hand–eye coordination, movement and balance.

confidence

Much of your baby's desire and ability to learn during her first year will be based on her confidence. A young baby demonstrates an innate self-belief from early on. The idea that a challenge may be too big is simply not a consideration. Watch your baby and you will see that she will always try to get to a toy beyond her reach and, if she wants your attention, she will continue to make a noise until you respond.

Your baby's self-confidence is essential for her motivation and ability to form relationships. It is important to boost her self-belief by praising her achievements. Be aware of her limitations, and be ready to comfort her when she cannot do something. Avoid her experiencing repeated failure. Step in when frustration or disappointment mount, and steer her in another direction until she is ready to try again.

Is your baby over- or under-stimulated?

As the first few weeks pass, you will gradually get to know your baby and will be able to tell if she is bored, tired or frustrated. You will also become more aware of her abilities and limitations. Have reasonable expectations of her development – most make steady progress. If you find it hard to gauge your baby's responses, here are a few indicators:

An **over-stimulated baby** may:
- Show signs of irritability.
- Find it difficult to concentrate.
- Show a lack of interest.
- Be unsettled when left alone.
- Have trouble sleeping.

An **under-stimulated baby** may:
- Show a lack of drive.
- Become passive.
- Become upset easily.
- Be less expressive.
- Complain less.

Q **My baby is 8 months old and gets angry when she cannot complete a puzzle toy. What should I do?**

A Encourage her to complete the task, but do not force her to do so. Let her see you struggle with a similar task, but stay calm. She will be persuaded to adopt the same attitude.

your baby's
development

Your baby notches up a terrific catalogue of 'first times' during his first year. His development is so rapid, and often subtle, that you may find it a challenge to keep track of all the changes. When it comes to learning, however, there are a few key areas on which to focus, where a good understanding of how your baby develops is important for helping him to move from one stage to the next.

'We used to think it was funny that Stephen put everything within reach straight into his mouth. I had seen other babies do it, so was not unduly worried. But when he was still doing it at 10 months, I felt the time was right to put a stop to it. Every time I saw an object heading for his mouth, I distracted him with something else. He would stop in his tracks and look at me for long enough for me to take away whatever he was holding. It did not take long for him to learn not to do it altogether.'

Heather, mother of Stephen (15 months)

shared experience

mobility

A baby establishes control from the head down: he can raise his head before he can sit, sit before he can crawl, crawl before he can walk. He develops from the middle of his body out: he can raise his chest off the floor before he can reach out accurately with his hands, and can pick something up with his hands before he can kick something. All new movements are small stages towards taking his first unaided steps.

dexterity

At the same time your baby is working towards walking for the first time, he is improving the way he uses his hands. As a newborn, he can do little more than wave his arms. Gradually he learns to bat at toys, then to grasp and hold them. He learns how to pass a toy between his hands and how to drop a toy on purpose, to see what happens or to give it to you. By the end of the year he is dexterous, being able to pick up items between thumb and index finger and manage moving parts on toys.

Your baby's dexterity develops so fast, she can grasp an object from 3 months.

The moment your baby realizes that he can make a noise by shaking a rattle, there is no end to the pushing and pulling, banging and squeezing that he will do.

speech

As your baby listens to those around him, he masters not only the basics of language but also the idea that people take turns to talk and listen to each other without interrupting. Incredibly, during this time he progresses from using different cries to attract your attention, to being able to understand and act upon simple questions and instructions and, eventually, to uttering a first word.

cause and effect

The pace of your baby's neurological development is linked to that of his physical development, and a major milestone during this first year is his comprehension of cause and effect. At around 9 months, he realizes that he has an element of control over his environment when he discovers that he can roll a ball by pushing at it or light up a toy by pressing a button. This is a significant advance in his learning, as it encourages him to play in another dimension, operating toys for himself and looking for activities that he can influence.

object permanence

Your baby also masters the idea of object permanence towards the end of his first year. Up to about 9 months old, he is unable to comprehend fully the fact that an object does not disappear simply because it goes out of view. As this concept dawns on him, he tries hard to locate a toy he has dropped or to find one hidden under a blanket or behind your back. He is starting to be able to apply his mental agility to complex ideas.

from natural reflexes to learned movements

When your baby is born, his movements are predominantly the result of natural reflexes – blinking, the Moro reflex and the palmar reflex are all involuntary movements caused by specific stimuli (see pages 17–19). Gradually, however, your baby learns to control his body so that, by the age of 3 months, he uses learned movements to turn his head to the direction of a sound, image or touch. From this point on he builds on his movement skills, fine-tuning the way in which he manoeuvres his body and improving his balance. Everything he does now is learned through experience and built upon, always moving forward to the next step.

learning
through play

During the first year, everything your baby learns is through play. She observes all that goes on around her and absorbs information at an impressive rate. It is through play that she sees her first colours, feels her first textures and hears her first sounds. She also discovers action and reaction for the first time and comes to terms with the idea of object permanence (see page 263).

Once your baby can raise her head, she will also begin to reach out for toys that are just out of reach.

0–3 months

Although your baby has little control over her body, you should encourage her to move as freely as possible. At this age, she is most relaxed when lying on her back, and this naturally provides plenty of opportunities for her to move her legs in the air and wave her arms about. As your baby grows, these movements will become more coordinated and stronger.

Despite her restricted movement, your baby will express a desire to reach out and touch things from early on. Placing toys within her line of sight will stimulate her vision, but may also encourage her to move towards them. Lying your baby face down on the floor with toys within reach will encourage her to lift her head, while changing her position from time to time will allow her to see her surroundings from different perspectives and to learn more about her environment.

playtime with a baby of 0–3 months

Take your baby swimming. This is a great activity, stimulating your baby to move freely and strengthen developing muscles. Skin-to-skin contact with you will also give a boost to the bonding process between you and your baby.

Hold a brightly coloured object in front of your baby – primary colours work best or those with bold, contrasting patterns. Once she takes an interest in the object, move it from side to side and encourage her to follow it with her eyes. Try the same exercise moving the toy up and down and watch her follow it.

Introduce your baby to a range of sounds. Play different kinds of music to her – some calm, some more energetic. Hold her in your arms and dance to the rhythm or beat of the music.

Get out the clean laundry in front of your baby and let her watch as you pull clothes out to hang them up. Touch them against her cheek so she can feel the sensation of wet and cold, then dry and warm.

Make faces at your baby. Blow wind gently into her face, screw up your eyes and wrinkle your nose. She will squeal with delight and, from 8 weeks or so, will try to imitate you.

look and learn

Visual stimulation is very important at this stage, so play games that encourage this. Your baby's vision focuses at around 25 cm (10 in), so make sure objects of interest are within her range. Her head movements are limited during the early weeks, but she will soon be able to turn her head to look at something nearby. Notice how she stares at a new toy, scrutinizing it as she tries to make sense of it. Don't over-stimulate her, but have two or three favourite toys in the pram or cot. She is able to distinguish between different colours, textures and sounds, so vary the toys. Play could include activities that focus on her body awareness and boost her sensory-motor development: try tickling her gently when you change or dress her and see how she reacts.

On a social level, your baby will delight in watching you go about your daily business. Take her with you around the house as you do the housework. The repetitive nature of hanging out washing or doing the washing-up looks like great fun to her. Later you will find her imitating these, and other, adult activities. The idea of role-play is important from early on, as this is how your baby learns to interact with others.

Q How can I best help my baby to learn and develop?

A It is quite simple – play with her. When your baby plays, she engages all of her skills. Movement and balance, hand–eye coordination and mental agility combine to make sense of the activities you provide for her. She has a natural aptitude for learning, having inherited a number of characteristics from you, but will also benefit from the stimulation of her surroundings.

‘At 6 weeks, we bought Michelle a mobile with simple geometric shapes in primary colours. She would lie staring at it for hours, literally mesmerized by the tiniest movement it made.’

Shelley, mother of
Michelle (3 months)

shared experience

A low-hanging mobile is an ideal toy to hang over a cot for your young baby to swipe at now and again in play.

4–6 months

By this time, your baby's increased control of his head and neck means that he can sit with support, and this presents an altogether different world to him. Prop him up on cushions so that he can see more clearly. Play games that involve bouncing him on your knee facing you or rocking him from side to side, both of which will help him to gain greater control over his balance. When he's lying down, play games that encourage him to roll over. When he does this for the first time, it will usually be from his stomach to his back, which is easier than the other way around.

Up to this point your baby has been relatively passive, simply looking at a new object placed in front of him. By 5–6 months he has greater concentration and control over his body and will actively seek new interest. He will be a natural explorer. Be prepared for this and set him tasks that make the most of it. Encourage him to look for things that are not within his grasp. Talk to him as you move around the house. This will encourage him to move his head, enhancing his head control and balance. Explain what you are doing as you go about your business. Give him toys to hold that offer different textures or sensations and explain when they are warm or cold, rough or smooth. Play games that involve passing a toy from one hand to another, or from him to you, and allow him to grab at things that he wants to investigate further.

playtime with a baby of 4–6 months

Prop up your baby on cushions and let him watch as you move around the room purposefully with a favourite toy. Leave the toy somewhere in the room – on the sofa or next to the television, for example – then ask, 'Where's…?' Watch as he scans the room looking for it. He may even make an attempt to move towards it.

With your baby lying on his tummy, position a toy above him and encourage him to raise himself up to reach it.

Visit a park to see other children playing or a farm to see animals, especially when they have their young. He will see how older children interact with each other and their parents, or how animals care for their offspring; both are a boost to his social awareness and lay the foundation for games that involve role-play later on.

Once your baby reaches 6 months and has good control of his head and neck muscles, place him on your lap facing you and support him by holding his hands. Play clapping or seesaw games. Turn him around to face outwards and, holding him firmly around the waist, take him for a little ride on a horse or a car journey. Pretend to move from trot to canter and to jump fences. Or rev the engine, speed up and slow down and turn corners.

Now that your baby is more aware of his surroundings, and makes an effort to examine toys for himself, he will marvel at any toy that makes a noise, despite not yet being able to make the connection that he is causing the noise to happen in the first place.

A baby of 4–6 months will have gained sufficient control of his neck and head that he will now be able to enjoy activities at the local playground.

7–9 months

Your baby will be sitting confidently without support by this time. You can leave him safely to play alone for longer periods, amid a range of different toys, some within easy reach and some that he will need to stretch for. Exploring toys for himself is a very important way for him to learn and develop, using both his brain and his body, and he will revel in his newfound abilities. Reaching for and manipulating toys will improve his upper body strength, movement and balance, as well as his dexterity and mental agility. His improved stability also means that there is more fun to be had at bathtime. Introduce pouring water from one cup to another, squeezing water out of a sponge or blowing bubbles for him to swipe at.

Your baby's desire to learn and explore intensifies once he is able to crawl. A natural curiosity leads him to find a distant object much more interesting than one close by. This, together with better balance and improved dexterity, widens the field for learning through play. He will respond well to hide-and-seek games, will love knocking down piles of blocks or bricks that you build and will start to grasp the idea of cause and effect – the fact that something happens when he presses a button, shakes or pushes something and drops toys on the floor (see page 263).

playtime with a baby of 7–9 months

Play 'come-and-get-it' games. Shake a box with something in it, then place the box out of reach. He will strive to get at it to discover what is hidden inside.

Work on the cause-and-effect concept, which is still alien to your baby. Let him watch as you hide a favourite toy under a blanket, then sit back as he pulls the blanket away to reveal the toy. Show him how rattles work, how to get a lid off a box and how to retrieve a toy hidden under a piece of fabric, such as a handkerchief or muslin square.

Sit on the floor facing your baby and pass toys to him. Hold the toy short once in a while so that he has to reach for it, or drop it just before he grasps it, letting him pick it up from where it has fallen.

Place a range of items in a cloth bag, each with a different texture, size and use – a spoon, a ball, a rag doll, a toy car. Show your baby how to feel the shapes through the bag, then encourage him to dip in and pull something out. This will appeal to his curiosity. Then talk to him about the item – warm or cold, smooth or rough, hard or soft, round or pointy.

Sit your baby on the kitchen floor with a range of kitchenalia – wooden spoons, plastic boxes with lids and saucepans. Encourage him to bash, shake and bang bits together to make noises, showing the different sounds he can make.

Sing nursery rhymes with repetitive actions or sounds, such as 'Old MacDonald had a farm' and 'Five little ducks went swimming one day'. These help to introduce him to a variety of new concepts, such as counting and animal noises.

Even if your baby shows little interest in bath toys early on, he will enjoy slapping the water's surface, often splashing himself.

Q **Is there any point expecting my 8-month-old baby to play quietly? She makes so much noise, it is often hard to get on with anything else.**

A Naturally, you do not want to discourage your baby from playing, but now is a good time to teach her that there are other people to consider. When she is particularly loud, ask her quietly to calm down. After a time she will learn to make less noise, without it affecting her enjoyment at play time.

10–12 months

At this age, your baby is on the way to taking her first step, and there is plenty you can do to encourage her. Play standing bouncing games on your lap to let her feel her legs under her. Use an entire room to get her to crawl greater distances. You could try having 'toy stations' in different parts of the room and letting her crawl and shuffle from one to the next, or making an obstacle course – complete with cushions to climb over or go around – that she must negotiate to get from one side of the room to the other. Entice her to 'cruise' around the room – pulling herself up on pieces of furniture and using them to support her as she moves from one to the next.

With her mobility increasing daily, your baby seems to shift focus slightly now and develops much greater concentration. She is willing to stay in one place for longer, taking the time to find out all there is to know about a toy. You will find that she is keen to look at books more closely now, rather than constantly trying to chew the corner or turn the next page. Take this opportunity to linger on each page and point at or name what there is to see.

When sitting, offer your baby inset puzzles, nesting beakers or a shape-sorter to play with. These are difficult toys and she may find them hard work at first. However, they are also great for building confidence at this age. Take time to help her and give her plenty of practice. Playtime gets a real boost from improved language skills (see pages 270–273) and your baby will love playing hand-activity games like 'incy wincy spider' or 'pat-a-cake'.

Messy play appeals to babies in their first year, who love to explore new and different textures and temperatures.

playtime with a baby of 10–12 months

Depending on your baby's crawling or walking ability, you can encourage her to use a baby stroller when moving around the room. Usually taking the form of a large soft toy or a trolley full of bricks, these have standing-height handles for babies to hold on to as they push them forward. You will need to support your baby in doing this as she gets used to the idea. Introduce a 'bumpsadaisy' element to cruising around the room. Perhaps fall over with your baby, or grab her before she falls in rough-and-tumble play. This will encourage her confidence so that she is less likely to be upset when things do not go according to plan.

Sit facing your baby with three balls of different sizes. Start by rolling a ball to her – see if she rolls it back. Then encourage her to crawl after one that goes wide, and so on. The different sizes of the ball offers a good exercise in hand control. Try something that is not round and see how she reacts to the fact that it will not roll.

Play messy games: introduce the idea of finger painting or making handprints. Or make some jelly with fruit in and let her fish out the fruit with her hands.

Now that your baby has grasped object permanence (see page 263), she will love to play 'peek-a-boo', which she is happy to do for increasingly longer sessions.

It helps if you are there to demonstrate a new, more sophisticated toy to your baby.

‘At 10 months, Susan suddenly became much more interested in games that involved specific interaction between the two of us: rolling a ball to one another; me building a brick tower and her knocking it down. It was very rewarding for both of us. ’

Clare, mother of
Susan (12 months)

shared
experience

listening and speaking

From the moment he emerges from the womb to the time he speaks his first word, your baby is constantly listening to and absorbing the sounds around him. He may not be able to communicate verbally himself, but he learns quickly how to attract your attention and express discomfort, fatigue or hunger. He is also able to distinguish various sounds around him.

Q **How can I encourage my baby to talk?**

A There is much you can do to aid your baby's language skills, not least by simply taking the time to talk to him. Explain what you are doing as you go about daily routines, and name body parts and items of clothing as you get him dressed. Make eye contact as you talk to him and repeat sounds or words for him to mimic or copy. He will stare intently at your mouth as you talk and make sounds, sometimes even mouthing back at you.

innate language skills

From very early on, your baby discovers that he can make a range of noises of his own. What he needs to learn over the next 12 months is how to make noise with meaning, which you can interpret and understand. This form of communication is known as 'expressive' language and his ability to use it develops gradually during his first year and beyond (see pages 272–273).

When he listens to sounds, your baby interprets them in his own way in order to make sense of what he is hearing. This analytical skill is referred to as 'receptive' language, and tends to be the dominant language skill during the first year, as your baby generally understands

Making eye contact with your baby as you talk to him engages his keen interest.

By the age of 12 months, your baby will sit through a story happily, listening intently to the words as you read them.

more than he can speak. To help him develop, you need to stimulate his natural ability to communicate, working in both expressive and receptive language.

communication

Your baby's language skills improve at a striking pace from about 6 months on, as he begins to understand more of the words he hears. You can talk to him and expect a considered response now – ask simple questions or give simple instructions. Encourage him to understand that people have conversations, each taking a turn to say something. He may even make attempts at conversing himself. When you talk to him, leave a gap for his reply and see what happens. Pick a sound that he makes – 'da', for example – and repeat it back to him, looking right into his eyes – 'dada dada'. This will make him feel good about himself. Start to name objects around the house with more precision. Talk in greater detail about his clothes as you dress him, or his food as you feed him, gradually introducing an increasing range of simple vocabulary.

Towards the end of his first year, your baby may speak a first word. It is likely to be simple   mummy, daddy, no, teddy or ball – but this marks the beginning of his ability to talk properly as a means of communicating. It is worth taking even more care over the language you use now. Singing songs and nursery rhymes will introduce the concept of sentence-making and help your baby to understand that words are not random but sequential. Take time to have proper conversations with your baby. He will have a few words and sounds that you understand well enough. Listen to him intently without interrupting, show him that you are interested and match his expressions when he talks.

the experience of sound

- From very early on, introduce a range of sounds to your baby – musical toys, rattles, the radio, your voice. Remember that all sounds will be new to him, and exposing him to them like this will help him learn to distinguish one from the next. When talking to a newborn baby, be sure to keep your face close to his (around 25 cm/10 in) so that he can watch your lips as you make sounds. Using your baby's name a lot and singing repetitive songs will get him used to the idea of language.
- Stimulate his listening skills by making sounds in different parts of the room and rewarding him when he turns to find the source, read stories to him and encourage him to react to music of different tempos. Take turns to say something with your partner. This will help your child get used to the idea of different voices.

Babies understand the concept of language from a very early age, and may make their first attempts at speech from as young as 2 months of age.

sign language

Sign language is an effective way of communicating with your baby before he can speak. It really comes into its own between 6 and 9 months, when he can appreciate that you use words to indicate particular objects or activities and has good control of his hands as well. Many education centres have classes that you can both attend, in which you learn basic sign language to enable your baby to tell you when he is hungry, thirsty, tired or needs a nappy change, for example. Most classes use action songs and rhymes to teach the signs, and the results are evident in as few as 4 to 6 weeks.

language: ages and stages

The building blocks of learning to speak are the same for all babies, and you can use these as steps in developing language further.

- Between 0 and 6 weeks, a baby can only communicate through **non-verbal** means – crying and various body movements. He will make eye contact with you, and will have a range of facial expressions. He will also wave his arms and legs when happy or distressed.
  Try this: Hold your baby in your arms and let him settle there. Talk to him softly and watch as he tries to move and turn his body in response to your speech, trying to tune in to the sounds that he hears you making.

- Between 2 and 4 months, a baby starts to **coo**, repeating meaningless vowel (and later consonant) sounds, usually when settled and content.
  Try this: Put your baby in his cot with a couple of toys and leave him to play with them. Once he is busy, talk gently to him. After a few minutes, he may start to make sounds of his own, such as 'na na', over and over again.

- From 4–5 months on, the cooing progresses to **random babbling**: your baby has greater control over his breathing and voice by now and is able to make a quite clear and distinctive set of sounds when he has your attention.

Try this: Talk to your baby, pausing every so often to let him get used to the idea of a two-way conversation. He will soon start to synchronize his speech with yours.

- Random babbling progresses to **controlled babbling**, with your baby responding to your talking, as if in conversation. He will start to string sounds together, such as 'papapapapa' or 'yepyepyep', in response to sounds you make.

  Try this: Chat to your child and listen very carefully to the sounds that he makes. Notice how he starts to link syllables to form a string of sounds, such as 'muh-leh' or 'ah-gah-gah'.

- Approaching 12 months, your baby moves towards early speech. He looks at you and makes varying sounds as if in conversation, often with a totally serious facial expression. He may even utter his first word at around this time.

  Try this: Sit your baby in a chair and move towards the door as if to leave the room. Turn round and wave at him, saying 'Bye bye'. Your baby may well wave back to you – he understands perfectly.

'My youngest child, David, seemed slower than my other children when it came to learning to speak and I started to worry that something was wrong with him. My partner thought I was making an unnecessary fuss, but I was not so sure. At 9 months, David stopped looking up when I came into a room or called his name and I decided the reason he was not talking yet was because he was having trouble hearing. I was right. When I got him checked out, it transpired that he was suffering from a partial hearing loss.'

Sally, mother of
David (12 months)

shared
experience

By 12 months, although your baby's own speech is limited to a handful of words, he is able to understand almost all that you say to him.

choosing toys

During her first year, your baby learns a huge amount through play, and the types of toys you provide are an essential part of this process. Whether it is using and manipulating her body to reach for something or applying her mind to difficult concepts such as cause and effect or object permanence (see page 263), play helps your baby to develop neurologically and physically in tandem.

above Soft toys are appropriate from birth, as long as they do not have loose fibres.

right Building blocks are a perennial favourite with babies from 5–6 months onwards, when they love to knock stacks down, right up to 12 months and beyond, when they are better able to build towers for themselves.

making a choice

When it comes to buying toys, it is easy to feel daunted by the sheer variety available (and the expense). Ask yourself a few questions before committing:

- Is it durable?
- Is it fun to use?
- Does it carry a recognized safety mark?
- Will it arouse my baby's curiosity and engage her?
- Does it reward my baby with lights, sounds or movement?
- Will it challenge my baby without frustrating her?
- How soon will she grow out of it?

The wealth of toys available for babies is tremendous. You will find all manner of soft toys, mobiles and rattles for this age as well as countless battery-operated, brightly coloured plastic toys. Ever popular are coloured bricks or cups for stacking and books with lift-up flaps.

It pays to buy toys that are age-appropriate for your baby, and the chart opposite provides a rough guide. Don't despair if your baby rejects a given toy initially – it may prove too much of a challenge, and she may well return to it later on.

Toys: ages and stages

Age	Stage	What toys?
1–2 months	A newborn baby can focus on objects up to 25 cm (10 in) away. She moves her arms and legs, but has little voluntary control over her body. She gradually gains control over her limbs. Her neck and head muscles strengthen.	Choose toys with bold shapes and sharp colour contrasts, striking patterns such as spots and dots or stripes in black and white or primary colours. Hang a mobile above the cot for her to look at. Give her rattles and bells with simple sounds. Soft toys.
3–4 months	Your baby begins to swipe at objects at random and she develops a good grip. Her eyes focus well now and she has a good comprehension of sounds.	A floor-based baby gym with hanging toys to bat and grab is appropriate. Give her a music box or wristband with bells on to encourage locating sounds. Bright colours and simple shapes are still popular, as are rattles that are easy to hold.
5–6 months	Your baby can now reach and grasp toys easily. She shows signs of improved concentration and can sit with support.	Graduate on to wooden blocks for stacking. Toys with different textures to stimulate her sense of touch are still fun, and she will enjoy those that make a noise when activated. Spend time listening to nursery rhymes or animal noises on CDs or cassette tapes.
7–8 months	Your baby can sit unaided. She begins to stretch for things out of reach, showing greater dexterity as her pincer grasp develops. She shows interest in language and the sing-song nature of daily conversation. She recognizes her reflection as that of another baby.	She will start to appreciate soft books with lift-up flaps and pockets. Keep her busy with toys that require dexterity, such as rings that stack on pillars. Give her balls of different sizes, empty containers, a baby-safe mirror and simple toys with wheels – car, train, duck.
9–10 months	Your baby is now sitting and reaching for things; she may even be crawling. She has an ever-improving understanding of cause and effect.	Look out for smaller toys for busy fingers, or toys with moving parts for manipulation, such as a plastic tea set. A jack-in-a-box is fun, as are push-along toys and balls of different sizes.
11–12 months	Your baby has a good grasp of object permanence. She starts to be able to sort items. She will be cruising and taking her first steps. Her skills of imitation are growing and she may say her first word.	Nesting and stacking beakers will stimulate her interest, as will inset puzzles and shape-sorters. Give her a toddler trolley with bricks and provide toys that imitate real life – telephone, iron, pots, cloth dolls and cuddly toys – to appeal to her growing interest in role-play.

Several toy companies produce flat-packed push-along toys for you to assemble at home.

Your baby will appreciate a simple, home-made mobile with brightly coloured shapes from a very early age.

making toys

Babies are fascinated by all that they see and are easy to entertain with the simplest of toys. They do not need a vast choice – a few will suffice, as long as they encourage a good range of activities. You can make a toy out of almost anything, from a piece of fabric to a paper plate. It is fun and your baby will benefit from watching you make something for her, even if she cannot join in. It can be a boost both to her confidence and her ability to bond with you if she feels warmth and love in the toys you make for her. Once your baby can sit supported, she will find endless ways of playing with a sheet of paper, an envelope or a cardboard box. Here are some quick and easy ideas:

Mobiles These are appropriate from birth. Make a simple mobile from a paper plate by making a hole in the middle and drawing a spiral from the hole to the outside edge of the plate. Cut along the line to make a springy spiral that you can hang from the hole in its middle.

Expressive faces Draw a large circle on a piece of paper and make it into a smiling face. Draw another on a separate sheet with a sad face. Babies from an early age will recognize the two emotions. Add more expressions as your baby gets older, frowning or sleeping, for example.

Shape-shakers Use clear plastic bottles for a range of different toys. Fill one with clean water and drop in some glitter, sequins or small plastic beads. Part-fill an empty bottle with dried beans, pasta or rice to make a rattle. Babies from 3 months onwards will enjoy both of these visual and noisy shakers.

Hats It doesn't get easier than rolling a sheet of paper and securing it with sticky tape to make a cone-shaped hat. Make one to fit your 6- to 12-month-old baby's head (or yours) and even one for a favourite teddy. Decorate it as simply or elaborately as you wish.

Masks A baby of 9–12 months will enjoy playing with a mask made from a paper plate. Cut simple shapes for eyes, nose and mouth, and decorate it any way you like – from tiger stripes to a clown's beaming smile. Secure the mask over the face using sewing elastic threaded through a hole in either side.

Hidden treasure Choose a small favourite toy and place it under one of three upturned plastic beakers (preferably different colours to start with). Encourage your 10-month-old baby to watch as you move the cups around, then ask her to find the toy.

Letter box Towards the end of her first year, your baby will happily spend hours posting toys through a slot cut in the front of a cereal packet. Position the slot about 2.5 cm (1 in) from the top of the packet and give your baby a range of toys to drop through it.

Push-along toy With a little more skill you could construct a simple wooden toy with wheels – a duck or train, for example. Attach a cord to the front for your year-old baby to pull the toy behind her as she moves about the room.

Q Is it better to give my 12-month-old baby a large or small ball to play catch with?

A She will be able to hold a small ball in her hands, but is likely to have difficulty throwing it. However, a large ball may block her vision when she holds it in preparation for throwing. The best solution is to choose an intermediate size, one that she can hold firmly between both hands, while still being able to see over the top of it.

Q How do I know which toys are safe for my baby?

A Most toys have a 'recommended age' sticker, which can help you to work out if it is suitable for your baby's age and abilities. All toy parts should be bigger than your baby's mouth to prevent the risk of choking, so check for small parts, buttons, ribbons or bows that your child could pull off and put in her mouth. Finally, never buy toys that don't bear the CE or Lion Mark, which shows that they meet recognized safety standards.

You can make a basic shaker by half-filling two plastic cups with rice or dried beans and taping them together.

starting to
explore

It is in your baby's nature to explore – his innate curiosity leads him to examine everything he comes across. For the first few months he is limited to what he can see around him, but when he becomes more mobile, his explorations will increase. Exploring is a very healthy part of your baby's development. Do all you can to encourage him to discover his environment.

exploring toys

Your baby does not have to be constantly on the move to explore. Give him any toy and he will stare at it, pull at it, shake it and mouth it. He is discovering what it smells or tastes like, how it feels, whether it is soft or hard, warm or cold. Every new sensation, sound or visual stimulation is a thrill to your baby – a completely new experience to be stored. Encourage him to examine the toys he plays with – show him how a toy works or how to hold it in different ways (see pages 274–275). Introduce new toys when you think he is getting bored with the ones he has already.

Q My baby shows little interest in the toys that I give him. Is there something wrong with him?

A Some children are more dynamic than others and have a greater desire to explore. If your baby won't reach for a toy and isn't very keen to explore, there is nothing to worry about. It is probably simply a case of him needing you to push him gently into more activities. To increase his motivation, bring toys to him, place them in his hands and stay and play with him. Check that his toys are suitable for his stage of development (see page 275). If they are more suitable for a much older or much younger child, he is unlikely to show much interest in them.

Much of a baby's early exploration is done using his mouth as he bites, licks and sucks objects within range in order to discover what they are.

Crawling offers your baby long-awaited forays into areas he could only dream about exploring before.

on the move

Once your baby is crawling, from around 9 months, there is no limit to what he will want to do and every corner of your house will be a temptation – that cupboard where all the toys are kept, the shelf holding DVDs next to the television, behind the curtains in the living room. Perhaps the biggest challenge of all is the stairs. These offer hours, even days, of excitement as he tries to find what lies beyond. Your baby is looking for adventure, desperate to find out more about his world and to add to his library of new experiences.

As your baby becomes increasingly adept at getting himself around the house, he is at greater risk of injury. It is in his nature to be lured by small, fascinating places that you would not expect him to notice, let alone access. Make every attempt to baby-proof your home and garden (see pages 224–227). It is a good idea to remove as many potential hazards as possible for these early crawling months.

It is also very important at this stage to be firm with your baby. Up to this point, he has mainly been exploring things that you have given to him. He has not been told that there is something he cannot play with or a place he's not allowed to go to. He cannot distinguish what is good for him to play with and what's not. It will come as quite a shock to him to discover that your china collection is out of bounds or that some liquids are not for drinking. You do not want to discourage natural curiosity, so the best plan of action is to remove anything harmful, fragile or precious, keeping it well out of your baby's reach. This way the issue never arises.

life's lessons begin

There will be times when you cannot avoid your baby trying to play with something unsuitable – say he grabs a tiny shoe from a sibling's doll set, or lunges for an electrical flex while you are ironing or using a hairdryer. In these instances, you need to take the item out of his grasp and try to explain why he cannot play with it. He has to learn that some things are dangerous. The fact that there are limits is an important lesson that will be built on throughout his life.

Q **My baby is 9 months old. I am worried he'll hurt himself one of these days when he tries to pull himself up. How can I keep him safe?**

A The only way your baby can learn new movement skills is by tackling new challenges and these always come with a small risk of injury. Rather than restricting him, stay close to him when he manoeuvres – that way you are better placed to prevent an accident from happening.

meeting people and making
first friends

Your baby develops on an emotional level from the moment she emerges from the womb. She rapidly adopts a range of expressions and mannerisms, and you can very quickly tell whether she is happy or discontented. Your baby has an innate need to be with other human beings, and her ability to interact successfully throughout her life is strongly influenced by her early relationships.

'Every time I went out, Sandra would burst into tears the moment the babysitter arrived, and would cling to me helplessly. A friend suggested I stop prolonging the ordeal with reassuring hugs and kisses and that, instead, I act firmly and leave promptly. I did this on three occasions, and each time Sandra showed decreasing signs of separation anxiety. After that she barely even noticed me when I was leaving the house!'

Stephanie, mother of
Sandra (14 months)

shared
experience

your baby and you

Bonding (see pages 58–59) is crucial for a baby's long-term personality, emotional stability and friendliness. The process is completely natural, and one for which both you and your baby are quite prepared. You cannot determine how long it will take, or whether she will develop a similar relationship with your partner at the same time as she does with you, but be assured – it will happen. The strong connection that is created by bonding gives your baby a tremendous sense of well-being. It also provides a solid foundation on which she will build future relationships.

Your baby will benefit from spending time in the company of other babies, even if they do not appear to take much interest in each other.

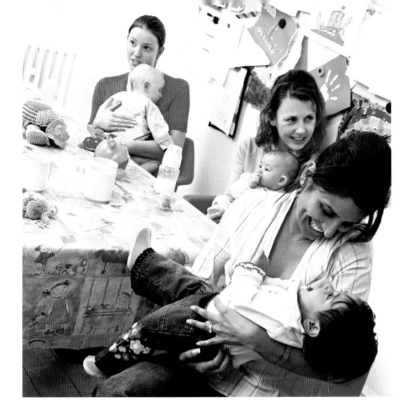

A parent-and-toddler group is the ideal vehicle for introducing your baby to children of different ages and gender.

The early months are likely to be dominated by you (and your partner) spending time alone with your baby. Take the opportunity to forge a strong relationship. She needs to learn as much about you as you do about her: that you will be there to soothe her when distressed, help her when she needs feeding or changing and cuddle her when she needs love. It is a good idea to introduce your baby to other adults early on. Grandparents, aunts and uncles are an obvious start, but friends and neighbours are also important. This enables her to get used to being held by other people, and to hearing their voices.

your baby and others

From around 3–4 months, your baby will demonstrate a desire to interact with others. She may be shy with strangers, but will respond quickly to a smile or playful interaction. She will benefit from being with other babies, toddlers and older siblings. Babies particularly love other babies and instantly recognize that they have much in common.

By about 7 months, your baby will make active attempts to respond to others. Although she cannot have a proper conversation, she will babble to anyone who talks to her. This is a good time to introduce her to a parent-and-toddler group. She is unlikely to play cooperatively with other children, but she will enjoy being in their presence.

Your baby's increased awareness of the world around her as she approaches the end of her first year may cause a temporary halt in her sociability. Her attachment to you may also intensify: she feels very secure with you and is more aware of strangers. At the parent-and-toddler group she will begin to benefit from seeing how other children behave. In snatching a toy from someone, she begins to make the link between her behaviour and another baby's disappointment or frustration. This is a major step in her emotional development.

that first smile

Babies smile at between 4 and 8 weeks. Social smiling begins when your baby makes a connection between her grin and the enthusiastic response of the person who sees that smile. Once she gets it, she will want to do it again and again. While they save the biggest smiles for those they love most, babies will generally smile at anyone until about 7 months, after which they stop smiling so readily at strangers. Some experiments have shown that the more parents smile and show positive affection towards their baby, the more likely she is to smile and interact with others.

index

acknowledgements

Alamy Agencja Free 153, Amy Lundstrom 155, Bart's Medical Library/Phototake Inc 254 above, Bubbles 152, Comstock Premium/Jupiter Images 17, Digital Vision 281, Eric Nathan 89, Glow Images 59, Image Box Uk Ltd 106, ImageState Royalty Free 80, Jacky Chapman/Janine Wiedel Photolibrary 230, James Clarke Images 42, Jann Lipka/Nordicphotos 34, Jupiterimages/BananaStock 73, 93, Jupiterimages/Pixland 127, Jupiterimages/Think Stock 245, Libby Welsh/Janine Wiedel Photolibrary 37, Loisjoy Thurstun/Bubbles 238, 241, M Plantec/Jupiterimages/Stock Image 212, Mikael Leijon/Nordicphotos 180, Niall McDiarmid 169, Peter Bennett/Ambient Images 13, Picture Partners 61, 64, 102, 201, 276 top, Profimedia International sro 68, 221, purewhite twins 36, Shout 16, 247 bottom, Shrikrishna Paranjpe/ephotocorp 39, Superstock 49, Tetra Images 78, 192, thislife pictures 53, 63, 101, TongRo Image Stock199 top

Babyarchive.com Catherine Benson 200, Claire North 228, Lina Ahnoff 205 above left

BananaStock Royalty Free 12, 23, 82, 100, 133, 136, 147, 171, 175, 202, 208, 239, 258, 267, 279

Bubbles John Powell 272, Loisjoy Thurstun 151, 252

Corbis A Green/Zefa 25, Bury/photocuisine 214, Fancy/Veer 137, Frank Lukasseck 237, John Fortunato Photography 90, Kristy-Anne Glubish/Design Pics 79, Larry Williams 10, Lawrence Manning 170, LWA-Dann Tardif 122, Olivia Baumgartner/Sygma 55, Royalty Free 188, Tom Stewart 114, Tom Stewart/zefa 269, Yellow Value RF 22

Creatas Royalty Free 88

Digital Vision Royalty Free 62, 173, 265, 280

DK Images Dave King 277, Ruth Jenkinson 181, Steve Shott 198, 276 below

Dreamstime.com Camptown 83, Dana 84 right, Lorna 227

Getty Images Alain Schroeder 113, Alan Powdrill 178, altrendo images 91, Ariel Skelley 270, Barry Willis 229, Betsie Van Der Meer 98, 125 left, Bruce Ayres 174, Camille Tokerud 110, Caroline von Tuempling 70, Daly & Newton 97, David Lees 121, Dorling Kindersley 43, Elie Bernager 259, James Woodson 213, John Howard 69, Kei Uesugi 210, Laurence Monneret 99, Lisa J Goodman 11, Lisa Spindler Photography Inc. 24, Macduff Everton 179, Marcy Maloy 123, Paul Vozdic 65, Philip Nealey 66, Regine Mahaux 41, Ross Whitaker 247 above, Royalty Free 120, Ruth Jenkinson 197, 264, Tony Metaxas 154, Victoria Blackie 116

istockphoto.com Hilary Brodey 249, Sharon Day 240, Vivid Pixels 184

Jupiterimages Babystock 86, Bananastock 92, 167, Brand X 48, Corbis 199 below, Dex 20, i love images 132, Image Source 52, Inspirestock 196, Pixland 75, Polka Dot 236, Radius Images 40, 72, Stock Image 273, Stockbyte 124, 125 right, Tetra 35, Workbook Stock 29, 33, 207, 266

Masterfile George Contorakes 50, Michael Mahovlich 142, Norbert Schäfer 119

Octopus Publishing Group Ltd 274 below right, Adrian Pope 60, 262, 263, David Jordan 209, Frank Adam 205 centre right, Gareth Sambidge 218, 274 above left, Lis Parsons 211, Nina Duncan 1, 9, 45, 57, 129, 130, 134, 138, 140, 144, 149, 156, 165, 183, 187, 189, 190, 217, 257, Paul Bricknell 85, Peter Pugh-Cook 176, 193, Russell Sadur 15, 26, 27, 54, 71, 74, 81, 103, 108, 150, 158, 160, 162, 163 above right, 166, 177, 182, 194, 195, 206, 224, 231, 232, 244, 250, 261, 271, 278, William Reavell 205 below right, 215

Photodisc Royalty Free 260

Photolibrary Anais Mai/Photononstop 111, George Shelley 112, Hervé Gyssels 115, BSIP Medical/LA/Ravonison H Am 222, Picture Press 56, 76, 225, 268, Pty Ltd Shoot 38, Radius Images 105, Royalty Free 58

Punchstock Brand X 242, Image Source 168, Polka Dot 159, Tetra 185

Rex Features Burger/Phanie 30

Sally and Richard Greenhill 51

Science Photo Library AJ Photo 31, 223, BSIP, Astier 28, Gusto Images 32, Ian Boddy 143, Ian Hooton 220, 233, 243, James King-Holmes 19, La La 235, Mauro Fermariello 18, Mike Devlin 254 below, Paul Whitehill 95

Shutterstock Adam Borkowski 7, AG photographer 117, iofoto 104, Jovan Nikolic 204, Najin 96, niderlander 77, Vladimir Melnik 2, Waldemar Dabrowski 226, William Milner 219

SuperStock Brand X 94

Tina Bolton 14, 46, 109

Tips Images Ltd John Powell 84

Executive Editor Jane McIntosh
Senior Editor   Charlotte Macey
Executive Art Editor Penny Stock
Designer one2six
Picture Researcher Zoe Spilberg
Senior Production Controller Manjit Sihra
Special Photography Nina Duncan